MW01094316

THE CAPACITY TO GOVERN

THE CAPACITY TO GOVERN

A Report to the Club of Rome

YEHEZKEL DROR
The Hebrew University of Jerusalem

FRANK CASS

LONDON • PORTLAND, OR

First published in 2001 in Great Britain by
FRANK CASS PUBLISHERS
Crown House, 47 Chase Side, Southgate,
London N14 5BP

and in the United States of America by
FRANK CASS PUBLISHERS
c/o ISBS, 5824 N.E. Hassalo Street
Portland, Oregon 97213-3644

Website: www.frankcass.com

British Library Cataloguing in Publication Data

Dror, Yehezkel, 1928–
    The capacity to govern : a report to the Club of Rome
    1. Political science 2. Public administration
    I. Title
    320'.01

ISBN 0-7146-5228-8 (cloth)

Library of Congress Cataloging-in-Publication Data

Dror, Yehezkel, 1928–
The capacity to govern : a report to the club of Rome / Yehezkel
Dror.
    p. cm.
    Includes bibliographical references and index.
    ISBN 0-7146-5228-8 (cloth)
    1. Political science. 2. Public administration. I. Title.
JA71.D76 2001
320'.01–dc21
2001002917

Typeset in 10.5/12 Baskerville by Cambridge Photosetting Services
Printed in Great Britain by
MPG Books Ltd, Bodmin, Cornwall

Contents

CONTENTS

Foreword by the President of the Club of Rome

The problem of governance is central to the concerns that led to the creation of the Club of Rome. The Club's founders were struck by the inability of governments to take a long-term view, being instead too absorbed in dealing with day-to-day problems and current political difficulties. This lack of vision and the impotence of governments and international institutions in the face of the extremely serious problems besetting the modern world (unemployment, underdevelopment, environmental degradation, the bloody conflicts raging in Africa and elsewhere, AIDS, and so on) raise fundamental questions about the structure and methods of governance, and the competence of politicians.

For this reason, the Executive Board of the Club of Rome asked Professor Yehezkel Dror to prepare a Report analyzing the root causes of the incapacities of governments to fulfill their responsibilities, and suggesting how governance might be improved and enabled to cope with the global transformations now under way. *The Capacity to Govern* presents the fruits of this labor.

This Report to the Club of Rome has been made possible thanks to the generous help of Circulo de Lectores and of the Bertelsmann Concern. Also most important was the cooperation and support of the Banco Bilbao Vizcaya Foundation in organizing discussions of drafts of this book.

Based on many years of academic and consultative experience, Professor Dror did an admirable job in preparing the text and meeting our queries. With the typical patience of a scholar he has subjected his Report to frank examination and critique by meetings of interdisciplinary experts. This was a condition of the Club of Rome for acceptance of the manuscript.

Reports to the Club of Rome are prepared at its own invitation and under its auspices by world-renowned highly qualified institutions or scholars. However, the authors are exclusively responsible for the final text.

The Club of Rome, which is sometimes known as 'The Conscience of Humankind', is an independent global organization. It was founded with one hundred members in 1968. Members are selected internationally from personalities with different ideologies and professions, all of them concerned with the problems of our world.

The Club of Rome focuses on closely interrelated problems of global scale which are critical for the future of humanity in the medium and long term. With its technical reports, study groups and numerous meetings, the Club of Rome tries to provide the public with bases for enlightened opinion formation, to give early warnings and to mobilize active interest. The goal is to prevent and overcome difficulties and afflictions which concern us all.

The present Report deals with a central aspect of this important endeavor.

Ricardo Diez-Hochleitner
President of the Club of Rome

Endorsement by the Executive Committee of the Club of Rome

The present volume has been discussed in detail by the Members of the Executive Committee of the Club of Rome and accepted as a Report to the Club of Rome.

The Club of Rome hopes that this Report will stimulate wide public discussion on one of the more critical issues of our time and indicate ways for coping with it.

Preface

My main thesis in this book is that all prevailing forms of governance are increasingly becoming 'dead ends', unable to perform changing crucial functions. This applies both to democracies and to non-democracies, though to different degrees. The view that markets, civil society, non-governmental organizations and other social structures can compensate for this inadequacy is a chimera. Some new forms of governance are emerging which better fit shifting requirements, the European Union being a prime example, but these too suffer from serious inadequacies. Radical redesign of governance is therefore required; otherwise, increasing social costs, even existence-threatening failures, are unavoidable.

This book is dedicated to an exploration of this claim and the development of governance redesign proposals.

This Report builds on the long-standing interest of the Club of Rome in governance, as well as life-long theoretical and applied work of mine on upgrading governance. It is situated within basic democratic values. But it suggests queries, exceptions, limitations, and caveats; and also raises some doubts about the extent to which Western liberal democracy, in its present forms, can continue – and whether it should pervade the whole world.

I focus on the capacities to govern and to build the future and on the improvement of states, supra-state structures, and global governance. This neglects other key polities (an encompassing term I use for all politically organized social entities having governance), such as communities, regions, cities, conurbations, 'megacities', the Catholic Church and others. I do so in part because of limitations of knowledge and space, but mainly because of my view that in the foreseeable future state governments will continue to constitute the dominant form of governance, though other governance levels are taking on larger roles and should become more important in the longer run.

Earlier versions of this book have been published in German, Spanish and Portuguese. For publication in English, the text has been updated and made more compact; and the book as a whole has been made more reader-friendly.

But the basic evaluations and recommendations have not changed, as they stood the test of time well. Continuous declines in the capacities of governance since the Report was first submitted to the Club of Rome, about ten years ago, have confirmed my main findings on the obsolescence of present forms of governance, and reinforced the need for radical redesign.

Many of the ideas proffered here may startle readers accustomed to thinking and feeling in terms of the political platitudes, ideological slogans and – to use an apt term coined by Francis Bacon (as discussed in Wormald, 1993) – similar 'idols of the market place' that dominate much of contemporary public discourse. To pick one example, at first glance the proposals to raise the levels of knowledge of elected politicians may seem insulting and anti-democratic. However, in order to meet the challenges of governance under conditions of global transformation many 'common-sense' views need to be revised and even overturned, within fundamental values but without being constrained by contemporary folklore, proverbs and slogans. Therefore, deconstruction and redesign must often go together to permit essential improvements in governance.

Many of the recommendations developed in this book are debatable. However, if we merely go on with 'more of the same', accompanied with some tinkering at the edges, governance capacities adequate for meeting the needs of global transformation will not be available. Conventional reforms of public administration and government – however useful for improving the performance of 'normal' functions, increasing efficiency and serving the public in the short run better – are quite inadequate for handling the future-building tasks facing governance at a time of global shifts and human metamorphosis. There must therefore be a readiness for some radical remodeling of governance.

In outlook, this book belongs to the literature of 'resistance', challenging many features of present and emerging realities and trying to suggest redesigns of governance that increase the collective capacity to influence the future for the better. In nature, this book belongs to 'frontier knowledge' rather than 'textbook knowledge' (Bauer, 1994). But I wish I were capable of better, following the maxim of Heidegger 'rigor of meditation, carefulness in saying, frugality with words' (quoted in Harpham, 1987, p. 269). But I have tried my best and hope the reader will forgive the many shortcomings.

Kinalizade Ali Celebian, a sixteenth-century Ottoman poet, policy intellectual and moralist, said that 'true friendship means looking at a friend's work with the eye of an enemy' (Fleisher, 1986, p. 43). May I invite readers to follow this adage and help me with my further work on governance by sharing with the author reactions, comments, criticisms and suggestions.

Yehezkel Dror
The Hebrew University of Jerusalem
Jerusalem, June 2001

Acknowledgements

This book and its revision have been long in the making and are much indebted to others. The direct impetus for this endeavor has been provided by the Club of Rome, starting with its Founder and First President, Aurelio Peccei, and reaching its fulfillment thanks to the support, help and friendship of the current President of the Club of Rome, Ricardo Diez-Hochleitner, who also made very important substantive inputs based on his rich experiences in government.

The generous help of Fundacion BBV and its director, Jose Angel Sanches Asiain, in sponsoring two meetings of Club of Rome forums to discuss drafts of this book, is acknowledged with much appreciation. Similarly great is my debt to many other members of the Club of Rome and to colleagues of mine too numerous to enumerate who freely offered their ideas. The many thinkers and scholars on whose work I build is acknowledged, though inadequately so, in the References and Further Reading. But the author owes no less a debt to governance practitioners, in his own country and in many others, who provided unique opportunities to observe the realities of governance from the inside. These realities are often quite different from scholarly narratives, which frequently reflect fantasies stimulated by inappropriate research methods. The readiness of senior politicians and officials to participate in workshops mentored by the author and, from time to time, acting upon his recommendations, provided me with further essential 'laboratory' experiences.

Let me also express my thanks for the many improvements of the English manuscript, in contents and style, suggested by Dr Ruth Hubbard, President of the Canadian Public Service Commission during my consultative and workshop mission there. Ms Ann Johnson, from the former Paris office of the Club of Rome, did an excellent job in editing the first version of the Report.

Taking care of the publication of this book is a demanding task. It is a pleasure to thank the publisher Frank Cass, the editors Andrew Humphrys and Jonathan Manley and all the staff at Frank Cass for undertaking this endeavor, devoting their energy to it, doing an excellent editorial job and producing the book so well.

Glossary

Thinking depends on concepts. Therefore, new concepts are essential for novel thinking. This book moves in the direction of a 'conceptual revolution' in governance. Accordingly, I necessarily coin a number of new concepts and use some unfamiliar ones. Each concept is explained when first introduced, but for the convenience of readers this glossary provides short explanations of the main new or perhaps unfamiliar concepts used in the book.

Akrasia:	A term going back to Greek philosophy and especially Aristotle, referring to incontinence, in the sense of weakness of will – internal inability to do what one knows one should.
Axial Age:	A concept proposed by the philosopher Karl Jaspers to refer to the period between 500 BCE and 100 CE, when radical changes in transcendental views and human self-understanding took place in parallel in a number of civilizations.
Blowing bubbles:	A metaphor referring to the creation of images unrelated to reality, as a main activity of politics much aggravated in modern and post-modern populist mass media democracy. Blowing bubbles includes what is often called 'spin-doctoring' but it is a broader concept which encompasses manufactured images of various aspects of reality and not necessarily political ones.
Constitutional dictatorship:	A legal arrangement going back to the Roman Republic which provides for special temporary regimes in periods of acute crisis, during which rights of citizens are suspended, authoritarian rule is instituted, force may be used more freely, and so on. Such regimes, taking the form of 'state of siege' or 'national emergency', for instance, are legally

recognized and provided for in many democratic countries as temporary but essential expediencies for special circumstances.

Continental governance: governance of multi-state and supra-state politics composed of countries sharing borders, interests and, often, values and a core civilization – as paradigmatically illustrated by the European Union.

Crazy state: A concept proposed by the author in a book first published in 1971 dealing with fanatical–aggressive governments, countries and groups armed with weapons of mass killing.

Critical choice: A choice making a real difference for the future, in the objective sense, or assumed to do so subjectively. The appropriate metaphor, as used in classical Confucian writings, is one of painfully facing crossroads leading into different futures, however uncertain.

Critical intervention mass: The minimum scale of activity necessary to make a significant difference to historic processes.

Future weaving: As used by Plato in *The Statesman*, the activity of using current materials and processes in order to build, or at least influence, the future.

Futuribles: A term coined by Bertrand de Jouvenel to refer to alternative possible futures.

Fuzzy gambles: A paradigm of choice proposed by me, with all decisions in the face of uncertainty being viewed eventually as 'gambles'; and choice in the face of radical, non-probabilistic uncertainty and inconceivability constituting 'fuzzy' gambling. Because of pervasive uncertainty and inconceivability in most domains of policy making and all domains of future weaving, governments engage necessarily in 'policy gambling', that is fuzzy gambling for high stakes. The notion also applies to the default option of continuing past policies despite changing circumstances.

Global Leviathan: Applying the idea of Thomas Hobbes to the global domain, the possibility and likely necessity, if lesser means fail, of a global semi-authoritarian regime to enforce measures essential for the survival of humanity, including *inter alia* preventing a global 'Behemoth' in Hobbes' sense of dangerous strife.

Higher-order tasks: In contrast to the 'ordinary' tasks of governance, such as collecting taxes, assuring security, transfer payments, providing social services, etc., higher-order tasks involve significant efforts to shape the future and put societies on a new trajectory. Illustrations include setting up the United Nations and establishing the European Union.

Humankindcraft: Statecraft as applied to the level of super-state and global governance and humanity as a whole.

Inconceivability: Future realities that are at present 'unthinkable' and beyond imagining because of their radically novel characteristics.

Law of requisite variety: Proposed by Ross W. Ashby, this law states that coping with a message requires at least the same degree of variety as in the message itself. Applied metaphorically to capacities to govern, this law requires in governments at least the same levels of complexity as in the realities with which they are dealing (see also meta-complexity).

Meta-complexity: Complexity on complexity, that is a higher level of internal complexity, such as in human minds and in governments, needed for comprehending and coping with external complexity. (See also law of requisite variety.)

Mirror for rulers: A proposed modern rendering of the classical literary genre of 'mirrors for princes', that is books of advice – moral and/or realpolitical – for those who govern. The best-known example is Machiavelli's *The Prince*, but this is only one work from a huge body of literature going back thousands of years.

Partnershipstate: This concept put the emphasis on the need for states to advance their capacity to cooperate with other states and with multiple forms of sub-state and supra-state governance. It stands in contrast to terms such as 'commerce state'.

Phase transition: A term taken from physics, referring to transformations, such as ice becoming water and water becoming steam, or more radically radium becoming energy. Phase transitions can take the form of a sudden mutation or of an aggregate end-result of a number of steps each one of which by itself is quite small.

Policy gambling:	See fuzzy gambles.
Raison d'humanité:	In line with the term *raison d'état*, as developed by Renaissance thinkers in Italy, *raison d'humanité* refers to the interests and needs of humanity as a whole as a proposed normative imperative.
Rulerscraze:	Tacitus discussed the tendency of rulers to become 'crazy' as a kind of professional disease. The term 'rulerscraze' is proposed to refer to this family of pathologies, as an English equivalent for the German term 'Caesaerenwahnsinn'.
Social guidance cluster:	A term coined by Amitai Etzioni to refer to the collage of main units and persons steering societies.
Subsidiarity:	A principle going back to the Society of Jesuits and Catholic canon law which postulates that authority to act should be allocated to the lowest level adequately able to do so, subject to strict directives and supervision. The European Union adopted the principle of subsidiarity in the sense of leaving and allocating authority at the lowest level able to act, but neglected the second part of the principle – which I include in the principle of subsidiarity as recommended in the book.
Supra-state continental governance/ government:	Supra-state and multi-state forms of governance and governments based on physical (and, perhaps, civilizational) proximity, as best illustrated by the European Union, but also emerging in South-East Asia and in South America.
Tragic choice:	A concept proposed by Guido Calabresi and Philip Bobbit referring to morally harsh choices between very important values some of which must be sacrificed in order to realize others.
True believer organizations:	Eric Hoffer's concept of 'true believer' applied to organizations sharing a deep belief system and a strong commitment to advancing it.
Virtual history:	A term developed by Niall Ferguson for a long-standing branch of thought experiments, speculations, surmises and theories on what paths history would have taken had some important event in the past been different, such as Hitler being assassinated in 1938.
Weapons of mass killing:	This term is proposed instead of the widely used 'weapons of mass destruction' (WMD), as more adequately expressing what is at stake.

Leitmotif: Redesigning Governance for Guiding Global Transformations

Throughout most of human history the human condition has remained relatively stable for long periods, disrupted and transformed from time to time by leaps and upheavals. In prehistoric times, for example, a drastic change occurred with the transition from foraging to settled agriculture. More recently, the end of the Bronze Age (Drews, 1993), the Axial Age[1] and the seventeenth century (Parker and Smith, 1978) were periods of rapid and major change.

We are now living through such an age of radical transformations, which is sure to accelerate in the twenty-first century: in demography, in science and technology, in consciousness and culture, in communications, in geo-economic and geo-strategic configurations, in regimes and in values (King and Schneider, 1991). The discontinuities in these and other fundamental 'drivers' of human existence interact and mutually reinforce one another, accelerating further transformations and deepening turbulence (Rosenau, 1990), and leading in the longer run to a future which is inconceivable to our present modes of thinking and imagining.

The plural of the term 'transformations' highlights the variety in both the nature and contents of the changes currently under way. This diversity needs to be stressed in order to counteract simplistic notions, now widespread, that regard present trends as moving rapidly towards a homogeneous and narrow range of liberal, democratic, capitalist, consumption-oriented societies (Fukuyama, 1992, to be contrasted with Gress, 1998).

Such views, often backed by hidden or explicit beliefs, or wishful thinking, as to the 'true destiny' of humanity, offer neither a correct picture of what is happening, a reasonable prognosis, nor an acceptable normative vision. In one regard most contemporary treatments of ongoing processes and the futures into which they flow do capture a unique feature of our times, namely the fact that transformations are global. But the fashionable term 'globalization' is very ambiguous and politically loaded, while other commonly used metaphors, such as 'global village' are misleading. Although in part similar processes occur all over the world, and some are shared by emerging global elites, many of the transformations differ markedly in their nature, rate and direction from one social and cultural setting to another.

This dissimilarity may be obscured by shared terminology and common features, especially technologies. More insidious is the way in which dominant global ideologies distort reality (Sklair, 1991), in tending to ignore divergent trends or minimize their long-term significance by regarding them as temporary. Yet, if we are to tackle the problems of governance properly, we must recognize divergent as well as convergent trends. This is especially important given the growing tensions within an increasingly integrated global system between strong centrifugal and not less strong centripetal forces. Therefore, it is advisable to think in terms of an emerging global umbrella-society together with diverse sub-societies and considerable cultural pluralism. It is also important to consider the prevalence of conflict, from cultural hostility (Huntington, 1996) and efforts to construct 'boundaries' (Singer and Wildavski, 1996) to chaos (Kaplan, 2000) and various forms of warfare (Creveld, 1991).

The state of flux in which we are living, in combination with rapidly increasing human capacities to influence the future by deliberate actions, creates serious challenges for governing capacities on all levels, from the local to the global. Thus, humanity as a whole faces critical choices in respect to science and technology and their uses, including possibilities to enhance human capacities; global economic and demographic processes and their regulation; the future of the environment; global equity; control of weapons of mass killing; and the future of global governance. Moreover states face vexing choices on employment, migration, infrastructure, and the integration of global processes and super-state polities.

It is the demanding nature of the issues which must be dealt with by governance, in their complexity and future-impacting potentials, which causes governments to be 'in over their heads' (Kegan, 1994). In the face of escalating needs, governance is increasingly obsolete, with a growing incapacity to govern caused by the relatively static nature of the main features of governance in contrast with rapid transformations in the issues with which it must cope. Hence the urgent need for a redesign of governance so as to ensure adequate capacities – with 'high-quality' governance being an essential minimum for coping with ongoing transformations and, especially, for fulfilling crucial governmental tasks in building the future. It is this capacity deficit, and ways to overcome it, that constitute the leitmotif of this book.

The challenge has been put very sharply by Bill Joy (Joy, 2000), himself a major information technology scientist and entrepreneur, who claims that the future 'doesn't need us' and that '[o]ur most powerful 21st-century technologies – robotics, genetic engineering, and nanotech – are threatening to make humans an endangered species' (ibid., p. 238). Even if his thesis is exaggerated, it clearly poses an existential requirement for humanity – namely, in my terminology, to improve its capacity to 'make the future' rather than being 'unmade' by it.

Accordingly, the main proposition of this book can be presented as follows: *Ongoing global transformations need guidance, to avoid very negative looming consequences and realize very positive potentials. Markets, civil society etc., however important, cannot be relied upon to provide the needed guidance; normatively and realistically only governance can do so. However, in order, to adequately fulfill crucial future-building tasks, politics must be revitalized, democracy must be refocused, and governance must be radically redesigned,*

The constraints on predictability, the ubiquity of uncertainty and the growing domains of inconceivability impose strict limits on the ambitions of this book and dictate some of its principal features. The discussion focuses on the more foreseeable future, roughly the first half of the twenty-first century, and an effort is made to reduce the sensitivity of my discourse to shifting details and irreducible uncertainties. Accordingly, this book concentrates on basic issues relating to the capacity to govern, with its main emphasis on the ability to build the future, and tries to cope with complex problems and proposals for improvement in terms of underlying principles. These are less susceptible to change and are likely still to be relevant, in part at least, in the second part of the twenty-first century.

This assumption is well supported by the history of governance, with many of its major features and problems arising from basic human characteristics and therefore being persistent, as is shown for instance by the relevance of classical Greek and Chinese political and social philosophy to contemporary concerns. However the history of governance also shows that unless innovations in governance – often radical ones – occur, obsolescence ensues, especially under conditions of rapid change in the main dimensions of human and social existence, with stagnation, decline and even catastrophe following inevitably (Eisenstadt, 1963). Indeed, *a major revision of theories of the rise and decline of states, societies and civilizations may well be in order, with more attention given to quality of governance as a critical, and partly independent, factor.*

This book does not presume to offer and elaborate such a reinterpretation of history. But its two main conclusions are based on some first steps in such a direction. Firstly, the quality of governance constitutes a major variable in shaping the future of societies, states, and humanity as a whole, including their very existence. This is the case despite contemporary illusions that free markets, civil society and so on can be relied upon to bring about by themselves a positive future. Secondly, the quality of governance is not overdetermined by other factors, such as modes of production, mass media, social values, globalization and so on but can be significantly improved by deliberate endeavor.

3

A moment of reflection will serve to put the subject into a context of both urgency and doubt. Let us return for a moment to the beginning of the twentieth century and compare ways of life and thinking as well as expectations at that time (Weber, 1986; Briggs and Snowman, 1996) with our circumstances and expectations. Obviously, living conditions and attitudes of large parts of humanity have changed beyond recognition and will change even more; political values and regimes have altered radically; and unprecedented events, which were regarded as 'impossible', did indeed happen, as tragically illustrated by the *Shoah* as a rupture in history (Cohen, 1993; Fackenheim, 1994). But, if we observe the inner corridors of power and the ways in which governments make fateful decisions, no significant changes can be discerned in the last hundred – or indeed thousand – years.

If one looks at the history of governance ever since states and rulers first appeared, a mixed picture emerges (Finer, 1997; Raadschelders, 1998). Over the generations, there have been radical innovations in its main facets, such as in legitimation, participation, goals and values, and machinery. However, regardless of how cosmologies and consciousness have changed (Collins, 1989), many core features of governance have been relatively very stable.

A crucial illustration is provided by the kernel of rulership, which, tragically, has remained in many respects the same since prehistory. Thanks to the *Memoirs* of Babur, the founder of the Indian Mogul Empire in the sixteenth century (Thackston, 1996), as supplemented by animal allegories of the Mongol court (Cowen, 1989), we can explore the thinking and choices of one who is often regarded as belonging to the small group of the more cultured rulers the world has known, while Hideyoshi in sixteenth-century Japan, illustrates an outstanding statesman and state-builder (Berry, 1982), as does Winston Churchill in his historical moment (Lukacs, 1999). Let us add to the picture the remarkable diaries of Richard Crossman on cabinet decision-making in Great Britain in the 1960s and 1970s (Crossman, 1975–7), studies of the court of Wilhelm II (Röhl, 1994, to be read in the context of Ferguson, 1998), and indeed, nearly all findings on top-level decision-making. The conclusion is clear: no overall progress can be discerned in the range of statecraft qualities.

This conclusion is supported by studies of governmental decision-making as a whole. Certain technical features, such as the storage and processing of information, have changed radically. Significant improvements also took place when reliable factual knowledge or theories provided a solid foundation for decision-making, as economic theory has done under some conditions. But the core features of critical decision-making are the same, including persistent serious weaknesses. This is not surprising in view of their grounding in human, group and organizational characteristics that are relatively very stable. However shocking this conclusion may seem to the uninitiated, a strong case can be made that there has been no progress in core processes of critical governmental choice, but this will not surprise acute observers of high-level policy-making.

This conclusion is made all the more ominous by its increasingly harsh consequences. To continue with the same basic modes of choice, with their many propensities to error, while the stakes grow by several orders of magnitude – this carries very high risks for countries and for humankind as a whole. It is therefore urgent that capacities to govern be radically improved, with special attention to the ability to make critical choices that influence the path societies and humanity take in the future.

NOTES

1. The concept of the Axial Age was first proposed by Karl Jaspers (Jaspers, 1949, pp. 15–106; Eisenstadt, 1986, p. 1). It refers to the radical changes in transcendental world-views and understandings of selfhood which took place, mainly between about 500 BCE and 100 CE, in several major civilizations, including early Judaism, classical Greece, early Christianity, Zoroastrian beliefs in Iran, early Imperial Chinese civilization, and Hindu and Buddhist civilizations.

Mission: Improving Capacities to Govern

This book deals with the capacity to govern, with emphasis on the ability to build the future as an expression of collective human will and choice, based on the human freedom to try and influence evolving history.

Plato, in his three books on governance, starts in *The Republic* with the utopian (or, in some views, dystopian) model of an all-knowing and wholly just philosopher-king supported by an elite of guardians detached from personal, family and material interests. Despairing of the model of philosopher-kings, apparently after his experience as an advisor and tutor to Dionysius II of Syracuse, he developed in *The Statesman* the idea of politicians as professionals, weaving the future out of the contradictory strands of human beings, their interests and groupings. Having lost faith is this solution too, *The Laws* proposes a system in which custom reigns supreme, with governments, rulers, and societies as a whole refraining from innovation.

Some modern schools of thought, such as more simple versions of libertarianism, market-economy ideologies, and civil-society populism, would also like governance to avoid future-shaping activities, though for quite different reasons from Plato. However, attempts to ignore or repress such activities by governance are not only futile; by causing governments to neglect a crucial task, they risk dire consequences. Such attempts also paralyze efforts to improve salient capacities of governments and thereby assure even harsher failures.

It is an irony of history that many free-market theoreticians seem to share the Marxist belief in the withering away of the state, forgetting that a hidden hand needs a body and brain behind and above it. Related to this is the fashionable view that business is more effective, efficient and trustworthy than governments, so that governmental functions should be transferred as far as possible to markets, with whatever remains of the public sector becoming business-like – as reflected in the fashionable term 'new public management'. Even qualified thinkers recognizing the roles of governments in managing markets (Yergin and Stanislaw, 1998) ignore their crucial future-influencing tasks, blinded partly by the 'economic view of governance', and similar frames of thought. Not surprisingly, even when belatedly recognizing the importance of governments, the World Bank and the United Nations Development Programme fail to focus on the most important issue, namely the need to radically upgrade the future-shaping capacities of centers of government. (See, for example, International Bank for Reconstruction and Development and The World Bank, 1997; World Bank, 2000, chapter 5; and United Nations Development Programme, 2000a, pp. 52–61.)

Markets can and should handle more of the service-delivery functions of governance, as well as decisions that can be decentralized, subject to 'market failure' limitations as compared to 'governance failures' (Wolf, Jr, 1996). But markets cannot and should not be in charge of critical future-shaping choices. Moreover, expanding markets themselves need to be regulated, and the future of the global economy depends inter alia on governmental policies (OECD, 1999).

This view in no way disparages the great importance of markets in producing wealth, nor the significance of grass-roots and communal governance, or the growing role of non-governmental organizations. Nonetheless, governments retain the authority to make critical choices and most of the instruments for carrying them out, even as the classical state is changing its nature and also, in some senses, losing power (Spruyt, 1994). This is demonstrated, inter alia, by the endeavor of non-governmental organizations and other public action bodies to operate largely by trying to exert pressure on the decisions and actions of governments, directly or indirectly.

It is enough to mention, at this preliminary stage of our discussion, the importance of state governments in shaping the future of the European Union, in managing transitions from command economies to market economies, in coping – or not coping – with new types of security threat and, more often than meets the eye, in engaging in 'social architecture', as visibly the case in Singapore (Sandhu and Wheatley, 1989; Chua, 1995; Yew, 1998) but true also in democracies, in order to deconstruct fashionable views on the 'hollowing out' of the state (Blockmans, 1997, pp. 372 ff.)

Study of the history of social institutions leads to a view of governance as produced by a dynamic mix between human and social characteristics shaped in the course of evolution, the specific histories and situations of various societies, prevalent ideas and ideologies, and a multiplicity of social forces and interests. But governance is also a human artifact, a deliberate 'work of art' as Hegel put it and Jacob Burckhardt said of the renaissance states in Italy. As such, it can to some extent be reconstructed deliberately so as to meet changing needs and aspirations; and many alternative ways of doing so are available within given basic norms – such as democracy and human rights – and given histories, societies and social forces.

Taking into account, on one hand, the long history of thought on shaping and reshaping governance and, on the other, the obvious predicaments of governance at present, it is not surprising that a lot of attention is given to improving governance. In part, these interests focus on values, such as broadening and deepening democracy and increasing transparency and responsiveness. In part, they are concerned with making governance leaner and more efficient. And to an extent certain institutions receive special attention, such as electoral systems and financing. However, all in all, most contemporary approaches to governance redesign are narrow. In particular, little attention is paid to the overall upgrading of capacities to govern, and even less is given to improving governmental capacities to build the future.

There are partial exceptions, such as the discussion on the reshaping of the European Union and its institutions; but symptomatic is the misuse of the slogan of 'reinventing government', as coined in 1992 (Osborne and Gaebler, 1992; better, though still too narrowly drawn in Gore, 1993). Many studies, global conferences and political declarations are devoted to it, but with a narrow focus having little to do with the real needs of redesigning governance – hence the proposed conception of 'refocusing' democracy, with future-building tasks being recognized as central. Doing so depends on 'resuscitating' politics, in the sense of putting it again in charge of making crucial choices.

Reinforcing this need is the misleading tendency to talk about 'ungovernability', rather than facing the real problem – incapacity to govern. The use of the term 'ungovernability' is not only often incorrect but also dangerous: incorrect because so-called societal ungovernability is frequently a result of governments' failure to adjust to changing situations; and dangerous because it provides an alibi for governmental inadequacies, putting the blame instead on societies. True, there are situations that are genuinely ungovernable without radical social transformations which no indigenous government can realize, such as in parts of Africa. But in most cases efforts should concentrate on improving capacities to govern rather than on blaming societies for being 'ungovernable'.

Some promising innovations are starting to emerge, such as the governance system of the European Union, and a few interesting ideas are to be found in public discourse and in literature. But, in general, existing governance patterns are increasingly obsolete, actual innovations in governance grossly inadequate, and available ideas for improving governance far from meeting urgent needs. Humanity therefore faces a critical challenge in respect to redesigning capacities to govern for coping with the unprecedented problems, dangers and opportunities of the twenty-first century.

A brief survey of contemporary discourse on democracy (as partially outlined in Dahl, 1999) and its performance (Lijphard, 1999) clearly demonstrates neglect of the most urgent of all issues – namely capacities to shape

9

the future. In the past, there was perhaps some sense in distinguishing between what has been called a 'Jacobin' view, regarding governance as one means of bringing about a better society (Eisestadt, 1999a), and more 'conservative' ones. But a main thesis of this book is that no such choice is open any more. *Because of the ongoing global transformation, governmental efforts to influence the future significantly are essential for preventing the bad and achieving the good – governmental passivity constituting not only a denial of democratic responsibility but a failure leading in all probability to very undesirable and perhaps catastrophic futures outcomes.*

But there is no guarantee that the challenges of shaping the future for the better can or will produce an adequate response. The possibility cannot be excluded that human beings, individually and collectively, have innate limitations preventing them from inventing and putting into operation patterns of governance capable of coping successfully with new, emerging types of danger, even when this failure may bring about the disappearance of *homo sapiens*. A less pessimistic view is that only a leap in human values and consciousness can create a governance system able to meet new challenges, but that such a transformation may well be caused only by the shock of a major catastrophe that does not completely destroy the human race. Alternatively, a moral jump producing novel capacities to govern might be the result of the emergence of a new major religion. More optimistic is the view that throughout history human beings have repeatedly demonstrated capacities to improve social institutions. Humanity may therefore possess the potential to make governance fit new challenges, though this cannot be taken for granted.

This book is based on the more optimistic view, together with the intellectual position that we do not know what are the limits of individual and collective human potentials, and the moral stance that we must do our best even if we have no guarantee that it will suffice. However, to have a chance to redesign capacities to govern so as to meet such needs, a new basis in political philosophy is essential – a requirement to which I will now turn.

2

Foundations in Political Philosophy

Political philosophies and political theologies (Schmitt, 1970, 1979) have served as groundings for governance and its transformations throughout history. This was as true for China and the classical Oriental states as for Greece and Rome; for the European Catholic states as for the Inca and Maya city states; for classical Japan as for modern Republicanism; for contemporary democracy as for the European Union. While states were often a product of power as well as technologies and historical accidents, governance systems have always been profoundly influenced by political philosophies and their normative grounding.[1]

As discussed in Aristotle's *The Nicomachean Ethics* and further developed by Martha Nussbaum (Nussbaum, 1995b), the application of political philosophy, as of other values, to concrete circumstances is in no way obvious and automatic. In all instances there is need for moral and political judgment, taking into account all the specificities of given circumstances and histories (Steinberger, 1993). However, in the absence of a political philosophy fitting the twenty-first century, judgment will be either too pragmatic and 'realpolitical', or swayed by incorrect philosophies and doubtful values.

If significant transformations in governance are needed, as they clearly are, then new political philosophies are therefore necessary to serve as one of their foundations. It is this dependence of radical governance redesign on new political philosophies that make the latter all the more essential for my endeavor – but suitable new political philosophies are sorely lacking.

This chapter does not presume to fill the void, but raises some of the main issues which political philosophy must address and indicates some possible approaches for doing so. It thus provides a normative basis for this book as a whole.

Political philosophy is evolving in association with moral philosophy, as illustrated by new points of view and values on human rights, gender equality, social justice, ecology, animal rights and more. However, fundamental issues facing humanity are not receiving adequate attention. These include, to give just a few preliminary examples:

- Implications and uses of science and technology and their regulation, especially in regard to interventions with human evolution.
- Conceptions of 'just war', including humanitarian interventions with armed forces.
- Global justice, such as growing disparities in material quality of life between countries.
- Moral implications of globalization and its regulation.
- Balancing freedom with needs to control new forms of private power.
- Coping with 'evil' actors armed with emerging weapons of mass killing.[2]

Innovations in values in such domains are essential as a basis for human choice, as are values dealing directly with politics and governance and their tasks. These are the main concerns of the present chapter.

New ideas in political philosophy on the very concept of the state and related ideas of sovereignty (Bartelson, 1995) are urgently needed. Without going so far as to predict the 'decline of the state' within the foreseeable future (Creveld, 1999, chapter 6 and conclusions), the state is nevertheless undergoing transformations. But political philosophy is a very poor source of foundational values both for emerging new polities, such as the European Union, and for global governance.

More difficult to meet is the need for novel foundations in political philosophy for the future-building tasks of governance, including discourse on the desirability of governmental engagement in this mission. Related issues include the right of a majority to make and enforce choices against strongly held views of minorities after offering a reasonable compromise so as to avoid a dictatorship of the majority, limits on permissible democratic resistance by committed pressure groups and ways of dealing with them, the appropriate scope of legal reasoning and court decisions on public issues, and more.

Also of pressing importance are issues involving the use of force. Not only is most of contemporary political philosophy mistaken in ignoring dilemmas on the use of force clearly foreseeable for the twenty-first century, but it fails to process the experiences of the twentieth century and to draw adequate lessons from them. Human propensities to extremism leading to evil (Hobsbawm, 1994) and even atrocity (Chirot, 1996), as prevalent in the twentieth century, have had little impact on political philosophy. Especially striking is the neglect of lessons to be drawn from the mass-based emergence and evil achievements of Nazi Germany. Instead of being recognized as an indication of the potentials of human evil under conditions of societal traumatization combined with technical efficiency (as will characterize many societies in the twenty-first century),[3] it is usually ignored or seen as an exceptional case. As a result, nearly all of contemporary political philosophy adheres, explicitly or implicitly, to an optimistic image of humanity. It concentrates on facilitating 'the good', while ignoring the necessity to make strenuous efforts to confront (Kekes, 1990) and disempower evil. Similarly, most of modern political philosophy accepts as true the pleasant delusion that all disagreements can be handled through discourse and 'building of consensus', without taking up in earnest the likelihood that stern measures may be necessary and justified to stop post-modern barbarism.[4]

To serve as an essential foundation for the future-building tasks of governance in the twenty-first century, political philosophy should, therefore, reconsider some of its basic assumptions and move into new areas.

Some of the contrasting normative alternatives on the nature of states and their basic norms and underlying assumptions emerge from a comparison of two classical Chinese political philosophies, as crystallized between the fourth and the third centuries BCE – namely, the Legalistic and the classical Confucian schools.

The Legalists based their position on the following basic values and assumptions:

1. Man is amorally self-seeking.
2. The people exist for the sake of the state and its ruler.
3. The people must therefore be coerced into obedience by rewards and harsh punishments.
4. Law is a supreme, state-determined, amoral standard of conduct and must be enforced inflexibly.
5. Officials must be obedient instruments of the ruler's will, accountable to him alone.
6. Expediency must be the basis for all state policy and all state service.
7. The state can prosper only if it is organized for prompt and efficient implementation of the ruler's will.

Conversely, the classical Confucians maintained that:

1. Man is morally perfectible.
2. The state and its ruler exist for the sake of the people.
3. The people must therefore be encouraged toward goodness by education and virtuous example.
4. Law is a necessary but necessarily fallible handmaiden of the natural moral order and must be enforced flexibly.
5. Officials must be morally superior men, loyal to the ruler but accountable primarily and in the last resort to Heaven.
6. Morality – specifically, the doctrines of good government expounded in the classics and manifested in the acts of worthy men of the past – must be the basis for all state policy and all state service.
7. The state can prosper only if its people possess the morale that comes from confidence in the ruler's virtue (Hucker, 1959, pp. 183–4).

Modern Western liberal democratic values are much nearer to the Confucian position, with four crucial differences. First, rulers are elected by the people and are expected, in one way or another, to represent and serve their will. Second, an individualistic view of human beings is substituted for a collective perception of 'the people', and a main concern is with individual human rights. Third, the moral purposes and moral foundations of governance are ambiguous, attenuated and relative; basic norms are limited to the values built into liberal democracy – the changing wishes of the majority, with much account given to minorities, in some admixture with constantly reduced doses of 'reasons of state', are seen as determining both law and governance; 'how' matters more than 'what'; and the emphasis is on rules rather than on virtue. Moral arguments continue to carry weight, but the values to be served by governance, within the basic norms of democracy as they change in the course of time, are decided by elections and justified in terms of the will of the populace rather than any absolute moral order. And fourth, less and less are rulers and officials expected to be of superior moral stature.

Let me add, as an introduction to the problem of the unavoidability and often effectiveness of 'dirty hands' in statecraft, that it was the Legalistic School which served as the basis of policies bringing about the successful consolidation of China into one powerful state.

To proceed to some crucial dilemmas of political philosophy relevant to the expected circumstances of the twenty-first century, let us start with the fundamental question: Governance for what? (Oakeshott, 1996).

The immediate answer is, 'in order to facilitate citizens achieving a good life', often modified by some allusion to the utilitarian principle of the greatest happiness of the greatest number. But this response raises more problems than it resolves; and it is not easy to specify substantively what it requires.

A first query is whether a 'good life' refers more to its moral significance, or more to its material standards, or to some combination relating to 'human development'. Extreme libertarians, and to a lesser extent also liberals, would argue that this question is irrelevant. It is up to each individual to define what constitutes for her or him a 'good life', within very flexible boundaries and as long as he or she does not cause direct harm to the right of others to do likewise.

Related to this is the question of how to understand 'causing harm to others'. An argument can be made that some ways of thinking 'natural' to human beings are increasingly causing harm to others, in a broad sense. Thus, it may well be that seeking enemies or overusing the environment is natural to human beings, whether as a result of evolutionary imprinting or otherwise. If so, than a longer-term view of the common interest of humanity may well require determined efforts to change some main features of human beings, including their views on what constitutes a 'good life' (Ruh, 1997).

To formulate the question somewhat differently: Should a goal – such as 'perfectionism', whether interpreted narrowly with regard to human nature or more broadly (Hurka, 1993, esp. p. 4), or 'fitting the long term survival of humanity', or 'its happiness', or 'well-being' in some sense (Griffin, 1986; Elster and Roemer, 1991; Dasgupta, 1993), or serving some transcendental values – be postulated for human beings, and by whom? And, if so, should its achievement be left to individual efforts, be supported and facilitated by collective action, or perhaps also be imposed upon individuals by collective controls? Or should no goal whatsoever be set for human beings, on the assumption that they should select their own goals with maximum freedom from societal influences, and subject to minimum restrictions? And, if so, should the task of achieving whatever goals are chosen be left to individual and grass-roots action, or be facilitated by collective processes and governance action?

These queries touch upon a central difference between a liberal democratic and a quasi-Confucian or classical Greek 'substantive morality' view of governance. In the first, every individual should decide what is for him or her a 'good life'; whereas in the second, some given value system or collective choice postulates the nature of the good life, which should then be promoted by governance as obligatory for everyone, or at least recommended to all and advanced through collective and governance action.

Within the first position, government can be required to be more passive or more active – either merely removing obstacles to achieving the good life, however conceived, or promoting it energetically. Thus, citizens can be helped to achieve their personal notions of a good life in a relatively passive way by being provided with certain minimum opportunities, or more actively through the assurance of wide opportunities for all to pursue whatever notion of 'good life' they wish.

An associated problem relates to the opposition between majorities and minorities, and to aggregate calculations of 'utility'. For example, let us assume that a majority wants to achieve a 'good life' for itself in a way that hinders a minority in its efforts to attain quite different notions of a 'good life'. Is the satisfaction of the wishes of the majority to be given priority over the wishes of the minority? Or are the rights of a minority to its notions of a 'good life' to be guaranteed, even at the cost of a 'good life' for the majority? And to what extent?

With respect to the second position, a weak form of state support for a collective notion of a good life would be to remove obstacles to efforts by other actors – such as a church – operating on a voluntary basis, to advance adherence to advocated moral notions. Active indoctrination and enforcement, on the other hand, would be a strong form of intervention.

All Western liberal democratic approaches share the value of letting each citizen make his or her own choice of his or her 'good life'. But this leaves open at least four difficult issues: the opportunity of future generations to promote their notions of a good life; the danger that a large number of citizens supposedly pursuing their notions of a good life may in fact be acting against their own interests, even self-destructively; the susceptibility of citizens to 'negative' influences in forming and reforming their notions of a 'good life', such as by the mass media, commercials and political marketing; and the problem of what to do about countries and cultures that wish to advance collective notions of a 'good life' of their own, such as living according to the tenets of a religion.

Acceptance of the right of future generations to choose their notions of a good life involves, first of all, recognizing that they are entitled to prefer ways of life different from our priorities and perhaps repugnant to us. This conflicts with our deeply ingrained desire to perpetuate our own values and have future generations follow in our footsteps, and is unacceptable to 'true believers' who sincerely and deeply feel that they know what is 'true' (Hoffer, 1951). Thus, it is hard to envisage passionately religious persons accepting the possibility that their descendants may be very anti-religious, and actively providing them with opportunities to be so, just as it is very difficult for passionate believers in the separation of religion from governance to consider the possibility that their children may support the establishment of a state religion.

Caring about the opportunities of future generations to realize their own, as yet undetermined and unknown, values leads to the major problem, which is crucial for all future-building endeavors, of allocating multi-purpose resources between generations (Sikora and Barry, 1978). How willing are people to reduce the chances of achieving a good life now in order to increase such chances for human beings in the future? And how should due weight be given to long-range considerations and inter-generational values in the face of pressing current needs and the demands of tight and very competitive electoral cycles, compounded by uncertainties about the future?

This quandary is compounded by a fundamental congenital defect of democracy, going deeper than 'paradoxes' (Eisenstadt, 1999a; Gerber, 1999) and taking instead the form of an irresolvable contradiction. The basic tenet of democracy is that those who will bear the consequences of decisions should have a say in them, or in electing those who make the decisions. However, many present decisions have weighty consequences for future generations, which clearly cannot vote now. Hence the need to *redesign governance so as to improve the capacity to make value judgments on time preferences and provide some surrogate 'representation' to unborn generations.* Such efforts require presently unavailable foundations in political philosophy.

Another question is posed by the possibility that a large number of individuals trying to maximize their private notions of a 'good life' may in fact damage themselves, even in terms of their own preferences. This is epitomized in game-theory models of the 'Prisoner's Dilemma' type, and in the classical problem of looking after 'the commons'. In such situations, sets of individuals who strive to make a good life for themselves, each one by himself, bring about results that are often counter-productive for many, though not all, of the same persons.

Coping with this problem requires some combination of three approaches. First, citizens' understanding must be improved, so that they can better consider the consequences of taking a narrow view of their individual interests. But this does not help much if, as is often the case, a real contradiction exists between promoting one's own good life and furthering some aggregate of good lives for the many individuals constituting the society of which one is a member. Welfare economy paradoxes and 'free rider' issues further add to the difficulty.

To overcome this problem, citizens must both be aware of the consequences of their individual acts, with all their uncertainties, and they must be willing to abstain from maximization of their own good life in order to give others a better chance to do so, even when this cannot be justified in terms of enlightened self-interest. For this condition to be satisfied, empathy, altruism, a sense of solidarity, some sense of 'decency' (Margalit, 1995) and similar moral impulses must be accepted as part of the notion of a good life by most, if not all, citizens. Alternatively, or in addition, the equivalent of such feelings must be enforced by governance action, preferably based on public support but, logically, not necessarily so.

A different and more interventionist and fundamental approach is to re-examine and re-evaluate ego-centered conceptions of a good life in light of psychology and ethics. The question then becomes: What subjective notions of the 'good life' are in the 'real interests' of human beings? Various fictions as to what people would really desire if they were fully informed, highly developed – not suffering from akrasia (weakness of will), or making choices behind some screen of ignorance concerning their future concrete circumstances – can help to deepen (and also obscure) the analysis (Rawls, 1999). But they do not change the difficulty of the questions that must be faced.

A number of steps may help. First, one of the tasks of governance should be to enlighten citizens and promote moral education so as to foster empathy with the needs of others, altruism and a feeling of global human solidarity – with governance elites setting an example. Second, the idea of human rights should be supplemented and completed by adding and institutionalizing the idea of human responsibilities and duties.[5] And, third, values of human solidarity and mutual responsibility can be viewed as a moral norm. This should be advanced either as a counter-ethics to self-centered individualism, based on a theory of reciprocal relations or, as proposed by Emmanuel Levinas, as a primordial component of human existence.

However, all this depends on the limitation of some of the values and assumptions of liberalism (Rawls, 1993) and the rejection of major forms of fundamentalism and sectarianism (Eisenstadt, 1999b).

To try and go one level deeper, we must take up the vexed issue of how far human beings have wishes and desires inherent in their humanity, which in some views are therefore entitled to a privileged position, as contrasted with socially conditioned wishes or temporary hedonistic desires. Speculation about evolutionary imprinting of preferences, whether taken as a constraint, a basis and justification for norms, or as a barrier to moral progress that must be overcome, add further complexities to the matter.[6]

One position is that human beings have some innate characteristics and capacities that shape their basic notions of a 'good life', with individual variations to some extent free from cultural and social influences. These innate propensities can be explained as resulting from neurological structures and biological needs, as shaped by evolutionary processes, or as stemming from a spiritual essence, as caused by transcendental creation. However, whatever the explanation may be, the shared conclusion is that being human involves some inherent notions of a 'good life', though the details will depend on particular situations and influences. Consequently, the notion of a 'good life that is becoming to a human being' is not vacuous, even if we lack instruments to specify its contents reliably.

A related position, but very different in its implications, is that human beings in one way or another suffer from 'original sin' and a propensity to prefer evil. If so, then a main duty of governance, or of governance-supported religious or other value-institutions, is to counteract what comes 'naturally' to human beings, so as to reduce vice and advance virtue.

The contrary position to these two was strongly put by Norbert Elias (Elias, 1978; on the context, Mennell, 1992), though the ideological extremes of Foucault should be rejected (Dreyfus and Rabinow, 1983). It claims that psychogenesis is largely shaped by sociogenesis. In this view, many features of the individual, including tastes, ways of expressing basic emotions, and modes of satisfying fundamental needs, are molded by social processes. Accordingly, as is also claimed by post-modern 'cultural politics' approaches (Jordan and Weedon, 1995), 'human nature' as such does not define the contents of a good life; rather, accepted notions of a good life, even if deeply embedded in individuals, are mainly the result of social processes and conditioning, and so do not automatically deserve a privileged position.

For the limited purposes of a political philosophy serving as a basis for redesigning governance, I suggest a selective synthesis of the three basic positions discussed above. The importance of social processes in influencing individual notions of a 'good life' must be recognized; thus, the daily realities of consumer societies bombarded by television salesmanship massively shape lifestyles and tastes, becoming part of the notion of a 'good life'. Therefore, the model of independent individuals with autonomous preferences trying to maximize their utilities is largely wrong.

However, as in part demonstrated by the dynamics of the breakdown of the USSR, there is a limit to how far desires can be engineered. Some inner essence of human beings will seek to break out, even if the chances and modes of doing so are strongly influenced by social and cultural forces and individual attributes and life histories. The limits of socialization are also shown by the existence of radical innovators and 'deviants' who transgress beyond dominant cultures and subvert controlling social processes.[7] But this inner essence of human beings is not necessarily all 'good'. It includes also a great potential for evil, as shown by the ease with which students can be motivated in experiments to inflict pain (Milgram, 1974), and, at its worst, in the willing participation of ordinary Germans in Nazi factories of death (Browning, 1992).

This proposed position has far-reaching implications for the tasks of governance. As well put by Elias:

> ...if in this or that region, the power of central authority grows, if over a large or smaller area people are forced to live at peace with one another, the molding of affects and the standards of the economy of instincts are very gradually changed as well. (Elias, 1978, p. 201)

The ramifications are radical: If we want to achieve changes in basic social realities, such as reducing human suffering, eliminating warfare, and increasing global equity, and if we want to do so democratically and in accordance with the will of citizens, governance must influence accepted notions of a 'good life'. For example, these must include much human empathy and solidarity.

The tendency to ignore and downgrade the importance of governance in facilitating a good moral life, however conceived, is understandable in view of liberal values, a belief in the innate goodness of human beings, and well-founded fears of opening a Pandora's Box by letting governments engage in value-inculcation. However, to rely on 'spontaneous' social processes and 'innate' human nature to assure high moral standards and an ethically justifiable meaning of the 'good life' is a chimera and a dangerous one at that. (Views of the individual and his fulfillment in terms of a postulated 'sovereign self' are, therefore, to be rejected morally, psychologically and sociologically [Broembsen, 1999]).

It follows that the various streams of 'communitarianism' (Etzioni, 1996) illustrate utopian illusions on the capacity of social processes and well-wishing actors to bring about in modern and complex societies a better moral order. Social virtues, such as 'trust' (Fukuyama, 1995) cannot be relied upon to develop spontaneously on a larger-than-tribal scale. Prophets can play an important role, but an unpredictable one, leading to evil as often as to good. An active role for governance in advancing moral notions of a 'good life' is thus an important possibility and, under some conditions, perhaps a necessity. But this depends on making governance itself more moral, and on imposing strict limitations on governmental 'soulcraft' (Will, 1983; Rose, 1990) activities.

Two premises lead to a contrary conclusion: that reducing the moral education efforts of governance will somehow help more moral notions of the 'good life' to emerge through various social processes; and that governance 'soulcraft' is sure to have negative effects, such as undermining democracy. However, in my estimation, the first of these premises has no strong empirical or theoretical underpinning, while the second is not compelling, though the risks of involving governance in moral education must be taken very seriously, and excesses strictly guarded against.

An additional consideration is that many social processes which may well become more pronounced in the first half of the twenty-first century carry a high risk of leading towards morally unacceptable, 'spontaneous' conceptions of the 'good life' being accepted by many individuals. Traumatization caused by globalization, xenophobia aggravated by culturally different immigrants, tribalist reactions to post-modernity – these are only some of the likely processes casting grave doubts on optimistic views of the expected standards of individuals free from the 'bondage' of moral education. To be added to this is the possibility that post-modern democracy may incubate anti-democratic and anti-humanistic values, as happened before the Second World War (Talmon, 1952; Sternhall, 1996). If this should happen, then the need for governance to engage in moral education, even through legislation (George, 1993), becomes essential for the protection of democracy itself. But this must be done cautiously, pluralistically and with strict safeguards.

Therefore, my recommendation is as follows: *subject to strict safeguards, governance should engage in a limited amount of moral education, facilitating pluralistic ethical notions of a 'good life', individually and collectively, within a pan-human context*. 'Moral education' should here be understood in a broad sense, including the inhibition of 'hate speech' in the mass media and internet, senior politicians giving an example of highly moral behavior, moral discussion in school curricula, and more.

Such activities should be based on a broad democratic consensus and the respect for minority views within broad limits. But the participation of governance in moral education should be immobilized neither by libertarian misperceptions of the 'sovereignty' of given human desires, by the ethical nihilism and exaggerated relativism of 'political correctness'; nor by blind reliance on diffuse social and economic processes as necessarily producing

highly moral individuals or an over-optimistic reliance on the innate goodness of human beings.

In order to enable governance to take a long-range view, to engage in
moral education and to fulfill in various ways its future-building mission, it
must be based on a sophisticated theory of democracy. A main requirement
of such a theory is that it recognizes that democracy, too, is a mixed regime:
democracies do and must include important components which are isolated
from popular pressures, electoral cycles and the dictates of the here and now.
Ultimate public control over independent parts of governance through constitutional amendments and similar extraordinary and difficult processes
preserves the integrity of 'sovereignty of the people' as a basic norm of democracy. But this norm in no way eliminates the necessity and legitimacy of
including in democratic governance some carefully constructed components
in the main beyond public and political direction.

A good example of this is the Supreme Court in the USA. While it is in
charge of some highly political decisions with broad policy implications, the
judges, once nominated by the President and approved by the Senate, are
nevertheless protected from the pressures of public opinion. Central banks
in charge of monetary policies, civil service commissions responsible for
senior appointments, electoral commissions controlling voting, tenured or
fixed-term high-level officials – these are additional examples of governance
bodies that are granted substantial autonomy from politicians and public
opinion. The Independent Election Commission in India is a prime example
of the necessity for such bodies, not only for strengthening long-term considerations, but also for the maintenance of democracy itself.

To improve capacity to govern, and in particular to strengthen future-
shaping abilities, *political philosophy should therefore recognize both the nature of democracy
as a mixed regime and the need to strengthen components enjoying substantial autonomy from
politics and public opinion, though ultimately subordinated to special democratic processes.*

Not only is a more sophisticated theory of democracy needed, but also a
novel one that refocuses democracy on the crucial task of building the future.
This was a main interest of early modern political thinking (Oestreich, 1982;
Collini et al., 1983; Fernandez-Santamaria, 1983), but has been excluded from
the center of modern discussions on democracy. However, ongoing global
transformations require governments to be active in guiding future-building
processes. To do so effectively, in terms of normative values, *a new democratic
political philosophy is needed. This political philosophy should re-assert the primacy of
politics and focus on the overall responsibility of governance for taking care of the future
in an open-ended way (not presuming to 'plan' it!), as far as is humanly possible.*

The cognitive requirements for trying to influence the future aggravate the
classical problem of the relations between power and knowledge. The tension
between an unwarranted trust in mass views and the increasing political

weight given to opinion polls, on one hand, and the growing ethical and cognitive complexity of major policy issues, on the other, cannot but reduce the quality of democratic choice processes. Further depressing the performance of democracy is the growing influence of economic power, together with the increasing impact of narrow interest groups and zealous movements and organizations. Exaggerated trust in populist movements, non-governmental organizations, market processes and an ill-defined 'civil society' further aggravate the downgrading of politics in contemporary political philosophy.

What is needed instead is a political philosophy which bases the long-term thriving of democracy on upgrading the moral and cognitive faculties of its main bearers. This should include the edification of the population as a whole, the advancement of new types of public-interest elites, and the upgrading of governance staffs and politicians – leading to what could be termed 'quality democracy' based both on morality and knowledge.

The importance of new elites in the proposed conception of democracy should be recognized. On an operational level, it is possible to work out proposals on developing and improving governance elites, and I will do so in Chapter Twelve. But working out a political-philosophy foundation for a novel concept of 'moral and knowledge elites' and their roles in governance – this requires another Pareto, Mosca, or perhaps Kant. However, let me at least remove a road-block by emphasizing that, from a political philosophy perspective, sophisticated democratic theory is compatible with a conception of plural governance elites in the role of quasi-guardians, provided that a number of strict conditions are met: governance should be transparent; governance as a whole must be subordinated to elections and other clear expressions of public preferences; governance elites must be open, representative, and pluralistic; rotation within them must be assured, and entrance into the elites should be based on elections and merit; election rules should permit the public to reach informed views on candidates; officials should be chosen and promoted on the basis of demanding criteria adapted to the needs of governance in a period of transformations; and a strict code of ethics should oblige the whole of the governance elite, including elected politicians, to meet exacting standards of quality, virtue and accountability, rigorously enforced.

Also, and most importantly of all, in order to maintain a democratic balance between governance and the people, attempts to improve governance elites must go hand in hand with educating the general public, so as to 'enlighten' and inform public opinion and empower people to exert more effective control over governance.

It is up to political philosophy to provide the foundation for a high-morality, high-knowledge democracy. Two essential elements of such a political philosophy are: firstly, vigorous efforts to raise the moral level of the public and popular understanding of complex issues; and, secondly, the development of moral and highly qualified democratic governance elites.

Let me return to the third question posed at the beginning of this chapter. What about societies that prefer, or at least those whose leaders claim that their societies prefer, to advance some collective notion of a 'good life', such as a religious one, rather than to give their citizens a free individual choice? Such societies pose to modern political philosophy the difficult issue of what is the correct moral stance when faced with fundamentalism and other ideologies different from democracy and liberalism, assuming that they pose no threat to the security and well-being of other societies and states.

If most of the population of fundamentalist or ideological countries share such a preference without being forced to do so, their choice should be respected. Provided that some minimum universal moral imperatives are met, such as respect for basic human rights, and they do not constitute a danger to others, no ethical justification exists for trying to impose Western liberal democratic values on countries wishing to live by some other faith or creed. A different conclusion is reached if we regard Western values as so compelling, eternal and universal as to imply a duty to impose them on all human beings, by force if necessary. But such a stance is not only historically, morally and philosophically unjustified; it is also abhorrent to democratic and liberal values themselves and would undermine their coherence and justification.

All countries should be induced to join in global consensus on a growing set of norms, starting with the prohibition of genocide and the Universal Declaration of Human Rights, and continuing with the treaties on economic, social and cultural rights, on women's rights, on children's rights, on civil and political rights, and more to come. But 'inducement' should be different from 'enforcement', and respect should not be denied to societies where there is consensus on following a different belief system, as long as they do not pose a danger to other countries.

This position is open to criticism and is but one of a number of starting points for discussion in political philosophy. A good argument can be made that all countries should be required and, if necessary, forced to respect norms on which there is broad global consensus; and many in the West will claim that Western liberal democratic values are so obviously superior that their supporters have a moral right and, indeed, duty to propagate them and convince others to adopt them, applying pressure when necessary. To strengthen such a claim, it may be argued that the apparent agreement by the inhabitants of a country to subordinate individual notions of the good life in line with Western thinking to some collective ideal is the result of brainwashing, underdevelopment, and ignorance. Therefore, so the reasoning continues, all societies should be pressed to adopt an individualistic and liberal notion of the good life, because this is the only 'reasonable' and 'moral' one conceivable, which all human beings are sure to prefer once they become 'enlightened'. The same applies to democracy as a political ideology to be enjoyed by all, and even imposed when this is not too costly (Macdonald, 1992; McDougall, 1997).

In my view, as already indicated, this is a wrong position, historically and anthropologically, psychologically and philosophically, 'realpolitically' and morally. Historically and anthropologically, the fact that other societies regard their values as superior, even though they look to us very strange (if not obviously wrong), should put us on notice that our values too may look bad to others, now or in the future. Psychologically, there is no strong reason to believe that current Western values are better than some other value systems in meeting basic human needs – insofar as this concept has a more than trivial meaning – such as with respect to existential anxieties, the meaning of life, and innate 'religious' feelings. 'Realpolitically', a condescending attitude towards values accepted by others cannot but increase tensions and hostility, with possible violent outcomes. Philosophically, major Western values can be seen as suffering from serious moral weaknesses – for example in adopting narrow egocentric and hedonistic views of the 'good life', encouraging greed and the enjoyment of affluence and conspicuous consumption even in the knowledge of the deprivation and suffering of others (Lipson, 1993; Solzhenitsyn, 1995). Morally, to impose Western values on others constitutes in effect, even if not in intention, a new form of cultural imperialism, often coupled with gross distortions of the realities of other cultures and belief systems (Said, 1979; Tomlinson, 1991; Said, 1993).

An ethics of tolerance and pluralism (Walzer, 1983; Kekes, 1993) prevents us from imposing Western values on other societies, with a very important but limited exception: namely, the condemnation, prevention and punishment of atrocities, such as apartheid, mass killing, the systematic use of terror and torture and other forms of the repression of basic human rights. Such actions violate moral imperatives that our conscience and values oblige us to defend and enforce universally, though in reality we do so very selectively and sporadically – a fact that further undermines the moral foundations of our claim to tell others what to do and not to do.

Competition between cultures, and the learning of one from another, contribute to the progress of humanity as a whole. Thus, propagation of one's own – and other – values can be justified as long as the methods are restrained. Moral judgments on others' values are also legitimate, as long as the rights of others to hold contrary opinions are acknowledged – including the rejection of extreme versions of 'political correctness' (Taylor, 1992).

Nevertheless, from a historical and global perspective and in terms of a pan-human, pluralistic political philosophy, no single value system can claim absolute, universal validity. However, we perhaps can, and certainly should, enforce what we regard as absolute moral imperatives. This obligation stands even when we know that others not only may resist our efforts, but might even be morally justified and also obliged to do so in terms of their own beliefs.

Closely related to this are the crucial issues in political philosophy posed by the need to develop what I propose to call *raison d'humanité*, understood as a constructive substitute for the concept of *raison d'état*. It expresses the idea that humanity as a whole has needs and aspirations that all forms of governance should promote.

In essence, *raison d'humanité* radically revises some fundamental principles and rules of political philosophy and their derivatives in public international law: countries that pose a threat to the needs of humankind as a whole should be kept in check; countries ruled by fanatics must be prevented from possessing weapons of mass killing; the 'global commons' must be regulated, and in part preserved and improved; crimes against humanity must be punished, including the individual leaders responsible; and so on, as further discussed in Chapter Nine. Here, it is enough to stress the urgent need for political philosophy to develop the idea of *raison d'humanité* as a major task.

The notion of *raison d'humanité* provides another perspective on the problem of societies wishing to live by values very different from liberal democratic ones. Even if we recognize and respect this right, the costs of some kinds of pluralism for humankind as a whole may be too high, because they may lead to dangerous cultural conflicts. However, *raison d'humanité* also implies that there should be a variety of value systems, so as to provide a greater range of possibilities for the future.[8] The risks of fanatical value systems must therefore be weighed against the costs of too little value pluralism, in the context of specific situations. It is easy to invoke arguments based on *raison d'humanité* in order to censure and attack societies whose value systems we happen to dislike, but which are not really dangerous to others; but there are also risks in being too tolerant of belief systems that may lead to dangerous fanaticism.

To sharpen the underlying issues of political philosophy, let us consider the argument that birth rates must be reduced if living standards are to improve, even though the increases in world population are expected to level off in the first part of the twenty-first century. Such a policy is regarded by many societies as immoral and contrary to religious imperatives, as an aggressive interference in private and intimate family decisions, an effort to prevent people from following what they regard as a moral obligation and as a gross infringement of the independence of states and the freedom of citizens. By contrast, the reduction of high birth rates is considered by many as essential for the future of humanity, because of the limited carrying capacity of planet earth (Hardin, 1993); countries that avoid effective measures against high birth rates can thus be regarded by proponents of birth control as 'free riders' who expect others to bail them out from economic and ecological consequences.

Governance for the twenty-first century must be able to deal with the scientific and political dimensions of such issues, with all their uncertainties, and enforce policies that a majority considers compelling and a minority as contradicting basic values. For this to happen, new institutions and forms of legitimization of global governance must be developed. However, on a deeper level, a political philosophy fully bringing out the moral reasoning involved in such dilemmas is a prerequisite for building up societal and governance capacities to deal seriously with such issues.

One of the most difficult moral issues facing humanity in the twenty-first century is that of global equity and justice. This includes the reduction of glaring inequalities in standards of living and human development; the assurance of minimum levels of security and human rights for all; the sharing of costs for taking care of the global commons (preserving the rainforests, maintaining biogenetic diversity, and so on); the assurance of equitable access to science and technology and their uses (UNESCO, 1994), and much more. In reality, such issues are handled (more correctly – mishandled) mainly in terms of *realpolitik*, accompanied by high-sounding rhetoric and inadequate expressions of worry about 'others' and the common future. The overall reality is a moral disgrace for humanity, with many enjoying luxuries while many more suffer serious deprivation, without the first doing much for the second or being deeply troubled by their misery.

A good example is the growing tendency in some Western literature to advocate de facto disengagement of the rich countries from the poor and turbulent ones (Rufin, 1991; Singer and Wildavski, 1996), leaving the latter more or less to their fate. (Not unlike the idea of a *cordon sanitaire*, as established by the West in the eighteenth century against the pestilence from the East [Hawthorn, 1991, chapter 2]). This illustrates the moral scandal resulting from the paucity of notions of justice and equity appropriate to the needs of the twenty-first century.

Ideas alone will not rectify this situation. But, though insufficient, convincing moral discourse is essential for injecting ethical considerations into 'realpolitical' thought and action, and for guiding well-intended efforts that at present are often misdirected.

Also essential is moral education directed at increasing human solidarity. There is no factual basis for supposing that people will be more sensitive to each other's problems as a result of growing mutual dependence. Empathy with the continuous suffering of others is probably rapidly replaced in most people by compassion fatigue (Spiaerenburgh, 1984). Hence the need for deliberate efforts to foster feelings of human togetherness. Commercial endeavors can also contribute much to meeting this need. The television program 'Star Trek', in its various continuations, is an example of the way high moral values and human solidarity can be dramatized in the mass media so as to attract and educate a mass audience, while also enjoying commercial success.

A vivid example of the need for new qualities of moral reasoning on complex global issues is posed by the hypothesis that the severe and lethal droughts of Africa are a boon for life elsewhere. This may be the case, since they probably supply vital minerals to plankton in the Atlantic Ocean and enrich nutrient-poor soils in the Americas so that vegetation there increases. A Solomonic judge, a Platonic philosopher-king, or a Confucian sage-ruler would be hard put to decide what to do in such a case. But it is up to improved moral reasoning and a novel political philosophy to at least supply guidelines for considering such increasingly acute issues.

It is interesting, as well as necessary for any progress in this area, to ponder the reasons for the backwardness of political philosophy and moral reasoning in dealing with issues of global equity, with the exceptions of a few preliminary explorations (Küng, 1991; Attfield and Wilkins, 1992; Nardin and Maple, 1992; Thompson, 1992; Dunn, 1993; Miller, 1993; Küng, 1995). One reason may well be the preoccupation with issues of equity and justice in certain countries; but I suspect that a main cause for this neglect, consciously or unconsciously, is the desire to evade conclusions that are anathema.

Any serious moral discourse on global equity cannot but reach the conclusion that there are strong ethical arguments for massive transfers of resources from the rich to the poor countries, subject to safeguards that these are used for human and economic development. The argument that charitable transfer of resources is often not really necessary, and may even be counterproductive if not done carefully, has some basis in fact (Fairbanks *et al.*, 1997). But it applies only to particular forms of transfer and in no way diminishes the moral seriousness of issues of global equity, and the unavoidable conclusion that the large-scale transfer of resources is a moral imperative.[9]

However, this conclusion is very unwelcome to the rich countries, imposing not only high economic costs but raising the very troublesome likelihood of immoral consequences of democracy if majorities prevent the transfer of resources, however morally imperative.

Whatever the reasons may be, moral discourse and political philosophy have not developed enough of the concepts, tools, methods, forms of reasoning and norms needed to cope with global issues. This is all the more serious a lacuna because notions of justice, once accepted by governance elites, do exert a considerable influence on state behavior (Welch, 1993), as Thucydides clearly recognized (Johnson, 1993, chapter 2 and conclusion), despite extreme versions of so-called 'realist' schools of international relations. Therefore, *the development of an ethics of global equity is one of the most important tasks awaiting political philosophy*.

Further demonstrating the inadequacies of political philosophy, as well as raising additional questions on democracy, is the issue of the applicability of democracy to emerging global governance. It is hard to imagine the Western democratic countries agreeing to a 'one person – one vote' basis for any global governance institutions, with the former becoming a minority; and it is doubtful whether by any moral standards they should agree to apply democracy to the global system, given present international realities. But the difficulties posed to democratic political philosophy by the non-application of democracy to humanity as a whole are serious, and ignoring them makes the matter even more problematic.

The World Federalists, and similar movements, are careful not to apply democracy on a global scale, but do so surreptitiously (Glossop, 1993).[10] Nor is the issue solved by the World Order Models Project (Falk, 1975; Falk, Johansen and Kim, 1993), by proponents of 'cosmopolitan democracy' (Archibugi and Held, 1995) and by other thinkers trying to deal with it (Held, 1995; Hall, 1996; Gorbatschow, Sagladin and Tschernjajew, 1997). Moreover, initiatives to call a 'Peoples' Assembly' at the United Nations, however interesting, in no way serve as a step towards 'global democracy' in any reasonable sense of that term.

However, once the principle of democracy is limited in applicability, its claim to universality is broken, opening the harsh question: Where are the borders between domains where democracy does and does not apply? Leaving aside the implications for the philosophy and theory of democracy, a new political philosophy applicable to a global regime is clearly required. In its absence, proposals for the improvement of global governance are ameliorative, but do not really touch on basic issues and real needs. The *development of a basis in political philosophy for global governance, including adjustments in the philosophy of democracy, is an urgent necessity*.

From the point of views of human values, one of the most distressing features of history is the lack of any positive correlation between the morality and immorality of behavior and consequent earthly achievements. Indeed, if any correlation can be discerned, a negative one seems more pronounced than a positive one. In theology this leads to the central problems of theodicy – the justice of God and the place of God in human history. In political philosophy the problem is especially acute, because any realistic treatment of statecraft must recommend a great deal of amoral, and even immoral, behavior. The issue of 'dirty hands' must therefore be central to political philosophy (Buckler, 1993; Scharfstein, 1995), all the more so since immoral behavior is often conducive, and also necessary, for the rise of nations, the thriving of societies and the success of politicians, and not only for dealing with 'foul problems'. These are problems which are inherently 'dirty' and immoral, such as whether to assassinate a terrorist who may be planning to use weapons of mass destruction while hiding in a country that refuses to extradite him.

A few aspects of the problem do receive some attention, such as lying in politics and the idea of a 'just war' (Walzer, 1977; Bok, 1979). But other essential dimensions are ignored, or else dealt with in ways that are both simplistic and hypocritical.

To put the moral issue of dirty hands into sharp focus, let us consider two test cases, one hypothetical but not unrealistic, and the second quite real. Let us assume, following the 'ticking bomb' issue suggested by Michael Walzer, that a group of terrorists has planted a nuclear bomb in a large city. The bomb will soon be detonated and is expected to kill millions of people. The only way to prevent this catastrophe is to force a terrorist who has been caught to reveal the location of the bomb and the code to deactivate it. How far should we go to get him to give us this essential information?

At first we would try humane arguments and routine psychological and light 'third degree' pressures. But assuming these fail, should we torture him? And, if this were to no avail, should we torture before his eyes his young wife and innocent young daughter until he reveals the information that will save millions of lives?

The second test case involves 'constitutional dictatorship', which may well be of increasing importance in the foreseeable future, but is nearly completely ignored in modern political philosophy.

In short, in some circumstances it may be justified to suspend democracy and human rights, and even use draconian measures in order to overcome Hobbesian situations, or enforce essential but very painful restructuring. An example might include a former communist country trying to move towards democracy and a market economy, but sliding into anarchy. Would it be justified to suspend the new democratic constitution for a couple of years and allow strong direct rule by a dictator – hopefully an enlightened one, although we can never be sure about that in advance? And what about summary justice against the mafia, who are enriching themselves, corrupting officials, terrorizing entrepreneurs and frightening away investors?

Another even more radical example would be the decision to subject certain countries to interim international supervision, perhaps even full-scale occupation, in order to deal with extreme situations such as those found in some areas of Africa.

Hence the need for an appropriate political philosophy which can serve as an ethical basis for modern versions of the classical Roman institution of 'constitutional dictatorship', and also 'humanitarian occupation', while suggesting strict criteria for applying such regimes. I will return to this very important issue in Chapter Twenty-One.

To serve as a strong grounding for future-building governance in the twenty-first century, political philosophy must take up additional issues. To give just a few illustrations:

- There is scope for developing a new idea of 'euergetism', a neologism referring to the duty of the rich to contribute their wealth to the public good and to public service (Veyne, 1990, pp. 10–13), in line with the founders of public interest foundations (Fest, 1997).

- Many currently fashionable slogans, such as 'sustainable development' and 'global village' need skeptical evaluation, in order to help counter misleading frames of thinking and wrongly postulated pseudo-values distorting deliberation.
- Substantial iconoclasm, along with the deconstruction of orthodoxies within political philosophy, as well as more attention to the irreducible aporia of politics (Beardsworth, 1996, for example p. 98) and governance are urgently needed, as essential bases for a restructured and, at the same time, self-critical and self-restraining capacity to govern.
- Going beyond the domains of political philosophy in a narrow sense, but still essential, is a renewed genre of utopias to propose ideals and explore issues of governance for and in the future. Such utopias are nowadays very few and of doubtful quality.[11]

Finally, and firstly, political philosophy must reassert the moral centrality of politics as part of its revitalization. Markets, civil-society actors, public interest groups, and so on, have important functions to fulfill. But none of them has the legitimacy of being democratically elected, and none of them has the right to claim to represent the public interest as a whole; only politics can do so in principle. Politics should therefore be in charge of collective action.

It is true that, in fact, much of politics is incompetent and corrupt and often inferior in intentions and deeds to the actions of other social actors, including some private enterprises. Furthermore, the damage to humanity caused by bad governance is often much greater than that caused by other destructive actors. Evil governments are a major danger to humanity – much more so than greedy enterprises and misguided individuals.

However, such realities must not block normative thinking, which clearly puts 'good' democratic politics on high moral ground when future-building is required. Only if one accepts the extreme position that there is no hope of achieving 'good' politics might another conclusion be reached. But such a position is both historically unjustified and fatal for the future of humanity, as no other social process can overcome the irreversible damage surely to be caused by bad politics and stupid governance, equipped as they are with the powerful instruments supplied by science and technology. Indeed, it is the very prevalence of bad governance that makes reassertion of the high stature of good politics all the more essential, so as to set standards and challenges for improvement and redesign.

One of the most insidious dangers of contemporary downgrading of the missions of politics and governance is an increasing acceptance of bad government as a 'fact of nature'. This leads to the reduction of the tasks of governments, the hypertrophy of control and accountability, and the increasing reliance on other processes and institutions, such as free markets and civil society. Up to a point this is a correct strategy, on grounds of both principle and practice. But it cannot be applied to crucial future-influencing tasks which only governments can handle. And, worst of all, it constitutes a self-fulfilling prophecy sure to make politics worse instead of improving their moral and cognitive capacities as normatively imperative and practically essential.

Modern Western political philosophy carries a heavy burden of guilt for this slippery slope.[12] Instead of renewing the idea of the 'noble science of politics (Collini *et al.*, 1983) and working out its implications for governance in the twenty-first century, it is captive to fashions, genuflexions before the idols of the market, and is passive in the face of the declining quality of much of politics.

A first task for political philosophy is therefore to reassert the primacy of politics and governance as in charge of collective choice, and to provide a normative grounding enabling them to fulfill their calling under the demanding conditions of the twenty-first century.

NOTES

1. To provide only two examples from the rich literature bringing out the complex relations between political philosophies and their underlying belief systems, social and environmental variables, chance factors and the evolution of governance, Gernet (1996) and Eisenstadt (1996) are recommended because of the rich historic panoramas they provide.

   Deuchler (1993) is focused on the specific impacts of new belief systems on society and governance.

2. The commonly used term in English 'weapons of mass destruction' (WMD) is inadequate, the proposed term 'weapons of mass killing' (WMK) expressing more correctly what is at stake.

3. Central features of Nazism are clearly related to details of the history of Germany and unique features of Hitler. The Third Reich was thus a unique phenomenon that will not repeat itself. But many of the social processes producing Nazism and other atrocious movements in the twentieth century will become even more acute in the twenty-first century, with a great likelihood of producing other grave forms of evil. This can already be seen in parts of Africa. Therefore, the tendency of Western public discourse and social sciences to assume 'goodness' as the most prevalent condition sure to accompany 'development' is wrong; and the refusal to draw general theoretical and practical conclusions from the case of Nazi Germany constitutes a dangerous case of collective 'mind blindness' (Kosslyn and Koenig, 1992, pp. 111–13).

4. Contemporary conflict studies and negotiation theories suffer from the same misconception, assuming that there is always a shared interest and that some agreement is possible. Applied to British cabinet decision-making after Nazi Germany overran France, such approaches would have resulted in Great Britain seeking an accommodation with Germany that surely would have been disastrous. As shown by a recent detailed historic study, this is not hypothetical 'virtual history' (Ferguson, 1997) but nearly happened (Lukacs, 1999).

5. The InterAction Council, the association of former heads of government, proposed in 1997 that the Universal Declaration of Human Rights should be supplemented by a Universal Declaration of Human Responsibilities (and, I would add, 'duties'). Similar proposals have also been made by the Club of Rome.

6. The subject is discussed in the growing literature for and against sociobiology, on 'human nature', cultural evolution, evolutionary psychology and so on. Texts illustrating different approaches include Budzieszewski, 1986, Maryanski and Turner, 1992, and Wright, 1994.

7. A striking example of the ability of a non-privileged individual to create for himself a different 'cosmos' is presented in Ginzburg, 1980.

8. This also applies to economic regimes, the present absence of any options other than free-market models being very undesirable, both on principle and because of possible growing costs, and also because of breakdowns of the single available alternative. The situation is all the more problematic because differences between so-called 'liberal economic systems' and 'social-democratic economic systems' are minimal and further diminishing. Declarations on a 'third way' lack as yet any concrete content posing an alternative to free markets (Giddens, 1999 and Giddens, 2000a). This is also true of declarations of heads of state that they are following a 'progressive option'.

9. This is the case even without taking up cases of what can be called 'historic accounting', such as compensation for the damage caused to the evolutionary potential of Black Africa by the slave trade, colonial occupations, the take-over of land, genocide in some areas, and so on.

10. I had opportunities to raise questions on global democracy with proponents of a world federation, peoples assembly etc. Their usual response was one of obvious embarrassment and displeasure at being forced to admit that democracy should not apply 'at present' to global governance.

11. For important surveys and discussions of modern utopias, see Saage, 1997 and Fil, 1997, esp. pp. 158-65. For a case study bringing out the importance of utopias and utopian thinking in bringing about new realities, see Elboim-Dror, 1993.

12. On the logic of slippery slope arguments, on which I rely several times in my argumentation, see Walton, 1992.

PART ONE
THE PROBLEMATIC

3

Unprepared Societies and Obsolete Governance

The situation of humanity in the face of global transformations can be summarized in two sentences: Societies are unprepared; Governance is unequipped.

People learn to use new technologies and alter their lifestyles with relative ease, and often with eagerness. However, as shown by many studies on acculturation of immigrants and on the meetings between traditional societies and modernity and post-modernity, this adjustment tends to be mainly instrumental, involving external behavior, rather than deep inner learning. This is even truer of many social institutions, which are usually quite rigid and often, with some important exceptions, respond to rapid change mainly by becoming entrenched in increasingly obsolete positions.

When change is slow, and human and societal adjustments occur gradually, then individual and institutional rigidities have their advantages, because they provide a sense of continuity and restrain recklessness. Even when change in some areas is rapid, lags in individual and social adjustment often do no harm and may serve to reduce trauma and maintain continuity in selfhood. Thus, the relatively long time it took to adapt to the invention of printing entailed costs in lost opportunities, but did not cause any lasting damage. The situation today, however, is dramatically different. The massive changes currently under way and likely to approach a mutation in the twenty-first century, open up new possibilities for social evolution, with enormous and open-ended prospects for the better – but also for the worse (Kirdar, 1992; Schwab, 1995). The unprecedented speed, scale and depth of these changes require that we learn to cope with them swiftly and effectively (Michael, 1997). Failure to do so will not only incur short-term costs, but increases the danger of serious consequences and of missing long-term opportunities.

The continuation and escalation of tribal warfare in Africa with modern weapons, coupled with atrocities in part caused by the erosion of traditional institutions and values without modern ones taking their place, serve as horrible illustrations of this possibility. But this is a relatively limited case in comparison to what is likely to happen if present incapacities continue.

35

Thus, high levels of population growth, rapidly increasing energy consumption, degradation of essential natural resources, disparities between rich and poor, cultural conflicts, and so on, carry huge risks. Apocalyptic visions (Meadows *et al.*, 1992) are exaggerated. But wars with biological or nuclear weapons, killing millions, remain a constant danger.[1] New forms of barbarism feeding on widespread traumatization and existential despair (Mestrovic, 1993) may turn the world into a high-technology Hell worthy of the imagination of a Dante. But most dangerous of all is an inability to guide the development and uses of new technologies that may undermine the very existence of *homo sapiens*, without an improved humanity taking its place.

To put it differently, societies and governments unprepared for radical changes are sure to get lost in shifting labyrinths dense with misery, with rapidly closing doors of opportunity, and even with 'killing fields'. High-quality thinking and action to cope with a very promising, but also truly precarious, future are thus more urgent than ever. Nevertheless, main social guidance clusters (Etzioni, 1968) can be relied upon to continue and speed up their 'march of folly'[2] unless radically redesigned – including, as already pointed out, the resuscitation of politics and refocusing of democracy and governance.

Admittedly, some parts of some governance systems appear ready and able to engage in adequate learning, as are some grass-roots initiatives and non-governmental organizations. At least one new governmental structure better suited to new needs has emerged, although increasingly it shows new incapacities: the European Union. Moreover, some governments do occasionally surpass themselves and adopt outstanding policies. However, in the main contemporary governance is obsolete and unable to deal fittingly with rapidly mutating problems and opportunities.

The chief inadequacies of governance in coping with the challenges posed by global transformations will be discussed in the first part of the book. The second part will propose some redesigns directed at upgrading capacities to govern, so as to enable governments to engage effectively with the main tasks, including future-building. These two areas are not, however, rigidly separated. In analyzing the problematic,[3] the foundations will be laid for the resolution; and in the resolution, further important aspects of the problem will come to light.

NOTES

1. The future of violence, including warfare but going far beyond it, and the challenges which its prevention, or appropriate use, pose to capacities to govern require a book by themselves. Inter alia, the nature of some wars as a cultural phenomenon with deep psychological roots – as distinct from the Clausewitzian instrumental-rational conception of the continuation of politics, must be recognized (Creveld, 1991; Keegan, 1993; Keegan, 1995).

2. I borrow this concept from Tuchman, 1984. But care should be taken in reading this book: some of the examples are incorrect, and no serious explanation for the failures is offered.

3. This being a Report to the Club of Rome, I am using its 'problematique' and 'resolu-tique' terminology. But the use of the latter term does not imply that the problematic can be 'resolved'. The redesign proposals can hopefully improve capacities to govern sufficiently for coping adequately with opportunities and dangers. However, no serious social problematique can be fully 'resolved' in the twenty-first century when problem areas will change all the time, often faster than any resolution.

4

Predicaments and Opportunities

Governance must function in the real world; it is not a matter of hypothetical systems existing in the abstract. Improvements in governance therefore have to be adjusted to existing and anticipated processes, institutions, traditions, cultures, values, resources, conditions and environments. Theoretically, also, no universally optimal model of governance does or can exist: Within given or accepted normative parameters – which also must change, in part, to fit changing environments, tasks and values – the preferable characteristics of governance depend on many variables, shifting with time, and in particular on its main missions and environments, which are dynamically evolving. Consequently, before identifying the tasks of governance and working out required redesigns, we need to look at the environments within which governance will have to operate in the foreseeable future and the problem domains with which it will have to cope.

But, first, it should be noted that in an epoch of transformations governance systems that have performed well in the past also require redesign to assure good performance under the different conditions of the future. *A fortiori*, this is the case with governance that has often performed dismally under relatively less demanding situations. In turn, redesigns which may fit situations in the next fifty years or so very well are sure to be in need of re-redesigns when conditions shift again beyond what has been foreseen and imagined.

It follows that different countries need quite different governance systems in terms of both principles and structure. Governance in such democracies as India and The Netherlands thus is and has to be different in significant respects. Countries with different political ideologies and theologies, such as China and Iran, have and require unique governance setups. Moreover, leaving aside sub-state governance, with which this book is not concerned, governments of states are different in crucial respects from higher-level governance, such as that of either the European Union or the United Nations system.

Nevertheless, all governments share major features and thus need redesigns based on the same or similar principles. This is the result of identical core components, such as top decision-makers and their staffs, and of shared tasks, such as assuring security, collecting and allocating resources, regulating the commons and engaging at least to some extent in future-building.

The increasing integration of the world system and the growing impact of globalization further augment the shared features of all states, enlarging the applicability of the design principles developed in this book. They need careful adjustment to particular settings, but largely fit all governments – although excluding areas lacking a functioning political process, such as parts of Africa, where first of all a working polity has to be established.

However viewed, preferable redesigns of governance depend significantly on specific situations, conditions and problems. Some exploration of expected realities is therefore essential. In this context, I concentrate on select features that are of paramount importance for the redesign of governance; I leave an overall discussion of alternative futures, uncertainties and unthinkable contingencies to the proliferating literature presuming to serve as a crystal ball into the future – though most of it is sure to be wrong, and all of it should be taken with a ton, rather than a pinch, of salt.

For our purposes, ten characteristics of global change are especially relevant:

(1) Rapid non-liner change.
(2) Increasing uncertainty and inconceivability.
(3) Globalization.
(4) Multiplying complexity.
(5) Powerful global actors.
(6) Growing prosperity coexisting with increasing inequality.
(7) Intense frustrations, trauma, despondency and unrest.
(8) The likelihood of harm and evil.
(9) A lot of conflict and violence.
(10) All the changes leading to mutations.

(1) RAPID NON-LINEAR CHANGE

Non-linear change is characteristic of human life and long-term history as a whole (Brown, 1995). But our epoch is distinguished by unusually rapid non-liner change, without the long intervals of relative stability, 'more of the same' or incremental change, change that was characteristic of most of human history. Even when some parameters seem to change in a linear fashion, such as population sizes, the curves change direction within less than one generation and the effects are even more non-linear, with qualitatively new attributes emerging once populations grow, or decline, or change in composition, beyond rapidly reached thresholds.

If a longer timespan is taken into account, change assumes a 'hyper-heraclitean' format: not only can we never bath again in the same water because it is constantly streaming, as Heraclitus is quoted as having said, but the river can become a volcano, and the volcano may suddenly bring forth pure water to become a river again.

Taken as a whole, the situation of humanity, its environments and artefacts, and the interface between them, is mutating, approaching a phase transition, or even a series of mutations – with crucial implications for required governance capacities. However, the 'wiring' of human beings is not changing, though the border lines between fixed 'hard wiring' and partly changing 'behavior and consciousness' programs, to use computer metaphors widely accepted in the modern cognitive sciences, are not known.

Governance must therefore amplify its capacities to cope with non-linear change, up to mutation, though many core features and potentials of the basic element out of which it is made, namely human beings, are unchanging.

(2) INCREASING UNCERTAINTY AND INCONCEIVABILITY

The future is always the product of a dynamic combination of necessity, contingency, chance and choice. In a period of global transformations such as the twenty-first century is sure to be, the part allotted to what human beings perceive as contingency and chance seems especially large. Interactions between various factors within complex systems (Jervis, 1997), such as demography, technology, values, etc., further increase the uncertainties inherent in each and add up to inconceivability, in the sense of results qualitatively different from what we expect and can predict.

Uncertainty and 'unthinkable' surprises increase the further ahead we try to look. But already the first part of the twenty-first century is difficult to predict, because some key factors are changing very rapidly and in a non-linear fashion. Observers of the sudden collapse of the Soviet Empire need no convincing that we are living through a period of extraordinary upheavals.[1]

Beyond uncertainty lies 'the unthinkable', when the very qualities of the future are beyond our conceptions and inaccessible to our minds, other than by sometimes wild imagination. A strong demonstration is given by Karl Popper: we can be quite certain that radically new scientific knowledge with profound implications for humanity will emerge; but the contents and impact of that new knowledge is by definition beyond our present knowledge – otherwise it would not be 'radically new' (in the sense of 'radical innovation' proposed by Hausman (1984)). Ergo, we are facing a kind of finding of ignorance. We know that it is certain that developments beyond our present thinking are sure to come about, and that 'much more is real than possible', to borrow a paradoxical formulation from the German philosopher Hans Jonas (quoted in Münz (1995), p. 75 in reference to the *Shoah*).[2]

However, in spite of uncertainty and inconceivability, there are underlying trends that allow us to make at least an informed 'guesstimate', to use a RAND Corporation term, and sometimes quite a reliable prediction of some likely predicaments and opportunities. Provided, therefore, that we make due reservations and think of the future also in terms of discontinuities and alternatives, no paralyzing nihilism is justified. However, to enable governance to cope well with often overwhelming uncertainty and inconceivability, radical redesigns are essential: *Governance must build up:*

(1) Ability to ponder choices in terms of uncertainty.
(2) Tolerance for ambiguity.
(3) High-quality professionalism in outlook.
(4) Decision methods reducing sensitivity to uncertainty.
(5) Propensities for rapid learning.
(6) Improved improvisation and crisis decision-making.

The implications of uncertainty and possibilities beyond imagination are even more radical. Because of them nearly all decisions aimed at having long-term impacts are in essence 'fuzzy gambles', sometimes for high stakes. This conception of governments as 'policy gambles' is of paramount importance, and is discussed in Chapter Fifteen.

(3) GLOBALIZATION

Thanks to modern information technologies, mass media and rapid transport networks – but also to increasingly shared economic systems, values, cultural factors (Featherstone, 1990), aspirations and the use of common terminology – the world is becoming more and more interactive. Interconnections become more dense, and links become tighter, with an increasing number of reality-shaping processes being truly 'global' in nature, as illustrated by financial markets, the drug trade and possible global warming. Social distances decrease, with global elites being formed. All this adds up to accelerated movement towards an intensely interactive global system – what is called 'globalization'.

This globalization is self-accelerating, being advanced by its internal dynamics and by special institutions, such as the World Trade Organization. Though a 'modern world-system' has been in the making for the last few hundred years (Wallerstein, 1974), globalization is new in its scope, intensity and penetration, and will become even more dominant in the twenty-first century.

Globalization exerts tremendous pressures on states, while also providing new opportunities. While the extent of state autonomy in the past should not be exaggerated, globalization further reduces it by imposing new conditions on 'competitiveness', forcing structural adjustments, increasing dependence on global economic institutions and limiting the scope of policy alternatives open to single countries. Furthermore, globalization is a major factor pushing towards the formation and strengthening of multi-national structures, ranging from common markets to continental and global governance.

For our purposes, the heated discussion on the advantages and dangers of globalization makes no difference.[3] Whether one is for or against globalization, it is a fact having far-reaching implications for governance. Certainly, globalization is one of the main phenomena requiring significant governance redesign, as will be shown throughout this book: *governments must adjust to globalization, including relinquishing some freedom of action, engaging in structural adjustments, coping with social consequences, and becoming increasingly involved in multi-state and global governance.*

However, very significant social and cultural differences between societies may grow (Kaplan, 1996) rather than diminish, so that it is misleading to talk about 'one world' or 'a global village'. Different histories produce quite diverse, and partly contradictory, versions of modernity and post-modernity, and the globalization process provokes many to say 'no' (Ishihara, 1990), and efforts to strengthen uniqueness.

One must therefore distinguish between two processes which are in a complex dialectic relationship: one, towards the creation of a global civilization, in which many social structures and cultural features are increasingly shared by an ever larger proportion of humanity, especially those with the greatest social and political influence; and a second, towards maintaining and strengthening specific social and cultural features. Japan is a prime illustration of both these processes in interaction, tension and competition (Ivy, 1995; Eisenstadt, 1996). The efforts of Judaism and of Israel to preserve their uniqueness serve as an additional and quite different example (Susser and Liebman, 1999).

The antinomies between these two processes, within and between societies and states and on a global level, can be constructive and lead to pluralistic social and cultural innovations, or can be destructive and lead to conflict. This poses one of the major challenges: *preserving many features of local society and culture and encouraging indigenous social and cultural creativity, while thriving within globalization and facilitating its positive features.*

Doing so demands substantial governance redesign, as will be detailed throughout this book. But some requirements can be derived from the very nature of the challenge: *to cope well with globalization, governments need to understand it, to develop outstanding negotiating skills for interacting with globalization institutions, to become creative in adjusting (while preserving) autonomy, and to concentrate democratic power to implement essential but painful restructuring.*

(4) MULTIPLYING COMPLEXITY

Not only is the amount and intensity of interaction increasing, but major processes are becoming more multifarious. Information technology, for instance, transforms the networks linking producers and consumers and financial markets in ways that are not well understood, and which often take a Kafkaesque form. This, in turn, increases uncertainty and inconceivability concerning the outcomes of essential governance interventions, with results that may often be both unexpected and undesirable.

As expressed by Norbert Elias in a somewhat different context: 'More and more perceptibly, every action taken against an opponent also threatens the social existence of its perpetrators; it disturbs the whole mechanism of chains of action of which each is a part' (Elias, 1982, p. 168).

Without a far greater understanding of complexity, and the development of instruments able to cope with it, well-motivated governance policies may prove counter-productive – even more so than in the past and with much higher costs. This requires a more complex architecture of governance itself for coping with external complexity[4] (for comparable ideas on corporate governance, see Gharajedaghi, 1999). Indeed, to cope well with growing external complexity requires meta-complexity – that is, a higher level of complexity able to cope with complexity. However, known methods for managing complexity (Cilliers, 1998) are inadequate, and complex governance easily degenerates into a bureaucratic jungle. Much reliance on the aggregate cognitive capacities of markets and social processes is therefore essential, subject to oversight and regulation, together with making 'central minds of governments' capable of coping with growing complexity, as detailed in the second part of the book.

The following is thus required: *governance must upgrade capacities to understand, map, analyze and cope with complexity. Maximum reliance on self-managing processes, such as markets, is necessary and somewhat eases the task. But this does not reduce the need for the governmental handling of growing complexity. Doing this requires some meta-complexity in the central minds of governments, care being taken to avoid degeneration into obfuscation.*

(5) POWERFUL GLOBAL ACTORS

The emergence of new, powerful actors is a major feature of ongoing global processes. These include individuals, such as media magnates and large-scale currency traders, and organizations, such as multinational enterprises and global non-governmental organizations and interest groups.

No less pronounced is the development of powerful global criminal actors, ranging from individuals who commit 'cybercrimes' to drug-related, money-laundering and terror networks.

Such actors, legitimate or criminal, are often beyond the reach of any government, operating in ways not covered by existing laws, finding protection in corrupt mini-states, manipulating politicians, avoiding taxes and hiding partly by dispersal and movement.

In addition, global networks are of profound importance, but are diffuse in nature and lack any dominant 'actor' or 'legal residence', with the web and internet being the most important ones, and many novel forms of 'virtual actors' emerging. These are by their very nature beyond the reach of any state, despite recent efforts by several countries to impose controls on them. Only global action can cope with them when necessary, such as for the prevention of hate-speech.

Many of the powerful global actors are an essential part of the positive sides of globalization, adding to prosperity and development, and can be left to regulation by markets. Some need no regulation, regulate themselves or are partly regulated by pressures of public opinion and non-governmental actors. But, overall, governance lags behind the development of powerful global actors. *Governance should therefore increase its capacities to regulate legitimate global actors and act against criminal ones. This requires increased cooperation between governments, the strengthening of global governance and invention of new forms of regulation, taxation and legal oversight.*

Due to the importance of this subject I will return to it in Chapter Eighteen, within the broader issue of governing private power.

(6) GROWING PROSPERITY COEXISTING WITH INCREASING INEQUALITY

The single most important feature of the present state of humanity is growing prosperity. The world is far from free of conflict and atrocities, hunger and malnutrition, sickness, disasters, repression and other afflictions. But the Four Horsemen of the Apocalypse have been bridled. More humans than ever before live longer under better material conditions, with greater access to education and health care and with more personal freedom and possibilities for self-expression. For all the difficulties involved in the concept when looked at closely in all its cultural variety, the quality of life (Nussbaum and Sen, 1993) for humanity as a whole is constantly improving by all measurable standards, and probably also according to most subjective perceptions.

This reality serves as empirical support for what can be called the optimistic school of the future. Julian Lincoln Simon, who died in 1998, is one of the better representatives of this view. Regarding people as 'the ultimate resource', he expects human ingenuity to be able to cope with all predicaments without very high costs. Thus when populations enlarge, more geniuses will be produced, solving problems stemming from high birth rates (Simon, 1995, 1996).

According to such views, as shared by many, prosperity can be expected to continue and expand and is likely to reach most of humanity in the twenty-first century. This outlook does not necessarily disregard the poverty, stagnation and relative decline afflicting large parts of the world, the limits to growth, and the potential for catastrophe; most proponents of the optimistic view support efforts to reduce suffering and inequalities and to prevent the worst from happening. Overall, however, according to this school the trend is clearly towards a better life for ever-increasing numbers.

An optimistic view on constantly growing prosperity has a strong basis in ongoing processes. It is strongly held by many thinkers and also by some international bodies (concisely so in International Monetary Fund *et al.* 2000). However, it tends to ignore – or not take seriously enough – many negative developments and threatening possibilities, such as the 'limits to growth', the psychological consequences of growth, and growing inequalities and their consequences.

'Limits to growth' may stem from boundaries imposed on energy consumption by the carrying capacity of the planet, water scarcities and other issues. Thus, it is not easy to imaging most of humanity using energy and consuming water at the rate of the USA today. New technologies will help, but redistribution and quotas may be necessary, and those are probably impossible to bring about without radical changes in global governance following serious crises and conflicts.

The psychological consequences of continuous growth, in the material sense of that term, are harder to pin down. One possible development may be constantly growing demand for even more consumer goods and services with increasing frustrations paradoxically caused by the improving material quality of life. Another possible development, which I think is very likely, is a search for new meanings in life, including fundamentalist ones, some of which may be aggressive and disrupt growth.

As distinct from such conjectures, the increase in disparities accompanying growing overall prosperity is a fact, with inequalities in material standards of living and other aspects of 'human development' growing rapidly (United Nations Development Programme, 1999, 2000a, 2000b). The optimistic school admits this fact, but claims that all share, or will soon share, growth in prosperity, though differentially so, and that this will be acceptable also to those moving ahead at a much lower speed than others. However, this is a very doubtful assumption. In addition to posing hard moral questions of social justice, growing disparities may easily produce social explosions, even if all are at least somewhat better off, because of growing relative deprivation and increasing feelings of hostility towards those countries and social groups that are the most prosperous.

The next two subjects sharpen the requirements from capacities to govern posed by growing prosperity with limits and disparities.

(7) INTENSE FRUSTRATIONS, TRAUMAS, DESPONDENCY AND UNREST

Despite growing material prosperity, frustration and despondency are likely to worsen. This paradox can partly be explained in terms of subjective relative deprivation, as mentioned above. In addition to expectation-escalating effects of growing prosperity, the global mass media increase the awareness of poor people everywhere of the the material affluence enjoyed by the more

45

fortunate, often seen in idealized images. The poorer naturally want the same for themselves, many of them becoming increasingly frustrated and angry when this expectation is not met, even if their standards of living improve somewhat. Some will look for 'enemies' who can be blamed for these glaring inequalities.

But this is too 'economic' an explanation, a more fundamental cause being various forms of 'future shock' (Toffler, 1971) and transformation crisis. Frustrations and anxieties will therefore grow in the rich societies too, and even more so in most of the societies in transition from one stage of development to another, as a result of harsh structural adjustments, demographic changes, pressures of migration, cuts in entitlements, unemployment and other factors.

To provide some further depth to the picture, let us glance at the mass psychology of rapid transformations, unaccompanied by unusual spiritual leadership leading to new belief systems providing a trusted anchor (Jaspers, 1960); or excellent governance action reducing traumatic effects. Cognitive vertigo and despair, swings between euphoria and depression, and the escape into the here-and-now, or new forms of aggressive fundamentalism, will be widespread reactions – even within major elites.

The non-linear and 'jumpy' nature of the change processes will cause much disorientation and trauma, even though many of their results are very positive, and despite large areas of stability. It is enough to think of three societies currently undergoing drastic transformations – namely the former Soviet Union, China and the Republic of South Africa – to appreciate how intense these traumas can be. But all human beings are likely to suffer transformation shocks and disorientation during this period of global upheavals, including in relatively stable countries (Reid, 1996).

We know little about the effects of large-scale disorientation caused by enormous change (still unique is Sorokin, 1942), but some conjectures seem well supported by available studies and experiences. Feelings of being 'lost' will increasingly lead to a search for simple answers, enemies to blame, reassuring leaders, fundamentalist beliefs, and 'weird' opinions (Shermer, 1997) such as belief in magic, astrology, doomsday cults and so on – even in so-called highly developed and 'educated' societies. Traditional norms and codes of behavior will be further eroded, with various forms of hedonism and nihilism partly taking their place. Short-term satisfaction will be preferred to investments in the future, and politics will become more and more a matter of images and emotions.

At the negative end of the spectrum, highly traumatized societies might well turn to some form of extreme populist regime, based on new forms of 'television-crowd' behavior and passions as whipped up by new types of 'image-heroes'. Established political creeds and incumbent elites might be discredited, and replaced by unrestrained power-seekers.

There will also be positive consequences of disorientation, such as greater creativity, thanks to both new stimuli and the weakening of traditional constraints. But most of the world is likely to suffer from the adverse effects of very rapid change during the twenty-first century, posing major problems for governance.

These effects will be accentuated by the disorientation and trauma of the governance elites themselves, who are sometimes more deeply affected than the rest of society. The world is increasingly 'over our heads' (Kegan, 1994), with given patterns of understanding and action becoming obviously obsolete. The consequences for high-level decision-makers can be very serious. They may limit themselves to short term improvisations; slip into 'maze behavior' (acting erratically and in an on-off manner, as mice in a labyrinth react to electric shocks); close their minds and become frozen in entrenched positions; or become reckless; and lock into increasingly vicious downward spirals, repeating their mistakes as failure follows failure.

Outstanding politicians can be stimulated by the breakdown of rigidities and initiate positive steps that previously were both inconceivable and impossible. But such accidents of history cannot be relied upon to happen when needed most; *hence the need for redesigns to enable governance in confronting frustrations, trauma, despondency and unrest, without depending on the timely appearance of political geniuses.*

(8) THE LIKELIHOOD OF HARM AND EVIL

If we could be sure of, or at least regard as quite likely, the correctness of the optimistic outlook in the long run, and that interruptions and disparities in human growth and prosperity will be temporary, the main tasks of governance would be limited. These would include prevention of events and processes that might disrupt the good trend, containment of the negative side effects of the overall rising curve, and coping with temporary growth slowdowns and crises. This is a view of reality widely accepted by adherents to the modern optimistic school. This school trusts the 'cunning of history' (as Hegel called it), evolutionary processes, the progressive effects of free markets and civil society, and the innate goodness and wisdom of human beings, to bring about a good future, with temporary interruptions at worst, which are not difficult to bridge. On this view, governance should engage in delivering some services that cannot be privatized; some infrastructure development that falls foul of market failures; helping to take care of essential parts of 'the commons'; assuring public safety; and motivating and assisting the deprived to help themselves. However, according to such a conception of the 'ultraminimal state' (Nozick, 1974, chapter three), governance should not engage in future-building.

My view is quite different. Without in any way jumping to the other extremes of apocalyptic visions and 'ultramaximal' states, my reading of history and of current processes makes me very skeptical of any deterministic optimism, as well as of rationalistic-materialistic-utilitarian views of history and the future. In my reading of past and the present circumstances, only ignorance of history and of the little we know on human individual and collective psychology can produce the illusion that 'progress' is assured.

It is enough to remember the hopes for the twentieth century that were widely current up to the First World War, which shuttered such optimism, to put us on guard against simplistic views of the future. A quote from Gladstone, from before the catastrophes of the twentieth century, fully illustrates this point:

> Certain it is that a new law of nations is gradually taking hold of the mind, and coming to sway the practice of the world; a law which recognizes independence, which frowns upon aggression, which favors the pacific, not the bloody settlement of disputes, which aims at permanent and not temporary adjustments; above all, which recognizes, as a tribunal of paramount authority, the general judgment of civilized mankind. (Quoted in Kissinger, 1994, p. 161)

One of the effects of post-modernity, with its overload of multi-media images of dramatic events in real time, combined with human yearning for reassurance in the face of the shocks of rapid change and the dislike for remembering terrible though not far-away evils, seems to be a cultural amnesia. This is a fatal handicap in trying to cope with the future.

Humanity and societies are not deterministically condemned to repeat the past; but neither are we deterministically assured that what will be is necessarily better than what has been. In place of such illusions, what is needed (albeit within an overall optimistic view of the future), is full realization of the deep grounding of the bad and also of evil in human history, and in the potential of human beings. This will prepare us for the likelihood of the bad and of evil in the future.

There is also a very active school of pessimists on the future, even entering apocalyptic visions. It would add nothing to repeat its scenarios, such as environmental degradation, global warming, nuclear terrorism, vicious conflicts between the poor and the rich, and so on (for a balanced discussion, see Karplus, 1992). It is enough for our purposes to admit that the future, even within the relatively short timespan of fifty to one hundred years, which is the maximum that can be taken into account in present choices, is in many respects unforeseeable and also unimaginable. But enough is known to reject all kinds of determinism and 'inherent laws of history'. Neither a benign nor a malignant future is assured. Ongoing processes have the potential both for very desirable as for very undesirable possibilities, with actual futures being likely to include both good and bad elements. However, the mix depends on a number of open-ended factors, with governmental future-building capacities playing a significant role.

PREDICAMENTS AND OPPORTUNITIES

In summary:

1. In exploring the future and trying to influence it, good and bad possibilities alike must be recognized.
2. While 'the hope principle' is to serve as a psychological basis for action, reducing the probabilities of the bad and of evil is a first priority, together with increasing the probability of the good (however 'bad' and 'good' are defined).
3. Coping with quality of life disparities, transformation shocks and traumatization is a main task of governance, also as a main way to reduce the probability of negative social developments including new forms of barbarism.
4. Early recognition of the possibilities of evil, and direct and forceful action to nip it in the bud, are a moral and realpolitical must.

Most of the redesigns developed in this book aim at meeting these requirements.

(9) A LOT OF CONFLICT AND VIOLENCE

A particular form of the 'the bad' requires special attention because it is important and because it has been neglected (especially by intellectuals) in over-optimistic global discourse. Much conflict and violence is sure to characterize at least the first part of the twenty-first century and probably all of it (Huntington, 1996; Tanter, 1999; Kaplan, 2000, CIA, 2000), including possible use of new instruments of mass killing such as biological weapons. This may well pose one of the supreme tests to capacities to govern, especially global ones.

(10) ALL THE CHANGES LEADING TO MUTATIONS

In summary, humanity is rapidly undergoing mutations, some cumulative and some rather sudden. These have open potential for better and for worse; and also for the unimaginable, posing crucial future-making choices. A fitting metaphor is provided by Xunzi, the main disciple and follower of Confucius:

> As Yang Zhu once lamented at a crossroad: if a man makes an error of half a step in the wrong direction, when he awakens to the fact, he will have made a blunder of a thousand *li*. (Knoblock, Volume II, p. 161)

Humanity and states are not facing a single and clear-cut crossroads. But the expanding evolutionary potential (this concept is developed in Hallpike, 1988) for better and worse poses many critical choices, choice sets and choice-nets which influence significantly the trajectory into the future.

It is this evolutionary potential, with phase transitions, transformations and mutations that may lead both to very positive and very negative futures, which pose the most crucial challenge and mission to governance. Were it not for this challenge, the revitalization of politics, refocusing of democracy and redesign of the capacity to govern would not be as fateful as this book claims. *It is the unavoidability of governance exerting significant influence on the direction of human trajectories into the future – by default, by mistakes or by considered interventions into historic processes – which makes redesign of governance capacities, with special attention to future-weaving abilities, into a fateful necessity.*

To return to a metaphor, governance may be worse off than the general in his labyrinth, as described by Gabriel García Márquez in his historical novel on Bolivar (Márquez, 1990), engaging in inappropriate action and inaction such as womanizing and thereby neglecting urgent tasks of government. He did so largely because of failure to understand changing realities, the missing of great opportunities and running of considerable unnecessary risks. To reduce such dangers of commission and omission, governments and the whole citizen body must be able to think and act in terms of transformations. This requires cognitive maps, namely subjective images of reality, and frames of thinking which fully reflect uncertainty, surprise possibilities and discontinuities – comparable to the innovative uses of a new cartography when it developed as a tool of governance and a reshaper of cognitive maps in early modern Europe (Buisseret, 1993). *Governance, and societies as a whole, require a new 'cartography' to comprehend ongoing transformations and their potentials and to serve as a compass for navigating through the dynamic labyrinths they present.*

NOTES

1. A striking illustration of uncertainties on fundamental processes is provided by the extreme shift in views by George Soros, within two years, on the future of capitalism. Compare Soros (1998) with Soros (2000).
2. Having used that term several times, I should explain that I am doing so because the term *Holocaust* is incorrect, meaning a kind of fire sacrifice.
3. The literature on globalization is expanding in leaps and bounds. Thus, in May 2000 Amazon Books offered 566 books in English with the term 'globalization' in their titles. The new emphasis of *Foreign Policy* is on 'global politics, economics and ideas', starting from September 2000. For our purposes especially pertinent – and adding up to a fairly balanced and up-to-date (though difficult to integrate) view are: Holton, 1998; Falk, 1999; Tomlinson, 1999; Vayrynern, 1999; Friedman, 2000; Giddens, 2000b, Lechner and Boli, 2000; and Micklethwait and Wooldridge, 2000.
4. On line with the law of requisite variety from information theory (Ashby, 1957, pp. 206 ff).

5

Political Culture Obstacles

Political culture changes with transformations in overall culture, of which it is a part. Thus, attempts have been made to distinguish between pre-modern, modern and post-modern parts of the world, and to understand the related implications for governments and the relations between states (Cooper, 1996). Different major civilizations lead to significantly dissimilar political cultures. Asian civilizations lead to quite distinctive views on governance, including other versions of democracy – so, at least, some of their leaders claim (Mohammad and Ishihara, 1995). A special case is the governance of the Catholic Church, which illustrates well the fundamental dependence of governance culture and institutions on the belief systems upon which they are based, especially when those are very coherent theologies. The Nazi SS State is an extreme illustration of a unique political culture based on an all-embracing Führer-ideology. Iran is a modern example, showing the collision between global political culture and local fundamentalist political theologies. And these are just a few illustrations of the many very different historic and contemporary political cultures which produce quite varied governance systems, and also sometimes prevent them from crystallizing, as in Africa.

The term 'political culture' has many meanings, as shaped by the cultural and linguistic context within which it is used. Here it is taken to cover the values, beliefs, norms and assumptions on governance and politics, together with the patterns of social relations inextricably linked with them (Thompson, Ellis and Wildavsky, 1990). These, according to Lucian Pye, give order and meaning to political processes. Almond and Verba add other elements: cognitive orientations (knowledge and images of the political system); affective orientations (feelings about it); and evaluations of it (Almond and Verba, 1963; Almond and Verba, 1980; Pye and Verba, 1965).

For our purposes, terminological issues are not directly relevant, neither will I delve into various possibilities of future political cultures, which may well be very different from our expectations and hopes.[1] In what follows, however, the reader is asked to keep in mind that there are many more possibilities for the future than we know from historic and present realities. In particular, as already discussed, Western expectations that there is sure to emerge a global culture in which Western-type democratic liberal political culture and institutions will dominate and, that such a global culture will last, are doubtful.

An illuminating example of the importance of political culture within its overall cultural embedding,[2] and the problems it poses to governmental capacities to build the future, is provided by Latin America. Fifty years ago Latin America was widely expected to be the next continent to 'take off', with South-East Asia not being seen among the candidates for economic breakthroughs. But realities confounded expectations: South-East Asia became one of the fastest growth areas the world has ever known, while Latin America remained relatively stagnant. True, there are signs of progress in some Latin American countries, including steps towards continental co-operation. But in large parts of the continent the situation is oscillating around a rather stagnant curve of underdevelopment and lack of real democracy. Inability to maintain high-level capacities to govern is both a main cause and a main symptom of repetitive failures.

Some Latin American countries are faced by inherently difficult situations, with a majority of the population being Indian, poor, uneducated and neglected for centuries. But incapacity to govern also characterizes countries having no such handicaps, but being on the contrary blessed by human and natural resources and a lack of enemies. Venezuela is a striking illustration. This serves to indicate that the causes of stagnation in Latin America as a whole are not only, or mainly, demographic and material.

It is important not to mix up causes with symptoms. Thus, political corruption is a striking symptom of the Latin American malaise, as is drug power in some countries. But these are surface phenomena, however malignant. The deep causes are largely cultural in nature.

Firstly, Spanish and Portuguese traditions, as transplanted to Latin America and still persisting there in much of political and governmental culture, constitute barriers to socio-economic success and political development (while continuing to make tremendous contributions to culture, literature, philosophy, style, etc. in Latin America). To overcome these traditions and move into modernization, Spain and Portugal had to become integrated into the European Union and thus become willingly exposed to an 'enforced' infusion of large measures of different socio-economic and political cultures. This has not happened in Latin America.

Let me be somewhat more specific with regard to Spanish–Portuguese political culture features introduced into Latin America and widely surviving there, which may well explain failure. These include strongly legalistic and formalistic approaches, combined with centralist and also autocratic features, together with quasi-aristocratic structures taking turns with populist ones. These contradict the requirements of socio-economic success under modern conditions and of democratic political cultures.

Secondly, Latin America has not passed through any deep process of 'constructive destruction'. No religious reforms or counter-reforms, or large-scale warfare, repetitive social revolutions, or penetrating foreign occupations, other than the original colonial ones, disrupted social institutions and networks enough to provide scope for, and to enforce, radical innovation.

Thirdly, there is a misfit in timing, with capital accumulation occurring after cultural internationalization of the economic elites, with the result that capital produced in Latin America moves out rather than being mainly reinvested there.

These are only some conjectures illustrating the deep causes of the failure of Latin America. All of them are cultural and all of them condition political culture, while also inhibiting serious efforts to upgrade capacities to govern.

It has been recognized for quite some time that contemporary political cultures pose serious problems to capacities to govern. These have often been described in terms of 'ungovernability' (Hennis, Kielmansegg and Matz, 1977, and 1979), with variants such as 'legitimation crisis' (Habermas, 1976), the 'crisis of democracy' (Crozier, Huntington and Watanuki, 1975), and more recently in terms of lack of trust in government (Kaase and Newton, 1995) and of major political processes leading to declining public participation (Judis, 2000).

But the most worrying aspect of contemporary political culture is the increasing domination of 'spin' and distributing benefits over weaving the future, as a result of the slippery slope towards what I call 'Pressure-Dominated Multi-Media Populist Democracy', to be contrasted with 'Quality Democracy'. The distribution of benefits, and politics as a circus, are not new – one has only to think of court politics in the absolutist states of Europe (Elias, 1969; Backscheider, 1993). But what is new is the growing impact of the mass media, displacing 'style' (Hariman, 1995) and, all the more so, content. This in turn encourages and even forces politicians to be even more obsessed by their media image (D. Morris, 1999b, ch. 20), the new principle being *videor ergo sum* ('I am being seen, therefore I exist'[3]). Accompanied by the growing importance of a new breed of political marketing and image professionals, the changing nature of political competition also multiplies corruption because of the growing costs of entering and succeeding in politics.

The situation is extreme in the USA (Morris, 1997; Reich, 1998; Stephanopulos, 1999). But it is becoming increasingly pronounced in all democracies, and also non-democracies. A remarkable illustration of the insidiousness of this development, and its metastasis into the professional levels of governance, is the requirement in the 1997 version of the Canadian guide for drafting memoranda to the Cabinet that these should include a

53

'Communications Synopsis and Communications Plan'. The guide states: 'Properly planned communications are crucial to the success of any policy initiative, and communications and policy people should work together from the beginning of the drafting process' (Government of Canada, 1997, page C3).

Such instructions to the professional policy staffs in charge of preparing and analyzing decisions for the cabinet, as distinct from the large public relations and communications staffs, are a clear symptom and sign of what may well be a very difficult challenge to governance redesign: *a very dangerous feature of present political culture is the slippery slope towards pressure-dominated multi-media populist democracy, with political spin and distribution of benefits, often corrupt, displacing future-building. Overcoming this feature and compensating for it are major imperatives for governance redesign, requiring some combination between changing political culture and insulating important parts of governments from the dominant political culture.*

Four additional problems caused by contemporary features of political culture include: domestic difficulties; tensions between external requirements and global needs; problems with spreading democratic culture; and the cultural prerequisites of global governance.

DOMESTIC DIFFICULTIES

Many domestic problems of governance stem from political culture, such as:[4]

- The legitimacy of the state and of political authority is less readily accepted than in the past; and holders of strong opinions are less willing to be bound by the votes of a majority.
- Pressure and interest groups have in part an increasingly powerful hold over governments, significantly limiting their freedom of action (in line with Lowi, 1979).[5] Building on widespread traumatization and anxiety, and on the idealistic search for better a world, even relatively small groups can organize mass action that forces apparently 'strong' states and international bodies to change their policies, as has happened with the World Bank and the International Monetary Fund.
- Related to the point above, non-governmental organizations are increasingly accepted as legitimate political actors and given much more weight than their public backing justifies, in terms of the tenets of quantitative democratic representation.
- The increasing costs of politics increase the power of strong financial interest groups, making politics and governance increasingly captive to money power.
- The authority of politics is undermined by its demystification and by growing cynicism about politicians based on hard evidence. Among the expressions and explanations of this trend are increasingly open government,

investigative mass media, a more schooled public, widespread and gross corruption and hypocrisy on the part of politicians, and the frequent failure of governments to deliver what is expected from and promised by them.

- The timescale of politics is becoming much shorter than the minimum time required to handle major issues. Some action groups, such as environmentalists, do advocate long-term perspectives. But, on the whole, agendas and priorities tend to be determined by short-term pressures and demands.[6] (Kingdon, 1995)

- Contemporary Western political cultures are based less and less on ideology, with most parties proposing similar policies on most issues. Even when electoral competition drives candidates to emphasize differences of opinion, the lack of real options on many issues has taken much of the fire out of ideological debates, to be replaced by televised duels between top candidates. Parties are losing their importance, but top politicians are occasionally committed to particular ideological stances which make quite a difference, as illustrated by President Reagan in the USA (Langston, 1992) and Prime Minister Thatcher in the UK (Seldon and Collings, 1999).

- All in all, the role of personalities in Western political cultures is increasing, in part thanks to the mass media. But other forces too are strengthening the positions of prime ministers and presidents, such as summit meetings (Dunn, 1996), and the need for coherent inter-ministerial policies. In addition, as already mentioned, disorientation and trauma push people to seek reassurance in authority figures and this, in turn, changes the way political cultures function, in directions that are as yet unclear but seem ominous – as further discussed in Chapter Thirteen.

- There is an increasing use of referenda for arriving at decisions on controversial issues, even in countries without a tradition of direct democracy. Such issues include joining the European Union, nuclear energy, term limitations, regional autonomy, and more. This further testifies to the inability of traditional political processes to cope with situations, and the lack of a satisfactory substitute. The impacts on political culture of referenda are numerous, including accelerating the movement towards populism, mass politics and mass-media dominance.

- One of the great successes of democratic political cultures has been their ability to tolerate 10 to 15 percent unemployment. Political stability has been maintained thanks mainly to relatively high unemployment benefits paid by the state. But the longer-term impacts of relatively large, chronic, and probably growing unemployment are unknown and may be extremely damaging, as indicated by the strengthening of extreme parties in a number of highly developed countries, including some with long traditions of tolerance and democracy.

- A number of pronounced malignant processes are at work, such as the growing hostility to immigrants, which also contribute to the growth of extrem-

55

ist parties (Bjoergo and Witte, 1993). Even more dangerous, in reaction to the move away from ideologies in combination with traumatization, there is a trend towards a 'politics of resacralization' (Samuels, 1993, chapter 1). These lead to strong emotions and attachments that are regarded as beyond the scope of tolerance and majority decisions, including new versions of vicious nationalism, tribalism, and so on, as already mentioned (Pfaff, 1993; Eisenstadt, 1999b). The economy also shows signs of accumulating theological meanings (Nelson, 1991) where markets are not regarded as tools but viewed with an almost religious faith. In combination with the possible anti-democratic potentials of post-modern cultures as a whole, the result may be new forms of political theology – even new forms of fanaticism – and even in countries with a long democratic tradition. The realm of the possible, even if not very likely, is well illustrated by various depictions of pro-ecological regimes, including dictatorships (Fleck, 1993).

- The already mentioned increasing power of capital may well become a major failure of liberal market democracy, leading on one hand to the undermining of real democracy by increasing plutocracy, while, on the other, producing ideological reaction (Wood, 1995) and various violent responses, both undermining democratic political culture.

Further difficulties with contemporary democratic cultures can be added, some of which are very significant, even as far as raising the question 'Was democracy just a moment?' (Kaplan, 2000, chapter 2). These, however, have to be balanced against the many achievements of democratic political culture and its growing strength – which, however, must not obscure the dangerous weaknesses of contemporary pressure-dominated multi-media populist political cultures.

TENSIONS BETWEEN EXTERNAL REQUIREMENTS AND GLOBAL NEEDS

One of the more serious weaknesses of contemporary political cultures is their dissonance with external requirements and global needs. In democracies, external policies always depend on internal support or, at least, acquiescence (Clinton, 1993; Rosecrance and Stein, 1993; Evans, Jacobson and Putman, 1993; Downs and Rocke, 1995). But changes in political cultures, as based on changing social values as a whole on one hand(Ester, Halman and Morr, 1993), and on external requirements and global needs on the other, increase the gulf between them into an abyss.

For instance, domestic pressures prevent the adoption of immigration policies needed to meet global pressures (as well as economic needs), public opinion hinders participation in international activities essential for maintaining peace, and the large-scale transfer of resources to poor countries is opposed by large majorities.

POLITICAL CULTURE OBSTACLES

In developing countries, the contradictions between domestic political culture and external requirements take on even harsher forms. Many developing countries are in the impossible position of being pressed by strong international actors – the World Bank, the International Monetary Fund and the leading industrialized countries – to adopt policies that are not feasible in terms of political culture and which will often destabilize societies, in addition to contradicting local values. This may also have contributed to problems in Russia, with economic reform being pushed by the West without regard for political culture and social stability.

PROBLEMS WITH SPREADING DEMOCRATIC CULTURE

Western pressures on non-democratic countries to move towards greater democracy open up further problems of political culture that help to determine its crucial importance.

Political cultures are the product of six sets of interacting and overlapping factors: indigenous histories of societies and civilizations; underlying belief-systems; socio-economic and technological structures; specific challenges facing a society; accidents of leadership and institutional innovators; the diffusion of ideas, willingly or under pressure.

Nowadays, the diffusion of ideas is the dominant factor, with the dominant global pressure and trend being toward Western-type liberal democracy, combined with a market economy. However, one must guard against reading too much into superficial factor and surface processes. There is a world of difference between the formal structure of democratic institutions and the way they operate in practice. They may function quite differently, depending upon the cultures and other specific characteristics of particular countries – mainly historical and cultural, but also related to the size and composition of populations, ethnic and religious structures, and traditional lifestyles. For example, although the Netherlands, Brazil and India are democracies, their political cultures and the actual workings of democracy within them are not at all similar: thus, the hierarchical social system of India (Dumont, 1981) produces a quite different type of democracy to the egalitarian lifestyle of the Netherlands.

Whatever the differences, and despite serious problems, India is a democracy and an impressive one. Another matter entirely, however, are those highly developed non-Western cultures that have not been subjected to long occupation by the West, the prime example being China. It is extremely doubtful whether Western-style liberal democracy could, or should, be transplanted to China and some other cultures, such as various Islamic countries (Roy, 1994). Even if formal democratic institutions were introduced, their meaning and way of working would be quite unlike the ethnocentric notions and expectations of the West.

Differences in political culture are therefore at odds with a Western expectation and desire to have Western-style liberal democracy adopted all over the world. Such transplants may bring about acceptance of some basic and very beneficial ideas and values, such as human rights and participation, even if practiced differently. But they can also be harmful, as in many parts of Africa, where the very notion of 'nation-state' has proved counter-productive (Davidson, 1992). Even in the case of South Africa, with its impressive democracy, it remains to be seen whether local history, traditions and conditions have been given enough weight in the new democratic constitution (Murray and Lane, 1996).

It should be emphasized that cultures unwilling or unable to absorb liberal democracy are not to be regarded as somehow 'inferior'. Johann Gottfried Herder's pluralistic concepts may well have been more correct than Kant's image of a cosmopolitan world (Brint, 1991, pp. 57–65). This conclusion is reinforced when the importance of religions or other fundamental belief-systems as ultimate anchors for political theologies is taken into account. Such is argued for within a modern context, albeit with somewhat different concepts, by Eric Voegelin (esp. Voegelin, 1952, 1974, and discussion in Sandoz, 1981).

Also to be taken into account is the view that basic institutions are hard to change deliberately, and usually evolve quite slowly, whereas secondary institutions that are easier to change may not be strong enough to change the essence of political culture (Dietl, 1993). This proposition is strongly supported by a thorough empirical study of regional democracy in Italy by Robert D. Putman, which he partly sums up as follows:

> This is one lesson gleaned from our research: Social context and history profoundly condition the effectiveness of institutions. Where the regional soil is fertile, the regions draw sustenance from regional traditions, but where the soil is poor, the new institutions are stunted. (Putman, 1993, p. 182)

This finding throws grave doubts on expectations concerning the assured and easy spread of Western democracy, which ignore the importance of political cultures and their diversity.[7] This has important implications for governance redesign: *Efforts to transplant political institutions, including Western democracy as a whole, without appropriate adjustments in them and in the political cultures of the receiving countries, may easily fail and even be counter-productive.*

CULTURAL PREREQUISITES OF GLOBAL GOVERNANCE

If there is to be harmony, or at least coexistence and cooperation – or even just compliance – in handling global issues, some shared elements of political culture must be developed to serve as a basis for global governance and the advancement of *raison d'humanité*. This is required also for rather minimalist views of global cooperation, such as those of the Commission on Global

Governance (1995) and the International Commission on Peace and Food (1994) – though in the main ignored by them. *In order to achieve adequate global capacities to govern important elements of a global political culture must be shared by all major countries and by most of the global population, combined with a pluralism in political cultures.*

Unless, therefore, global interactions and the spread of ideas and technologies produce a political culture shared in large part by the vast majority of societies, including all states who carry weight (which is very doubtful in the foreseeable future), it will be necessary to resort to 'global cultural architecture'. The deliberate development of at least some essential elements of a common global political culture is a very difficult task, especially in the absence of a global civil society in any reasonable sense of that term (Featherstone, 1990; Tester, 1992; Robertson, 1992; Tomlinson, 1999). But it is an increasingly important 'new imperative of high politics' (Doran, 1991).

Rulers and spiritual leaders should devote effort to building up a global political society based on increasing feelings of human solidarity, as part of their educational tasks – discussed further in Chapter Thirteen. Another important means of fostering a global political culture is via the use of symbols, defined by Clifford Geertz as 'tangible formulations of notions, abstractions from experience fixed in perceptible forms, concrete embodiments of ideas, attitudes, judgments, longings, or beliefs' (Geertz, 1973, p. 91). Since they both express and form emotions (Edleman, 1964, 1971 and 1998), inventing and transforming symbols is an important way of influencing feelings, as history clearly shows. We therefore need to use all our imagination and creativity to devise symbols to express global solidarity and other humane values constitutive of a global political culture as required, such as a flag, an anthem, commemorations (applying Gillis, 1994 and Boime, 1998), and so on. Given the impact of paintings and architecture as political symbols (Starn and Patridge, 1992; Warnke, 1984), a new iconography of a global political culture should be promoted.

Language has an even more potent influence on human minds. Zamenhof, the inventor of Esperanto in 1887, was right in recognizing the value of a shared language for all of humanity, though he was wrong in underrating the emotive and cultural significance of languages, necessarily missing in an artificial one (Nichols, 1992). For this reason, and in view of the practical problems, it would be pointless to suggest creating a universal second language, such as Esperanto. But some terms that express a shared global political culture, such as *raison d'humanité*, must be introduced into all languages with fitting adjustments.

Another set of factors with strong impact on human emotions is participation. People should be encouraged to engage in global thinking and activities, directly or through intermediary organizations. Representative groups of citizens could study global issues in depth. The apex of participative institutions is some kind of Global People's Assembly, however non-representative in terms of political democracy.

The combined effects of global transformations, as impacting on the sensation and experience of politics (Kaufman-Osborn, 1991) may provide openings for new social psychologies of politics (Harre, 1993, ch. 10). These may strengthen participation and democracy in forms appropriate to different political cultures, also providing a shared global political culture. However, no less realistic are pessimistic scenarios leading to very harmful forms of mass politics and to escalating conflicts between opposing political theologies.

This brings us to a major vicious circle: Upgrading capacities to govern depends a lot on changes in underlying political cultures that are unlikely to come about on their own. Therefore, governments must engage in political-culture architecture, including moral education as already discussed. However, to do so for the better, very high-quality capacities to govern are essential both morally and cognitively, which in turn depend largely on the existence of the yet-to-be-achieved political cultures.

How to get out of this double bind, and achieve reforms sufficient for required radical change are challenges which will keep us agonizing when relevant redesigns are presented, without the presumption on my part that I have a ready solution. However, the need is clear.

NOTES

1. For example, the basing of governance on what is in essence an environmental political theology and culture, as depicted in Ophulus, 1997 and Fleck, 1993.
2. Modern liberal democratic cultures can only be understood within the context of Western culture – this being a fundamental reason for serious problems concerning its fit with other societies having different cultural histories. A good sense of the cultural rooting of modern Western political cultures can be distilled from better histories of the latter, such as Harold Bloom, 1995, Harold Bloom, 1999, and Barzun, 2000.
3. I am grateful to Professor Gerhart Bruckmann for helping me with the Latin phrase, adjusting Descartes' classic formulation to modern politicians.
4. Relevant books going beyond textbook banalities include Brantlinger, 1983; Brecht, 1978; Eisenstadt, 1999a; Fuller, 1991; Held, ed., 1993; Jänicke, 1990; Powell, Jr, 1982; Putman, 1993; and Zolo, 1992.
5. Especially interesting are findings that in the USA citizen groups are becoming more effective in bringing about change, while economic groups tend to preserve the status quo (Gerber, 1999. For a different view, see Broder, 2000).
6. Pronounced in its neglect of future-building tasks, and thus in effect justifying short-term agenda fixations, is Moore, 1995.
7. I leave aside extreme views of Western intentions as 'conspiracies', such as those by Noam Chomsky (Chomsky, 1994). Neither do I take up the more complex question whether some Western policies are driven by an underlying anxiety about 'decline' (Herman, 1997; Luttwak, 1994), or revised conceptions of empire and mission fitting contemporary sensitivities (Pagden, 1995).

PART TWO
REDESIGN REQUIREMENTS

6

Gearing for Higher-Order Tasks

Our discussion in the first part of this book can be summed up as follows: *Humanity is undergoing transformations and approaching phase transitions with a large potential for both good and bad – even evil – outcomes. The actual trajectory into the future will be significantly influenced by both action and inaction on the part of governance, including critical choices that no other social institution can or should make. However, present governance is not equipped for weaving the future for the better. Therefore, radical governance redesigns are essential in order to upgrade capacities to govern and, in particular, to influence the future for the better.*

This part of the book, which serves as a bridge between these conclusions and detailed redesign proposals, works out some overall redesign requirements. In this chapter the main prerequisites of higher-order tasks of governance are explored, while the next elaborates a 'feature model' of high-quality governance.

But first a distinction is necessary between 'ordinary' tasks of governance and what I call 'higher-order' tasks. The ordinary tasks of governance include satisfying the needs and wishes of citizens, service delivery, maintaining public order, making transfer payments and so on. These receive quite a lot of attention in 'new public management', 'reinventing government' and similar fashionable schools of thought.

The ordinary tasks of governance are very important. Unless they are adequately fulfilled, societies and individuals are harmed and governance cannot engage in its higher-order tasks. Moreover, serious failures in the ordinary tasks can undermine the very fabric of society and of governance. Thus, the collapse of tax collection or the breakdown of public order paralyze the whole of governance and grievously damage society, leaving no scope and resources for the higher-order tasks. Efforts to improve the performance of governance in fulfilling its ordinary tasks are therefore very important.

However, given a minimum standard of success in its ordinary tasks, and in view of the phase transitions in the human condition as reflected in all societies and countries, the higher-order tasks of governance should receive much more attention and priority. What is therefore needed is a conceptual revolution, focusing on thinking, improving and acting in terms of 'influenc-ing the future', 'intervening in history', 'setting trajectories into time' and so on, in addition to and partly instead of efficiency, effectiveness, value for money and the like. This is all the more necessary because efficient execu-tion of the ordinary tasks within wrong or absent endeavors towards future-building will result in bad outcomes. Thus, more efficiently collecting taxes to be used for building an environment-endangering dam or financing a crimi-nal war is not an 'improvement'.

In order to be able to engage well in its higher-order tasks, governance must meet a number of prerequisites, including: the will to 'weave the future', perseverance, critical intervention mass, tragic choice abilities, strategy-mix for coping with turbulent environments, creativity and innovation-readiness, governance auto-redesign propensities, and democratic power concentration. These, as explored next, together with the feature model of high-quality governance presented in the following chapter, will serve as foundations for the resolution developed in Part Three.

THE WILL TO 'WEAVE THE FUTURE'

'Decisionism', a term apparently coined by Carl Schmitt, in the sense of decisions being mainly a matter of will and determination, has to be strictly avoided. Also to be shunned are other views emphasizing will, as inter alia stimulated by the popular misreading of Friedrich Nietzsche's *The Will to Power* (which, it should be remembered, is a doubtful combination of various fragments from his literary inheritance never approved by him for publication). Instead, judicious action based on the best deliberation that human beings, groups and institutions are capable of is the only method for trying to 'weave the future' which can be justified in terms of an ethics of responsibility (Jonas, 1984) and on pragmatic grounds in terms of results.

But 'will' is essential for weaving the future – both the overall will to have governance engage in doing so, and the specific will to engage in particular future-directed endeavors. The capacity to crystallize 'will' is thus a main requirement. It involves, in all societies and particularly in democracies, mobilization of some combination of support, enthusiasm, intense commit-ment, and acquiescence. It depends heavily on features of politics and culture, as well as on the personality and will of top-level governance elites and indi-vidual rulers.

Most difficult of all is the crystallization of will on the global level. Rely-ing on a consensus of the willing (Cleveland, 1993) is inadequate when impor-tant interests are at stake; neither can a post-modern political order with no one really in control (Cooper, 1996) satisfy requirements. This presents the need to make global governance more resolute.

PERSEVERANCE

But short-term will is inadequate, because weaving the future requires long-term efforts. Perseverance is thus another requirement of future-building capacities. However, stubbornness must be avoided, as constant learning and readiness to change one's mind are also essential in an epoch of rapid change.

The perseverance requirement is difficult for governments, and especially democratic ones, because of shifts in public opinions, short electoral cycles (Tufte, 1978), preoccupation with the 'blowing of bubbles' and so on. The already discussed lack of representation of future generations compounds difficulties. A main directive for governance redesign is therefore to seek institutions, processes and staffs that strengthen perseverance in future-weaving endeavors without becoming rigid and obdurate.

CRITICAL INTERVENTION MASS

It is not enough to have the will to weave the future and to persevere in doing so. In order to have an impact on the future it is necessary to intervene in historical processes with a critical mass of resources and efforts sufficient to influencing the future in desired directions (Schulman, 1980).

Illustrations include vast physical projects, nation building, movement from a command economy to a market economy, and other tasks in 'societal architecture'. These can be successful only if a critical mass of efforts, time and resources is concentrated on them.

Schumacher's phrase 'small is beautiful' (Schumacher, 1973) is widely repeated and has become an article of faith for some movements. Sometimes indeed small is optimal. But, as often 'small' is too inconsequential to achieve significant impact on robust processes. Efforts to preserve rain forests, to protect populations against floods, and arms control measures are additional illustrations falling into the category of requiring large-scale action.

Large-scale policies usually involve considerable uncertainty. However, when refusal to undertake a large project or significant societal architecture is sure to cause great harm or forgo much potential good, then the policy gamble to engage in them may often be justified. This applies also to major physical projects, such as large-scale flood control and irrigation projects, which the current Western policy orthodoxy tends to dislike and to try and inhibit.

A large-scale activity is not always required for achieving impact, much depending on the dynamics of the targeted processes; if these are fragile, then small interventions may suffice for changing their direction. Certainly, no 'comprehensive planning' is implied. Instead, weaving the future must be targeted on critical factors and lead sectors and aim sometimes to produce strong and even shock effects, in line with the ideas of Albert O. Hirschman (Hirschman, 1986 ch. 1) and my concept of 'selective radicalism'.

65

'TRAGIC CHOICE' ABILITIES

Efforts to weave the future involve a number of very difficult and highly controversial 'tragic choices' (Calabresi and Bobbit, 1979), in which incommensurate absolute values strongly held by various actors must be weighed against one another. This also applies to efforts to specify the 'national interest' (Commission on America's National Interests, 1996), *raison d'humanité*, and so on. 'Tragic choice' abilities are thus a central requirement without which higher-order tasks of governments cannot be properly engaged in, other than on a rhetorical level.

To make this point, it is enough to mention again the issue of global justice and equity, the ethical problems posed by genetic engineering, the needs of today's poor versus those of unborn generations, and the quandary of whether to invest large amounts of resources in order to prevent environmental risks that may not materialize. Every daily newspaper is full of more examples – such as controversies over abortion, disagreements as to how many soldiers of one nationality to put at risk in order to provide security to others, and many more, all demonstrating the need for tragic choices and their difficulties.

The difficulties of tragic choice are aggravated by an increasing lack of agreement on many issues, and the weakening of consensus on procedures for making judgments on divisive value issues, such as by majority vote. The weaknesses of political philosophy with its inability to provide useful ethical guidance for coping with new policy areas, as discussed, further aggravates the tragic choice difficulties facing governance.

When we take into account the fact that tragic choices are faced also with respect to time preferences and attitudes to uncertainty and risk, the need for redesigns to cope with tragic choice is accentuated. Redesigns should enable the better development of new values and their application to new problems, renewed consensus building, crystallization of political will, and much improved moral reasoning in governance. But redesigns meeting such requirements are difficult to specify and implement, all the more so as this is a much neglected subject in discourse on governance.

STRATEGY-MIX FOR COPING WITH TURBULENT ENVIRONMENTS

Another requirement is the capacity to handle turbulent environments. This involves some combination of five strategies, all of them demanding for governance:

1. Anticipatory adjustment, with prediction of how the environment is changing and measures geared in advance to cope with new situations, including seizing novel opportunities. This is always difficult and often impossible in a period of global transformations.

2. Rapid adjustment to changes that have already taken place, with swift diagnosis of ongoing processes and comprehension of new realities – which is also difficult, because of cognitive rigidities built into human beings, governance and societies (Margolis, 1992; Rosell, 1999).
3. The building of membranes around one's society, to try to reduce the undesirable impact of environmental changes, such as threats to cultural uniqueness, and to permit at least some aspects of society to evolve relatively independently of ongoing processes in the environment.
4. Efforts to strengthen indigenous characteristics so that they can successfully withstand external challenges and competition.
5. Efforts to influence the environment instead of being forced to react to it. This is an attractive strategy, but it requires a critical mass of appropriate capabilities, qualitatively or quantitively, which is hard to achieve. This is a major advantage of continental groupings, such as the European Union, because as a bloc their ability to influence outside actors and global environments is greatly enhanced, while those of individual states are becoming more limited (but Ohmae, 1995 is exaggerated).

But all these strategies require a capacity to read ongoing processes, develop new policy options, and – hardest of all – change oneself and one's own society, each in turn depending on innovative governance redesign.

CREATIVITY AND INNOVATION-READINESS

There is a widely held view that if governance were not corrupt, stupid or controlled by narrow interests, and if populations were enlightened, then the major problems facing societies and humanity would not be difficult to solve. This is, however, a delusion. While interesting ideas abound, most of the policy proposals proffered as 'solutions' in the literature and political debate are quite inadequate for the more important problems facing individual countries and humanity as a whole. Reliance on the flawed logic that 'X *must* be solved, therefore it *can* be solved', or belief in some *deus ex machina*, add to the fantasies surrounding many of the so-called solutions proffered for the problems of the world.

The blunt truth is that even if the world were ruled by a highly moral Platonic philosopher-king who had at his disposal all of present human knowledge and understanding, he would be hard put to come up with useful policies on many issues. To give just a few examples: no sound approaches are known for coping with the widespread use of hard drugs, persistent unemployment, the possible negative consequences of developments in science and technology, bloody anarchy in Africa, and so on and on.

A major requirement is therefore to invent and develop new policy options and to be able to implement them. However, creativity and innovation-readiness depend on the advancement of novel knowledge and theories, iconoclasm in respect to accepted policy orthodoxies, and other processes that cannot survive in governance. A main requirement is therefore for governance to encourage and facilitate policy-directed creativity throughout society, and to utilize it better.

As well put in an OECD study of innovation policy, reading 'century' for 'decade' and extending the coverage to all countries, not just the 'advanced' ones: 'The tasks confronting all advanced countries over the next decade call for a culture of flexibility and adjustment, a culture of innovation' (OECD, 1986, p. 30).

However, more is involved: If present political cultures and interest structures are taken to be permanent, the space open for feasible policy options is often too small to permit predicaments and opportunities to be faced properly. Consequently, governance must overcome the tyranny of the status quo (Friedman and Friedman, 1984) and avoid the trap offered by the definition of politics as 'the art of the possible'. Instead, governance must try to make the necessary feasible by educating the public, through improvements in political culture and new modes of mobilizing democratic will.

Free societies can deal successfully with many problems, but they must themselves undergo change in order to thrive during global transformations. This is a difficult and painful process hindered by societal rigidities (Olson, Jr, 1982). Capacities to encourage societies to be innovative and to transform themselves are therefore required in governments, as a major dimension of weaving the future – including the facilitation of such actions by society.

GOVERNANCE AUTO-REDESIGN PROPENSITIES

All that has been said leads to the requirements for governments to be able and willing to redesign themselves, so as to be able to carry out higher-order tasks successfully. This is all the more demanding because of the many forces in governance and around it which resist governance redesign or direct it into wrong channels.

Redesign of governance should therefore not be left to governance alone, because it is often incapable of 'exiting itself' and finding ways to overcome organizational, bureaucratic and political rigidities. Consequently, a variety of societal actors have crucial functions to fulfill in encouraging, demanding and supporting governance redesign and in developing salient proposals.

DEMOCRATIC POWER CONCENTRATION

Let me sum up the conclusions of this chapter thus far: *In order to build up required capacities to govern, governance redesign is needed for overcoming weaknesses in respect to will to weave the future, perseverance, critical intervention mass, 'tragic choice' abilities, handling turbulent environments, creativity and innovation-readiness, and governance auto-redesign propensities.*

However, one main requirement is still missing – namely, the need for democratic power concentrations. 'Power', in the classical double meaning of ability to influence the activities of individuals, groups, organizations, societies and countries, and of determining 'who gets what, when, and how' (Lasswell, 1911) is essential for all governance actions, with 'weaving the future' requiring especially large amounts of power. This prerequisite is unpopular in contemporary thinking on democracy and neglected in the current theory and practice of reform. In view of the abuses of power in the twentieth century there is much justification for being suspicious about power, and for prioritizing limits on power and ways to restrain it. However, fears of governance power and a preference for diffuse and consensual modes of action, which do not require power concentrations, must not undermine essential capacities to govern. Moreover, these depend on adequate power concentrations to make and implement critical future-shaping choices in the face of increasingly widespread action inhibitors and veto rights by various types of committed but unrepresentative actors and groups, with often rather narrow views.

Accordingly, *upgrading capacities to govern requires an increase in the abilities of government in their democratic mobilization, retention and deployment of power, especially at the level of central government, multi-state governance and global governance, which are in charge of weaving the future.*

In view of such requirements it is clear that governance redesign as discussed in this book is not a primary technical matter, but must take up controversial issues of politics which are at the core of capacities to govern. But before moving on to these, let me further introduce the redesign approach by framing it within a 'feature model' of high-quality governance.

7

A 'Feature Model' of High-Quality Governance

It is not difficult to develop different proposals for improving governance. However, in doing so, recommendations can easily be chosen or overlooked by accident, and different suggestions can readily contradict and cancel one another. Moreover, without clearly enunciated redesign proposals, guidelines are lacking for developing further improvement proposals, tailoring general recommendations to fit specific circumstances, or setting priorities.

Ideally, a paradigm for improving capacities to govern so as to cope with local, regional and global transformations is needed, but no viable general theory that can provide such paradigms yet exists.[1] In the meantime, we must rely on surrogates. The first of these is the set of prerequisites in the last chapter. The second, presented in this chapter, is a prescriptive 'feature-model' of high-quality governance that can serve as grounding for specific redesign proposals within a coherent and explicit system.

It must be stressed again that there can be no abstract model of 'optimal' governance and no universally valid operational conception of 'the best capacities to govern'. This is because the desirability of different forms of governance depends on values, histories and on the situations within which governance is operating. Thus, the pace of change is a key factor, since a certain system may perform well in relatively stable conditions and poorly in times of rapid transformation. For instance, governance institutions that tend to be conservative and overly prudent are quite well suited for situations of stability; whereas in a period of upheaval, governance systems 'wired' so as to innovate and experiment will achieve more.

Our age of transformations therefore demands a paradigm of 'high-quality' governance that is different, in part, from those we have inherited. When changing values are also taken into consideration, the concept of 'high-quality' governance becomes even more subject to periodization. Thus, historically given models as well as many fashionable opinions require very close re-examination.

Without claiming to offer a revolutionary new paradigm, the proposed model focuses on nine facets required in order to achieve governance adequate for its higher-order tasks in a time of global upheaval and transformation. However, the requirements specified by the terms 'minimum' (see Cherniak, 1986) and 'adequacy' are very demanding. *The minimum qualities governance needs for adequately fulfilling ordinary and higher-order tasks in the twenty-first century, so as to avoid very costly failures, take advantage of fleeting opportunities and influence the future for the better, are far superior to what we have now or had in the past.* Indeed, the highest quality that governance is capable of achieving may be barely adequate.

The proposed model focuses on qualities. This leaves open the question to what extent governance must realize these qualities in order to achieve adequacy. However, since the proposed model serves as a guide to redesign, it is enough that it sets directions in which governance should evolve, as it is both theoretically impossible and practically unnecessary to quantify the facets in the form of an 'optimal' model.

Albeit, one quantitative specification will make the model more useful for applied governance upgrading: the more a governance unit engages in higher-order tasks, the more it should satisfy the requirements of the model. Top politicians and the offices of heads of governments should therefore meet the facets as maximally as possible, while much less will be enough in local service-delivery units. From a global perspective, the central minds of governments of powerful countries which have significant impact on the future of the world should meet the requirements more than is necessary for peripheral countries – though their populations may need the best governance possible. Countries facing threats to their existence or daunting development challenges need higher-quality governance than do highly developed and relatively stable countries. However, given the challenges, promises and dangers of the twenty-first century, all countries need high-quality governance, with special emphasis on the core units of central governments, multistate governance and global governance in charge of critical future-influencing choices and actions.

The model includes ten facets of high-quality governance, in addition to the prerequisites discussed in Chapter Six: *Governance should be moral, knowledge-intense, future-committed, consent-based, high-energy but selective, deep-thinking, holistic, learning, pluralistic, and decisive.*

'Moral' implies much more than that governance should observe certain basic norms, such as freedom and democracy, and then act as a neutral arbiter of societal forces and individual preferences. Instead, moral governance demands an active stance to push for higher standards, of democracy, for example and of human rights. It also means seeking to improve the values on which governance is predicated, such as working out what is involved in *raison d'humanité*, as well as engaging in moral education as already discussed. Furthermore, governance itself must be ethical in its behavior and that of its individual members and personnel, including senior politicians.

Governance must of cause be moral as a normative imperative; but there are also instrumental reasons. Governance must be moral in order to enjoy essential legitimacy, to cope with emerging predicaments and opportunities, and especially to be able to raise the moral standards of citizens, and of humanity as a whole. But 'moral' governance can become a nightmare unless great care is taken with the nature of the values that it holds. In particular, fanaticism must be rejected, as must any inclination towards 'evil'.

If the only choice were between governance actively serving evil or merely being passive about values, the second would clearly be infinitely preferable. Similarly, if the choice were between rulers wholeheartedly committed to evil or rulers engaged in corruption and debauchery, the second would be much less bad. But if these are the only options open for human governance, then prospects for the future are very dim indeed.

Bringing about more moral governance requires great effort, both to clarify desirable values and to build institutions that improve the prospects for value-intense governance. This is certainly the most difficult and dangerous, but also the most essential challenge for the redesign of governance.

'Knowledge-intense' denotes a rather obvious requirement, though amazingly it is ignored in most of contemporary thinking on governance improvement. Accelerating the movement towards knowledge economies and the beginnings of an advance towards knowledge societies makes it all the more essential for governance to be knowledge-intense. Quite a number of the redesign proposals in Part Three aim at the realization of this feature which, while neglected, is relatively less difficult to accomplish than other more complex and politically sensitive ones.

'Future-committed' is a feature closely related to the need for will to influence the future, as discussed in the last chapter. But it also incorporates giving much weight to the thriving of future generations as against a pre-occupation with responding to current needs and pressures and being fixated on electoral competition.

The need to be 'consent-based' could be subsumed under the term 'moral', because for governance to be truly moral it must, according to democratic values, ultimately be founded on the consent of the people – though not all the time and in all matters. But this aspect is so important that it should be recognized as a separate dimension of the model.

This requirement obviously reflects traditional democratic values, but it also permits alternative forms of consent appropriate to different values, cultures, societal traditions and situations. It also permits active endeavors by governance to mobilize consent, as indeed required for coping with painful necessities and for long-term policies, as long as this is done within the basic norms of democracy.

The consent-based requirement is placed deliberately after the moral imperative, which must have priority lest societies give their consent to what by the common values of humanity is 'evil', as happened in Nazi Germany. In such cases, international intervention would be needed to restore the moral basis of governance, despite the adherence of a majority to evil. Therefore, being based on consent is a necessity but not sufficient by itself. Consent in doing evil is not acceptable.

'High-energy but selective' governance stands in contrast to a minimalist and passive conception. If other processes could be relied upon to perform the most essential tasks, including weaving the future for the better, then a minimal 'Night Watch' state and parallel low-energy governance would be preferable, so as to avoid the risks inherent in all forms of high-energy governance. However, our analysis leads to the inescapable conclusion that spontaneous processes and 'zero-governance' institutions cannot by themselves adequately serve human progress. Thus, free markets can easily be taken over by monopolies, may collapse (Gray, 1998), and indeed themselves need high-energy governments to support them and provide essential infrastructure (Maddison, 1991; OECD, 1999). This is also increasingly recognized by pro-free market global economic governance institutions (World Bank, 1993; International Bank for Reconstruction and Development and the World Bank, 1997; World Bank, 2000). High energy is therefore an essential attribute if governance is to cope with its long-term responsibilities.

However, this is not the same as saying 'the more the better'. To ward off the danger of governance becoming overactive, the requirement to be selective must be added. The model does not imply that governance should engage directly in a wide range of activities, but rather that it should concentrate on main tasks that cannot be adequately fulfilled by other social processes and institutions, with special attention to the higher-order ones. There is certainly no suggestion of *dirigisme* or a command economy, in any of their old or new guises.

The *'deep thinking'* facet is related to knowledge-intensity but is different, because governance can be dense with knowledge but use it mainly for surface thinking directed at pragmatic needs. The deep thinking requirement adds the need for action-oriented contemplation trying to deal with issues on their more fundamental levels, rather than focusing on symptoms, as governance usually does.

Furthermore, governmental thinking, choice and action must be *'holistic'* (6, 1997), in the sense of considering the main issues within a systems perspective (Jervis, 1997) and trying to achieve synergy between its various endeavors. However, as already noted, no comprehensive planning is implied – this would not only be futile but also counter-productive because of its rigidities and disregard for uncertainties and unforseeable circumstances.

'Learning' also deserves special emphasis because of its critical importance in times of rapid change (Michael, 1997). It is also a main pathway to creativity and innovation, as already discussed.

73

The remaining pair of dimensions, *'pluralistic'* and *'decisive'*, need to be examined with close attention to the way they interact. At first sight, they seem banal, but further exploration reveals weighty implications. Pluralism in governance includes multiple levels and types of agency, multiple skills and multiple cultures – in line with the requirements of complexity and also meta-complexity (namely higher-level complexity capable of understanding and managing complexity) for coping with complex environments and issues. Fostering pluralism requires adding new forms of governance to existing ones. For example, new regional and continental levels of governments and novel types of policy-development and moral deliberation units. Pluralism also relates to the already discussed principle that democracy, too, must be a mixed regime, with non-democratic enclaves and layers in part to be strengthened rather than suppressed.

However, pluralism can easily prevent holistic perspectives and lead to stalemates, blocked governance and powerlessness. The conventional idea of checks and balances acknowledges this possibility, but regards it as an advantage rather than as a fault. Our only answer to the question posed by Cicero, 'Who shall guard the guardians?' is to construct a pluralistic governance system within free and pluralistic societies where powers offset one another. But when transformations require incisive governance action, even in the face of strong resistance, the tendency of pluralism to produce inaction must often be considered a drawback.

Hence the critical importance of decisiveness. This facet requires that the various elements of governance reinforce yet correct one another and result in a clear choice, rather than neutralizing each other or producing counter-productive over-compromises. This requires workable rules for decision-making, controlled hierarchical authority, and – as discussed – democratic power concentrations. These should be combined and balanced with pluralism, but not paralyzed by it. Accordingly, competition among the components of pluralistic governance should be organized so as to increase energy levels and stimulate creativity.

Improvements of different governance layers, processes and components must therefore be kept in balance: raising the quality of elites must go hand in hand with empowering the people; and strengthening global governance should be parallelled by enhancing local governance. To prevent paralyzing stalemates in the face of critical choices, there must nevertheless be ways to focus overriding authority and power.

Equipped with this model and the prerequisites of higher-order tasks, we are now ready to take on the 'resolution', with detailed redesign proposals; but first the proposed approach to redesign needs explanation, which will be undertaken at the beginning of the next part.

NOTES

1. Unusual in modern literature is the comprehensive theory proposed by Friedrich Hayek (Hayek, 1979). But however brilliant in its own terms, his approach is narrow in its underlying assumptions and values and does not take into account the requirements posed by global transformations. Worst of all, as do nearly all modern treatments of democratic governance, he ignores the compelling reasons for refocusing democracy and revitalizing politics as essential for governmental future-building – given the emerging opportunities and dangers that cannot be handled by other processes and institutions.

PART THREE
THE RESOLUTION

8

Approaches to Redesign

Having examined the problematic and some overall requirements and facets for the task of weaving the future, we now move on to specific proposals for the redesign of governance. Since it is impossible to treat the subject comprehensively, the proposals concentrate on levels and aspects of governing capacities that are most significant for future-building. How to overcome serious inadequacies and upgrade essential capacities with the help of 'leverage factors' – this is the challenge to which the redesign proposals are directed.

Four main approaches to developing redesign proposals are available. The primary approach is normative, and aims to make governance operate in accordance with higher values. All major belief systems provide moral directives for governance, including what is called 'political theologies' – that is, theological norms and prescriptions for governance. Examples include the demands of certain religions for governance to be subordinated to heavenly law and its representatives on earth, the ethical conception of governance put forth by classical Confucianism, the requirement of rule by or on behalf of the proletariat by communism, and the norms of human rights and equalities on which liberal democracy are based. These norms are a central concern of political philosophy and public debate, from Pericles and Plato in classical Greece to contemporary discussions on feminism, justice, communitarianism and libertarianism. As discussed in Chapter Two, these themes serve as the deepest normative grounding of governance and its redesign.

A second and very different approach to governance redesign is that of 'debugging'. This approach starts by identifying the principal weaknesses of governance and its propensities to error, either by scientific investigation or from practical experience, and then develops counter-measures. For instance, one well-documented defect of governance is 'groupthink', where group deliberations tend to provide mutual agreement at the expense of effectively tackling problems (Janis, 1982; Hart, 1990). To take a different example, 'misuses of history' are prevalent among the highest echelons of governance, already brilliantly discussed by Nietzsche (Nietzsche, 1874) and

79

THE CAPACITY TO GOVERN

further investigated by modern researchers (May, 1972; Dermandt, 1978; Nolte, 1991). Another example includes the barriers to learning that prevent governance from drawing lessons from experience (Etheredge, 1985). The departmental structure of governance causes another serious weakness, namely the fragmentation of issues that ought to be treated together – a weakness that governments repeatedly recognize and try to overcome, but usually without much success (HMSO, 1972). Even more serious is the pressure on governance to 'focus on the present issues and avoid more distant, but frequently more fundamental matters' (King and Schneider, 1991, p. 3), and so on.

Once identified and understood, such weaknesses can in part be remedied. Thus, appropriate group structures and group management can minimize groupthink; misuses of history can be reduced by including sophisticated historians in high-policy staffs and by teaching senior decision-makers to 'think in time' (Neustadt and May, 1986); learning can be enhanced with the help of evaluation and feedback units; lengthening periods between elections and strengthening non-democratic enclaves within democratic governance can extend the time horizons of governance (Stone, 1996).

A third basis for reform is that of prescriptive (that is, instrumental rather than normative) models of 'optimal', or 'preferable' governance, as illustrated by the feature model presented in Chapter Seven. Such models can, in part, be based on various domains of knowledge, such as philosophy of action and judgment, different notions of 'rationality', market models, welfare economics, public choice theory, cognitive science, cybernetics, general systems theory, organizational theory, and other disciplines of the sciences and humanities. Also relevant are various design theories (Goodin, 1996), organization theory (March, 1988; Brunnson and Olsen, 1993) and parts of political science (Sartori, 1996). The wealth of experience with attempts at the reform of governance throughout history and in different settings can also be reinvestigated (Corkey *et al.*, 1998) to yield important, though less formal, prescriptive models. Also very important, though underrated nowadays, are models derived from informed contemplation of statecraft, as is well illustrated by parts of the classical genre of 'Mirrors for Princes'.

The fourth approach stresses imagination and creativity, leading to the invention of new designs for governance. This approach includes a variety of bases and components ranging from envisaging utopias and dystopias to proposals invented by experienced and imaginative practitioners and professionals, and also by more eccentric thinkers.

Much more imagination and creativity are essential because existing ideas for improving governance are interesting and promising, but inadequate. Accordingly, one of my hopes for this book is that it might stimulate fresh thinking on ways to improve governance better than my own.

As already noted, the 'resolution' presented in this book does not presume to 'resolve' the issues of governance, this being inherently impossible; but I develop a series of redesigns aiming at upgrading capacities to govern, and especially those related to future-building. They are grounded in a mixture of the four approaches presented above, within fundamental values of democracy and human rights broadly interpreted to fit a variety of cultures and value systems (for earlier versions of some underlying notions and models, see Dror, 1983, 1988b). Another important basis of the redesigns is the personal experience of the author as an adviser to governments.

The proposals are presented in accordance with the following principles:

- They are formulated in general terms, so that they fit a variety of settings. However, they are intended to be operational and efforts are made from time to time to illustrate their application to particular governance systems.
- They try to follow a middle path between the mundane and the utopian. Some of them distinguish between minimum and preferable specifications – the former being easier to implement but less useful, the latter being more demanding but promising better results.
- Some of the proposals are crash programs intended to achieve rapid improvements, while others are long range, requiring considerable lead times and implementation cycles.
- A few proposals stand alone, but most form clusters that are interdependent, supporting and reinforcing one another.
- The recommendations are presented in their essentials, as succinctly as possible.
- The recommended redesigns are a sub-set of those that are necessary and possible. They were selected according to their importance in terms of impact and feasibility, but inevitably also reflect my own personal interests, biases and limitations.

The recommendations need to be carefully tailored to apply to specific settings. Thus, although the suggestion may be universally valid that citizen participation in governance should be improved by increasing public knowledge and awareness of policy complexities, its application depends very much on the levels of education and the ideologies of different societies. Nonetheless, many recommendations, such as creating enclaves of excellence in policy professionalism around rulers, are relevant to nearly all governments, even though the details must be adapted to particular personalities, political institutions and cultures. Application to particular circumstances is left to those readers willing and able to put the redesigns to the test, whether in their own minds or, hopefully, in the real world.

Most of the proposals are multi-purpose, with the same recommendation aiming to improve several dimensions of the capacity to govern, although certain clusters of reforms are targeted specifically at one dimension or another.

Relating the different chapters to the feature model may help orient the reader and make clear how the recommendations are integrated into a coherent set. Fostering *raison d'humanité* and virtues and vices (Chapters Nine and Ten) directly relate to making governance more moral. Future-commitment is also served by those chapters, as well as by refashioning governance elites, deepening policy reflection, becoming qualified in 'fuzzy-gambling', improving the central minds of governments (Chapters Twelve, Fourteen, Fifteen and Sixteen) and strengthening the autonomy of high-quality government (Chapter Twenty-Two). High-energy but selective governance is to be achieved in a variety of ways: empowering the people with public affairs enlightenment; refashioning governance elites; restructuring governance architecture; governing private power; making global governance more resolute; and gearing governance for crises (Chapters Eleven, Twelve, Seventeen, Eighteen, Nineteen and Twenty-One). Deepening policy reflection, becoming 'fuzzy-gambling' qualified, improving central minds of governments, and empowering the people with public affairs enlightenment (Chapters Eleven, Fourteen, Fifteen and Sixteen) aim at raising standards of policy reflection, learning and creativity. Empowering people with public affairs enlightenment while refashioning governance elites, restructuring governance architecture, and augmenting oversight (Chapters Eleven, Twelve, Seventeen and Twenty) increase pluralism. Greater decisiveness is achieved by rulership, restructuring governance architecture, governing private power, making global governance more resolute, gearing governance for crises (Chapters Thirteen, Seventeen, Eighteen, Nineteen and Twenty-One), and strengthening the autonomy of high-quality government (Chapter Twenty-Two).

Additional links between the model and specific redesign proposals will become clear in the course of the discussion, as will their relation to the prerequisites of higher-order tasks as detailed in Chapter Six.

9

Fostering *Raison d'Humanité*

The single most important – and also most radical and difficult – change required in governance is to make it more moral, above all in the sense of increasingly serving ever higher conceptions of *raison d'humanité*, with special attention to values concerning the future. This is both a moral imperative and an essential basis for engaging well in weaving the future. *Raison d'humanité must become a main moral driving force and decision criterion increasingly guiding all levels of governance, especially in their efforts to weave the future.*

But caution is of the essence. One of the paradoxical advantages of the term *raison d'humanité* is that, by reminding us of *raison d'état* it serves as a warning against misuse. 'Reasons of state' has become pejorative because it was often wrongly invoked to justify evil acts (even though historically the idea was quite progressive, putting the duty of rulers to promote the collective good above dynastic and personal interests (Meinecke, 1957)). *Raison d'humanité* is an essential concept for statecraft and what should be called for lack of a better term 'humankind-craft' in the twenty-first century, but there must be safeguards against its misuse.

However, the real danger is for *raison d'humanité* to remain an abstract dream. To become an applied norm, *raison d'humanité* must be widely accepted by large publics and many political cultures and become central to the concerns of political elites and rulers. Social actors outside government can and should exert their influence to make *raison d'humanité* a main concern of governance, while governance has a key role in educating people about *raison d'humanité*.

On a deeper level, *raison d'humanité* requires quite a transformation in individual ethics (as advocated, for instance, by P. Singer, 1995). Otherwise, essential public support for democratic governance giving increasing weight to *raison d'humanité* will be lacking. This returns us to the tensions between governance influencing the values of citizens and making them more 'moral' (George, 1993) and being subordinated to them.

Developing the ideas and advancing the application of *raison d'humanité* is a task for social processes and actors, including intellectuals, spiritual and religious leaders, political philosophers, scientists and professionals, community leaders, ethical and ideological forums, and groups of concerned persons. The general public must also be brought into the debate, with the help of the mass media and grassroots organizations, in addition to the governmental 'moral education' as already discussed. Representative deliberative forums might also contribute, as suggested in different ways by Bertrand de Jouvenel (Jouvenel, 1967), James S. Fishkin (Fishkin, 1991) and others (for a balanced discussion, see Elster, 1998).

The major world religions have a key role in helping to define and spread the concept of *raison d'humanité*. When reconsidering and reformulating their doctrines, they may wish to emphasize general human values and to call for human solidarity, as was done by Pope John Paul II in his 1993 encyclical *Veritatis Splendor* (The Splendor of Truth).

In view of the radical changes in conceptions of national independence and interests needed for the acceptance and realization of expanding notions of *raison d'humanité*, incremental progress may be the best that can be achieved until the shock effects of serious calamities bring about deep changes in values. This will probably occur together with the decline of the state as the dominant form of polity (Creveld, 1999), together with the strengthening of global governance.¹ However, to try to advance *raison d'humanité* as much as possible and be ready for opportunities to expand its applicability, it is essential that the idea of *raison d'humanité* be clarified. This is a main task awaiting moral and political philosophy, as pointed out in Chapter Two.

As we have seen, a lot of work has been done on certain ethical issues, for example the environment. But central problems, such as global equity, are as yet seldom subjected to serious thought. Moral reasoning, as well as public and political discourse, on coping with radically new possibilities provided by science and technology, is very simplistic; and much of the thinking on relatively well defined issues, such as protecting the environment, is superficial and even plainly wrong in its reasoning and principles.

The provisional and constantly changing contents of large parts of *raison d'humanité* add to the demanding nature of this concept. With changes in social values and in the problems, opportunities and dangers facing humanity and its sub-divisions, the contents of *raison d'humanité* will and should undergo revisions. New human capacities are raising novel and increasingly perplexing moral issues; science and technology, globalization and other processes will have a substantial impact on actually accepted values, including notions of *raison d'humanité*. Values that seem to us now to be 'eternal', such as those concerning human rights and responsibilities, will also acquire new meanings and require significant reformulation. Therefore:

Contemplation, philosophical discourse and theoretical work on the meanings and contents of raison d'humanité should be advanced and applied to a growing domain of issues.

This work should not be bound by narrow conceptions of feasibility and realism; instead, it should adopt a level of 'realistic vision'. But it should not go to the extreme of vision-ary utopianism (though well designed utopias, sorely lacking at present, have an impor-tant contribution to make).

Moving to some preliminary thoughts on the structure, nature and substance of *raison d'humanité*, it is to be noted that it should be oriented more toward consequences than intentions, but without necessarily adopting a utilitarian position. It is not enough to be very 'moral', even in the extreme sense of being ready to give up one's life for one's values, but consequences must be weighed up in terms of *raison d'humanité*.

The distinction between 'intentionalism' and 'consequentialism' is funda-mental to ethics (Pettit, 1991. For a concise discussion, see Audi, 1999, pp. 176–7) and need not be explored here. For our limited purposes it is enough to mention the hypothetical discussion by R.M. Hare, featuring a Nazi true believer who is highly 'moral' in terms of his 'values', which he believes in sincerely and for which he is willing to sacrifice his life (Hare, 1963, ch. 9). This thought experiment makes the point that, rather than the intensity of subjective 'moral' intentions, their actual or probable conse-quences are central to moral judgment in *raison d'humanité*. Having good intentions is not a sufficient justification for action that can have significant impact on human beings and humanity. This point needs emphasis in view of the many global action groups which may have the best of intentions, but who may be quite destructive in terms of the likely consequences of realiz-ing their beliefs, as illustrated by some of the 'deep green' movements.

A distinction must be made between the values applicable to human beings considered as individual persons (and perhaps other sentient beings, such as animals (L. Johnson, 1993)) and those applicable to groups and to humanity as a whole. Examples of the first kind are human rights in a narrower or broader sense, including for a start the rights recognized in the Universal Declaration of Human Rights, in the International Covenant on Economic, Social and Cultural Rights, and in the International Covenant on Civil and Political Rights.

Examples of values applicable to groups, and especially to humanity and its global habitat as a whole, should again start from a minimal core. This includes the human concerns recognized in major global agreements, such as the UN Convention on International Trade in Endangered Species, the UN Framework Convention on Climate Change, the International Tropical Timber Agreement, various agreements on the Law of the Sea, the begin-nings of various international criminal tribunals, norms prohibiting certain weapon systems, and so on.

To go one step further, *raison d'humanité* requires more emphasis on 'species-collective' values, concerning humanity and its future as a whole, as against both individual and national values and interests. This leads, for instance, to an emphasis on individual responsibilities and duties as against individual rights, within an overall devaluation of egocentric values as contrasted with human solidarity.

As already mentioned, the notions of human rights should be balanced and supplemented by a sense of human responsibility and norms expressing responsibility. But to translate this idea into operational principles raises complex issues as to the meanings of 'responsibility' for and to oneself and others (Lucas, 1993), and of relations between responsibility and community boundaries (Smiley, 1992). Clearer in principle, but politically even more difficult to realize, is the requirement to give more weight to global values and the interests of humanity and its future as a whole, as against national interests – with the latter having to include more and more of the former. The debates on the International War Crimes Tribunal illustrate the difficulties of proceeding on the road towards *raison d'humanité* against narrow and self-centered perceptions of 'national interest'.

A different illustration is provided by the notion of 'cultural rights', to be protected against excessive globalization. Thus, neglected in present global discourse is the danger that, of the 6000 languages spoken today, about half may disappear within a century (Moselley and Asher, 1994; Grenoble and Whaley, 1998).

Other major issues involve values concerning time and risk preferences. To start with the time factor: genetic experimentation with human beings, including human cloning and genetic engineering, or investments in very expensive scientific projects, may be beneficial for the long-term future of humanity as a species; but they do not help, and may even do some harm, to human individuals and collectives in the shorter term. Different attitudes to risk also give rise to difficult choices, such as within biotechnology, which may provide terrible weapons for fanatics and/or cheap and safe ways of cleaning up the biosphere. Present tendencies in both political and moral discourse (Jonas, 1984) tending to prefer risk-avoidance, making it all the more necessary to be careful in such judgments and not to be overwhelmed by fear of the unknown and inconceivable.

To go one step further, there is a major tension, as well as an overlap, between values directed at improving the quality of life (in one sense or another) of humans as individuals and groups, and improving the future fate and civilization of humanity as species. As sharply put by Walter Benjamin: 'there is no document of civilization which is not at the same time a document of barbarism' (quoted in Jay, 1984, p. 36), and, vividly, by Ernst Block: 'the mansion of culture was built on dogshit' (ibid., p. 19).

This tension is sharply posed by the history of warfare. Despite some romantic notions, war is obviously a painful and deadly tragedy for individual human beings and human groups. War must clearly be eliminated to satisfy both human values and – since the invention of nuclear weapons and the potential of other mass killing instruments of violence, such as biological weapons – 'humanity values' (as classically discussed in Jaspers, 1958 and Schell, 1982). Yet warfare and its consequences have throughout history made essential contributions to the achievements of humanity (Chanteur, 1992, Part 1 and Lewin, 1967). Therefore, the question must be faced: What if any substitutes are needed for the positive functions fulfilled by warfare in the past which continue to be important for the progress of humanity in the future?

No less vexing is the question of what value costs may be involved in eliminating warfare. Seeking enemies and engaging in warfare, and even enjoying the excitement and anxiety of battle (Bohrer, 1983 and H. Bloom, 1995) has much deeper roots than 'conflicts of interest', 'miscalculations' and 'fundamentalist fanaticism'. It may well be that a liking for war is wired into our mind, having been evolutionarily useful since the emergence of *homo sapiens*. Reversing such deeply rooted propensities now, when they become dysfunctional, may require the equivalent of radical surgery, without the benefit of anesthesia. Thus, it is not impossible that the only way to stop humanity-endangering conflicts with mass-killing weapons will prove to be the establishment of a 'Global Leviathan'. Inter alia, this may take the form of authoritarian rule by a coalition of superpowers using brute force to eliminate war and destroy all weapons of mass killing owned by countries other then themselves. If so, then *raison d'humanité* may require movement along this path, though the cost in terms of many essential values, including human rights, is very high.

Another vexed problem is that of global equity, as discussed in Chapter Two. It is quite inconceivable that all the growing populations will achieve a more or less equal or equivalent material standard of living within the foreseeable future. One means of trying to reconcile the rich and poor in ways which might reduce human suffering, while avoiding very costly conflict, may be to create more what can be called 'global spheres' (I am applying Kaus, 1992), in which all humans can participate on an equal basis. This should be taken together with the assurance of constantly growing minimum standards for 'human development' for all, as conceptualized, for example, by the annual United Nations Development Programme *Human Development* reports, starting in 1990, within a multi-dimensional understanding of 'inequality' (Temking, 1993). But these are temporary measures at best, leaving open fundamental and very conflictive issues of global equity, which are further aggravated by the already-discussed impossibility of global democracy and the possible need for global authoritarian regimes if consensual processes prove inadequate.

To further explore some issues related to *raison d'humanité* let us engage in a thought experiment (in line with Sorensen, 1992) in three stages.

In the first stage we assume ideal circumstances. We suppose that political cultures all over the world care deeply about *raison d'humanité*, are imbued with a real sense of human solidarity, and are ready to promote the long-term good of humanity at the expense of other considerations and desires. We also assume that governance is completely overhauled so as to serve *raison d'humanité*, to which it is fully committed, enjoying almost universal support in doing so, controlling substantial resources, and acting optimally for the future. In such conditions the stumbling block takes the form of the crucial question: What, after all, is *raison d'humanité*?

It is not difficult to establish minimum criteria and to delineate some evils that should be avoided, as indicated above. Thus, *raison d'humanité* will clearly include preventing a major nuclear war and avoiding the depletion of irreplaceable global resources essential for human survival.

However, when we turn to more complex criteria, such as global equity, human development, or assuring a good life to a growing proportion of humanity, salient concepts prove controversial, relative, dependent on perspective and *Weltanschauung*, and to some extent even meaningless and vacuous. This is most apparent when we consider the controversial space between avoiding evil and achieving good. For example, is production by genetic manipulation of a modified (hopefully 'superior') human species a danger to be avoided or highly desirable, as the only chance to overcome the limitations of present humankind?

Another illustration of the vexed questions surrounding *raison d'humanité* is the concept of 'sustainable development', apparently first coined by Barbara Ward in 1972 for the Stockholm Conference on the Human Environment. The concept was taken up and put into common use by the World Commission on Environment and Development in its famous report *Our Common Future*, and is today widely relied upon as a standard for action. The idea of 'sustainability' makes sense for essential life-sustaining resources as long as they are not easily replaceable and no substitute for them is available, such as forests, water systems, and so on. But its canonical application to development as a whole, not to speak of nonsensical uses such as 'sustainable government', becomes very misleading (for a critique from a contrary point of view, see Porritt, 1993).

A central definition of the term is 'development that meets the needs of the present without compromising the ability of future generations to meet their own needs' (World Commission on Environment and Development, 1987, p. 43). But this glaringly raises the question of how 'needs' are to be defined – given that the concept is cultural and has no inherent meaning, once minimal biological requirements have been satisfied (Springborg, 1981). It is even harder to answer the question: Why should present needs receive priority over future needs? For example, an alternative formulation of 'desirable development' could be 'development that ensures the satisfaction of potential future needs, even if this involves some sacrifice of satisfaction of present needs'.

Most doubtful of all is the 'play safe' value implicit in the sustainable development formulation, combined with the fallacy that human development can at all be a smooth and broadly linear process. The question is whether *raison d'humanité* should be risk-averse, in the sense of seeking a stable level of need satisfaction over time; or whether it should be more adventurous, willing to take serious risks in order to seek a superior future with partially unknown parameters? This presents, as already mentioned, a major value judgment issue. The advancement of potentially risky but very promising areas of science, the investment in vast projects to change the physical habitat of humanity, the toleration of ideologies that may threaten the status quo – these are only a few illustrations undermining the concept of 'sustainable development' and its implications of stasis as a preferred state of the world.

If we look at the history of the human race with the little understanding we have, it is clear that had any sustainable development imperative been accepted in the past it would have frozen human progress at some stages which, by present standards, would be extremely undesirable. It is true that human, change-endeavors are now potentially more hazardous and therefore need some limitation, but not within the mental cage of 'sustainable development', which in any case is sure to be stormed. No 'stable state' should be aimed at, nor can any supposed 'equilibrium' of humanity be more than a temporary phase, certain to be disrupted by the energy and dynamism characterizing human history (see Postrel, 1999). For this reason, the terminology of 'sustainable development', when misapplied as a *raison d'humanité* principle to the advancement of humanity as a whole rather than to a few particular projects and resources, must be rejected. It inhibits the advancement of humanity by postulating that any given line of development followed now should be sustainable in the long term, instead of viewing humanity as moving through changing dimensions of development, none of which needs to be sustainable for very long. Therefore, *a formulation such as 'catastrophe-avoiding dynamic development directed, inter alia, at enhancing the evolutionary potential of future generations' should become a core value of raison d'humanité, instead of 'sustainable development' – which should be dropped as a misleading, fear-driven slogan.*

Returning to our thought experiment, let us now move on to its second phase and assume that the contents of *raison d'humanité* are quite clear to governments, who are willing to be guided by them. Democratic governance can, however do little to foster *raison d'humanité* if political cultures are resistant and public support lacking. Thus, if *raison d'humanité* (even if reinforced by enlightened self-interest) requires that rich countries transfer substantial resources to poor ones, and absorb large numbers of immigrants from the

latter, it is more than likely that present political cultures will stop governments from acting accordingly. This is true even in the not very likely case
that many senior politicians are convinced that the demands are both just
and serve the long-term geo-strategic interests of their countries.

Also relevant are issues of problem perception (Dery, 1984), as shaped by
political cultures. Thus, while interviewing most ministers in Brasilia in the
1990s, during one of my consultative activities, I asked them to identify the
five most important issues facing their country. None of them mentioned the
future of the Amazon – which from a *raison d'humanité* perspective is surely
one of the most important ones.

Emergent properties of the global political system as a whole lead to the
same results, because of interactive mutual expectations. As put by Jervis:

> Some arrangements of connections will make a system resistant to
> change ... When one element or relation cannot change unless several
> others do, small and slow adjustments will not be possible; each element
> has a veto over all the others. In international politics the most important
> case is that each state might be glad to abandon a pre-occupation with
> power and narrow self-interest if its rivals did. But for anyone to change
> everyone must change, which means that Realism may exist because it
> exists: Once it is in place, no individual state can alter it ... This dynamics
> also means that we cannot infer desires from behavior: An or all states-
> men could prefer a world governed by norms and justice to one dominated
> by power politics and yet act according to the precepts of the latter.
>
> (Jervis, 1998, pp. 19–20 and footnote 47)

This statement underrates the ability of outstanding statecraft to change systems and bring about radical transformations, as occasionally illustrated
throughout history. But conditions must be ripe for such changes, and
whether they are feasible or not can often only be determined in retrospect.
For all we know about social systems, present and expected transformations
will provide many opportunities for radical shifts brought about by a few
actors – because of destabilization processes which reduce systemic rigidities.
Still, to move towards *raison d'humanité* becoming a main consideration in
governance will require many and difficult changes in present political
cultures, structures and propensities.

This brings us back to the need to imbue political cultures with commitment to *raison d'humanité*, chiefly in the big powers with the greatest influence
on global policies. This means encouraging feelings of solidarity and growing
'concern ... with the good of other people whose lives are distant from ours'
(Nussbaum, 1995b, p. xvi), and hence significant changes in consciousness in
order to facilitate the switch from tribalism to globalism. Cultural identities
and pride in ethnic character should not, and need not be sacrificed. But self-
awareness as an individual and a member of a sub-set of humanity must be

combined with a strong sense of belonging to the human race (still relevant is Meinecke, 1969, first published in 1907).

A major question for governance redesign is therefore how to bring about the changes in political culture necessary for governments to foster *raison d'humanité*.

There are three main approaches to coping with this question – one clearly wrong, the second doubtful, and the third promising, though limited and not guaranteeing success. The first approach adopts the logical error of assuming that 'what must and should happen to ensure human survival will somehow happen'. This approach lacks any historical basis and misperceives the cosmos as benevolent in human terms. It is also wrong in terms of teleological beliefs, almost none of which is committed to the indefinite earthly survival of humanity in its present imperfect form. As noted, only philosophers postulating the 'cunning of history', such as Hegel and, in a different way, Marx, felt certain that what they regarded as desirable mutations in history would in fact occur. Modern believers in 'progress' (Nisbet, 1993) and 'the end of history' (Fukuyama, 1992) continue to claim that what they regard as desirable is bound to happen. But this position is nothing but an irrational act of faith without the benefit of claimed revelation.

The second approach puts its hopes in the grass-roots. It expects positive human transformations to grow from the bottom up (Jantsch, 1975), fertilized and led by prophets, charismatic leaders, intellectuals, young people, and so on (see Richter, 1997, esp. ch. 13). As the history of the major religions shows, this has indeed been an important source of radical change in human development (as well described, for instance, in Cahill, 1999). A revolution in human consciousness developing in this way is therefore not impossible, although it should be remembered that extremely evil ideologies have also emerged by the same route and might do so again in the future.

However, there is a big difference between regarding a positive mutation in human consciousness as not impossible and considering it likely. To judge by contemporary trends on the grass-roots level, ranging from consumerism everywhere to growing xenophobia in Europe, positive signs of an emerging new and much better human consciousness are not pronounced, to put it relatively optimistically. Therefore, to base hopes for the future on the assumption that grass-roots forces will soon bring about significant changes for the better in political cultures in the direction of *raison d'humanité* is to construct castles on quicksand on a stormy seashore.

The third approach, as already indicated, is to engage in 'cultural architecture' and 'soulcraft', through deliberate action guided by avant-gardes (note the plural) operating partly through and in governance.

The term 'avant-garde' is not a popular one. It seems undemocratic, denigrating the worth of the masses, and was misused by the communist regimes to send people to the gulag or be promoted into a corrupt nomenclature.

However, sophisticated interpretations of democracy and liberalism as mixed regimes recognize the importance of pioneering intellectual and political elites, as long as these are open and pluralistic, avoid arrogance, and are committed and subordinated to democracy.

There is a risk here of relying on a *deus ex machina* in assuming the emergence, or at least possibility, of influential democratic avant-gardes, clustered into global elites committed to working out and actualizing in stages complex versions of *raison d'humanté*. But this is perhaps a less remote aspiration than the other two approaches criticized above. Some promising proto-elements of such an avant-garde already exist and are active, for example in very important global non-governmental organizations, constituting growing global networks and providing a core for expansion and development. Deliberate action to develop governance and global elites oriented toward *raison d'humanité* is possible in ways to be suggested later, even though difficult and without the assurance of success.

The need for global networks of avant-gardes and global elites committed to raison d'humanité, *and working to change political culture and democratic governance accordingly, should therefore be frankly recognized. Efforts to foster the development of such avant-gardes and elites, in part overlapping with governance elites, are urgently required.*

However, structures are crucial too. This leads us to the third and last phase of our thought experiment. Let us assume that the ideas of *raison d'humanité* have been clarified and that political cultures are receptive to them, but governance is not geared to becoming more moral. The question now is: What redesigns are needed to make governance serve *raison d'humanité*? This is all the more important a question as governments committed at least in part to *raison d'humanité* are essential to making political cultures more receptive to it and to move towards applying it in concrete decisions and policies.

This fundamental problem of making governance serve *raison d'humanité* as one of its major considerations underlies and connects the resolution proposed in this book. Governance capacities to think and plan in terms of *raison d'humanité* must be improved; political will and power to act in accordance with *raison d'humanité* must be crystallized; *raison d'humanité* must become a major concern and commitment within the central minds of governance at all levels; rapid steps must be taken towards creating a decisive global governance system and making it serve evolving *raison d'humanité* as it constantly evolves; and emergency measures to meet the most urgent requirements of *raison d'humanité* are essential.

However, the redesigns, as elaborated in later chapters, are unlikely to succeed in making governance serve *raison d'humanité* unless high governance elites have strong moral commitments to the future of humanity as a whole. This requirement brings us to the essential, albeit 'delicate' and repressed,

92

subject of the virtues and vices of politicians, senior officials and other govern-ance staffs, discussed in the next chapter.

Before taking up that subject, let me correct any impression that my argu-ments above on what 'must' happen, is 'essential' and so on, imply that I think such necessity is sure to produce results satisfying it. As explained, this is neither the logic of history nor the nature of the universe. Fallback positions are therefore needed for the quite likely possibility that none of the ways dis-cussed above to make *raison d'humanité* a reality will work out.

One possibility is that following catastrophes humanity and governments will learn and adopt crucial parts of *raison d'humanité*. A second fallback possi-bility is, as already mentioned, the emergence of a Global Leviathan – that is, a constellation of superpowers enforcing out of self-interest those norms of *raison d'humanité* essential for assuring the survival of humanity as essen-tial for their own success.

These fallback possibilities will appear several times in the following chapters, because of the serious impediments to adequate learning on the part of human beings and governments without shock effects, but this makes no difference to my main arguments. Optimistically, essential redesigns may be adopted before calamities; pessimistically, redesign proposals should be ready for the time when shocks create a demand for them.

NOTES

1. An alternative is to expect transcendental interventions, as believed in by some fundamentalists. An interesting utopia presenting such a vision is O'Brien (1996). Needless to say, this is not a basis on which governance and policies should be predi-cated. This is also the view of sophisticated Christian and Jewish theology which rejects human reliance on heavenly action as far beyond the capacities of the human mind to comprehend.

10

Virtues against Vices

Corruption in governance is endemic and expanding (Little and Posada-Carbó, 1996). In some countries, traditional loyalties, such as to family and clan, have moral priority over ethics in governance. In countries in transition, old ethical codes lost their force while new ones take a long time to develop and become accepted, leaving politicians and officials in a moral vacuum. In democracies, electoral competition is becoming increasingly costly for parties and candidates, unavoidably causing dishonesty and corruption.[1] Cut-throat competition pushes enterprises to look for every advantage they can gain, including bribing officials when useful (see Reno, 1995). In many countries, low salaries further motivate politicians and officials to seek additional income. Overtly corrupt rulers are widespread in some types of countries (Ayittey, 1992). Mafias, drugs traders and other criminal organizations combine offers of large bribes with physical intimidation, putting governance staffs under intolerable pressure. Market economies are often brought in rapidly, before essential cultural adjustments can be made, with corruption becoming rampant, and so on.

The depraved episodes at the highest level of the European Union Commission exposed in March 1999 and leading to its resignation further demonstrate the prevalence of corruption and the ease with which it infects senior politicians even in Western countries – without any special circumstances of cultural transformation, low pay and so on.

This problem is receiving quite a lot of attention. Some helpful ideas on how to contain corruption are provided in the literature (Klitgaard, 1991; deLeon, 1993). The World Bank, OECD and other international organizations devote increasing efforts to fighting it. Some countries, especially the USA, have made it a criminal offense for companies to give bribes in other countries. International agreements against some forms of corruption are being signed, such as the Convention on Combating Bribery of Foreign Public Officials in International Business Transactions, agreed in 1997; Transparency International is an example of anti-corruption initiatives by non-governmental organizations; efforts are being made to limit money-laundering and secret bank accounts; accounting practices are being improved in ways constraining corruption; codes of ethics for civil servants are being reformulated. Large-scale corruption can evoke public anger leading to efforts to reduce it, as illustrated by the Italian *mane pulite* ('clean hands') crusade, attempts at reform in Japan, and by some developments in Indonesia following economic meltdown. Investigative journalism, closer monitoring by special control bodies, vigorous prosecution of criminal acts and similar control processes are increasing. Efforts are being made to control the costs and money-raising modes of politics, and more. While such measures should not be expected to reduce corruption significantly in the absence of changes in public mores, political cultures and reduced costs of politics, at least the problem is on the public agenda and some efforts to contain it are being made.

The situation is quite different in respect to the underlying broader and even more significant issue of the virtues and vices of senior governance elites. There is little hope of making *raison d'humanité* a major concern of governance, or of making governance more moral and legitimate and having it engage in responsible moral education, unless its elites behave according to high standards grounded in personal virtues (on related needs for a public morality, see Schmidt, 1998). This applies in particular to the higher echelons, which shape the overall style of governance and which exert considerable influence on political culture and on society as a whole.

Especially malignant is the issue of virtues and vices of senior politicians. No amount of anti-corruption laws and other anti-corruption instruments will achieve significant impact unless the virtues of senior politicians are improved. The damage caused by the vices of senior politicians goes far beyond that of 'corruption' as this term is usually understood, however harmful. It makes achievement of high-quality moral capacities to govern impossible, damages political cultures and has very negative impacts on all social values. Efforts to improve the ethics of lower-level governance elites are in vain unless the virtues of senior politicians are first improved.

To bring out the main problem, let me distinguish between 'surface corruption' and 'root corruption'. Surface corruption includes all the forms routinely discussed when the subject of corruption is taken up, which are serious enough. 'Root corruption is different – more insidious and deeper. It is the corruption of the body politic, in the Greek sense of the term exemplified by the accusation, however unjust, against Socrates: 'to destroy utterly, spoil, harm, lead astray, corrupt, ruin, bribe or seduce' (quoted in Euben, 1990, p. 168. See also Euben, 1998). It is grounded in the vices of senior politicians, whether character-bound or brought about by environmental influences. To counteract such root corruption the virtues of senior politicians must become a main subject for evaluation, consideration and improvement.

This imperative brings us back to the classical concern of political philosophy with the duties, character, virtues and vices of politicians, which are all the more important when capacities to govern need radical upgrading. But broad issues of virtues and vices, and of the character of senior politicians, are very seldom addressed nowadays. This modern blind spot contrasts with the preoccupation throughout history with the virtues and vices of ruling groups, from Plato, Confucius, Cicero and Augustine, to the many moral 'Mirrors for Princes' texts written and debated in literate societies throughout history up until 'modernity'.[2]

Classical thought on politics and power recognized the deep sources of the vices of senior politicians, namely the insidious effects of power as first clearly discussed by Tacitus as leading to what I propose to call, following the apt German term *Caesarenwahnsinn* (Hentig, 1924), 'rulerscraze' – a kind of very malignant mental lack of balance, even 'madness', caused by wielding great power. A more modern formulation is the saying by Lord Acton that 'power corrupts and absolute power tends to corrupt absolutely'.

Modern factors aggravating the situation include elections which increasingly become a televised circus, the rising costs of politics forcing 'rational politicians' to sell themselves, and the corrupting impacts of public apathy, legitimized greed, unrestrained competition, norms favoring consumption and hedonistic culture.

Some counter-forces are at work, such as democratic oversight, legal and other controls, and mass media investigations. These may help to contain surface corruption, but not root corruption – which is less visible, but even more malignant.

There is much variation between countries and cultures and between persons, with quite a few exceptional senior politicians avoiding root corruption. But, *all in all 'root corruption' of senior politicians is one of the most serious pathologies of contemporary governance. Therefore, a crucial challenge for governance redesign is to raise the morality of senior politicians on the fundamental level of virtue and character.*

An essential first step is to recognize root corruption of senior politicians as a crucial issue. The present nearly universal lack of interest in the character, virtues and vices of the senior governance elites is, therefore, all the more morally disturbing and practically destructive.

Not only does practical politics ignore the issue, but so does contemporary professional discourse on governance. Some philosophers are showing renewed interest in virtues and vices (Foot, 1978; MacIntyre, 1978; Wallace, 1978; Guardini, 1967), and in character (Kupperman, 1991; French, Uehling Jr and Wettstein, 1988). But, with a few exceptions,[3] little attention is paid to moral requirements from senior governance elites (but see Budziszewski, 1988).

In terms of the history of ideas, this strange omission seems to stem from seven main causes, which constitute major barriers to trying to improve virtues in governance:

1. There is a widespread delusion that elections are a guaranteed way of finding adequate politicians in terms of both their intellectual capacities and, even more doubtful and dangerously, their moral character. Consequently, politicians' failings are blamed on weaknesses either in the electoral system or other governance structures, which can be remedied without taking up the real issues of the vices of politicians.

2. Modern Western culture is witnessing a general erosion of demanding moral concepts such as 'duty' and their replacement by quite different ideals, such as 'self-fulfillment', 'having fun', the 'sovereign self' (Broembsen, 1999), and permissiveness. Modernity and post-modernity seem quite impervious to conceptions of virtues and vices. It is enough to compare, for instance, the *Essays* of Montaigne (a recent translation is Montaigne, 1991) and Sartre's *Notebooks for an Ethics* (Sartre, 1992) to get some insight into the differences between traditional and modern attitudes: the concepts of virtue, vice and character tend to be ignored or repressed, especially in respect to politics. As one of the results, transgressions by members of governance elites are frequently regarded as 'stupid', 'illegal', 'distasteful', and sometimes 'criminal', but only seldom as morally wrong and 'sinful'.

3. The adoration of *homo economicus*, the regard of 'self-interest' as a major moral force, and the utilitarian and commercial ethics of the market (Jacobs, 1992) curb the moral demands made on governance.

4. The emphasis on human rights, without much concern for human responsibilities and duties, applies also to senior politicians and all governance elites. For instance, the right to privacy hinders probing into the personal behavior of senior politicians. Moreover, when investigative journalism does reveal cases of reprehensible behavior, the culprits resent what they see as unfair intrusion instead of feeling ashamed. Indeed, shame, frank admission of guilt, and repentance are scarce commodities in contemporary public life.

5. The widespread erosion of consensus on the moral standards to be followed in public life, linked to a relative moral vacuum in private life, inevitably also affects the norms of senior governance elites.

6. Our egalitarian democratic culture regards senior politicians and civil servants as 'ordinary people', and rejects special moral demands as 'elitism'.

7. The widespread view is that 'performance in office' and 'personal behavior' are different spheres that do not influence one another. This is fully reflected in widespread public apathy on immoral behavior by top politicians.

The combined effect of these and additional cultural and societal characteristics is to make the very idea of demanding virtues from senior politicians and governance elites look archaic. At the same time, these factors erode the behavior of governance elites from within, weakening any sense of duty or honor that might require them to aim for higher standards. Indeed, any obvious stance of moral superiority may even damage political careers, because it can appear condescending; and, perhaps, because of the guilty feelings it evokes in colleagues and voters.

On a more theoretical level, senior governance elites in Western democracies share in widespread social anomie, in Durkheim's sense of 'passions getting out of control'. The exaltation of self-interest, however enlightened it is supposed to be, as a perfectly valid motive for human behavior, cannot but have a strong adverse impact on senior governance elites (for a contrary view, see Burke, 1993). The rejection of any measure of asceticism, with its resistance to temptation (Harpham, 1987), further characterizes realities that undermine virtue in politics and do not even expect or demand it.

A vicious downward spiral is the result, with weaknesses in social values reinforcing vices in governance, and the latter aggravating the decline of social values. Unethical governance elites and unethical political cultures thus reinforce one another, making public life increasingly immoral and even anti-moral and 'root-corrupt' in the fullest sense of the term.

However, an important counter-argument must be faced, which is widely accepted implicitly and sometimes explicitly, though seldom acknowledged openly. After all, so the counter-argument runs, many types of immorality and corruption in government do no great harm. What we call corruption in governance was widespread in Europe while industrialization and democratization progressed by leaps and bounds, and the same may hold true today. Certainly, action must be taken against evil rulers who kill and torture their subjects or wantonly attack their neighbors, the argument continues, but making a lot of money by selling favors and having a good time by abusing power can very well go hand in hand with sound policies. Examples can indeed easily be adduced for such a claim – for instance, presidents who engage in immoral personal behavior, but follow sensible policies that benefit their countries.

A sophisticated devil's advocate can produce additional and more complex arguments, reminding us that the sale of offices, which to us looks very corrupt, played an important role in modernizing Europe by opening the way for the better educated into positions previously reserved for the hereditary aristocracy. Similarly, the argument continues, it may well be that in some countries what seems to us to constitute corruption is in fact a way to accommodate the transition from traditionalism to modernity. Some psychologists might add the argument that human being are, after all, 'multiple' (Elster, 1986) and glaring vices in some domains may well go together with good performance and even virtues in others, perhaps even helping the latter as a kind of 'mental hygiene'.

These are serious counter-arguments, which cannot be rejected out of hand on the basis of abstract principles alone. However, relying on historical experience opens the way to many contrary experiences of failures caused by the corruption of rulers, and also to the hypothetical counter-argument that much more might have been achieved if rulers had been more virtuous, if civil services had moved ahead more quickly to meritocratic patterns, and so on. Against the 'multiple self' argument, the unity of character must be taken into account, with vices in one domain probably reflecting and aggravating vices in personality as a whole. Most important of all, while many vices of senior politicians can go hand in hand with good performance of the ordinary tasks of governance, when 'weaving the future' and moral education are at stake, outstanding virtues are essential.

The practical need to present a facade of morality so as to preserve governability and power can perhaps be satisfied tactically by more skillful manipulation of the image of governance, with senior politicians busying themselves even more with what I have called the 'blowing of bubbles'. However, the nature of the future-building tasks faced by senior politicians and governance elites requires them to have many substantive virtues.

In psychological terms, virtues such as fortitude, forbearance, persistence, seriousness, commitment, resoluteness, self-restraint, and toughness are needed to deal with difficulties and opportunities. For creating and analyzing policies, detachment, open-mindedness, creativity and a capacity for deep thinking are required. Crucially, the value judgments involved in critical choices, together with the need to advance *raison d'humanité*, require moral virtues. These include a strong sense of personal responsibility, an intense feeling of duty to humankind, compassion, a sense of obligation to the long-term future, an ability to resist temptations and disruptive passions, and total dedication to the *res publica* even including a readiness to sacrifice oneself if necessary.

Making senior politicians more virtuous is thus essential for improving capacities to govern and 'weaving the future' for the better (Dror, in preparation). Indeed, without improving the virtues of the senior governance elites other proposals for upgrading capacities to govern may be counterproductive, by providing instruments for doing more efficiently what is wrong, such as better logistics for an immoral war.

Radical improvement of the morality of senior governance elites, and especially senior politicians, is therefore essential, with virtues becoming more important than 'being nice' and 'smiling a lot'. Without progress in this direction, other improvements of capacities to govern are likely to fail or to be misused.

Many related issues remain open. For example:

• The question of whether and how far the personal lives of top governance elites should serve as a positive example for the general public, or whether some latitude may be necessary as a release for drives that may otherwise interfere with governance functions.

• The danger – well recognized by Adam Smith – that misguided virtue may turn into dangerous fanaticism, with the risk of more serious consequences than selfish greed at its worst.

- The balance between morality based on Kantian and neo-Kantian conceptions of duty, and morality based on desirable passions, will and emotions, as propounded by Schopenhauer.

A situation that brings to the fore some of the issues of virtues and vices in politics and their links with other important problems of governance is that of sick rulers. This issue is receiving renewed attention (MacMahon and Curry, 1987; Macalpine and Hunter, 1991; Gilbert, 1993; Green, 1993; and Post and Robins, 1993). Various institutional arrangements have been proposed to deal with it, including provisions for scrutiny, procedures for transfer of authority, and arrangements for continuity. But little has been done.

Especially worrying from the perspective of vices and virtues is the fact that few top politicians resign even after they know for certain that illness, or age-related decline (McIntyre, 1988), is depleting their faculties. This is a sign of serious moral weakness, and no country has institutionalized effective ways for dealing with this problem.

These are only a few out of many specific problems, which require multiple measures. A determined effort must be made to raise the ethical standards of senior governance elites; codes of ethics for senior politicians and officials should be prepared; strictly enforced rules and laws directed against quasi-criminal behavior, gross conflict of interest and similar transgressions of minimum standards, are essential; political structures and processes, such as elections, have to be redesigned so as to reduce pressures and temptations to engage in inappropriate behavior; rules to remove incapacitated top politicians are needed; remuneration of senior governance elites must be high enough to reduce pressures to augment salaries illegally;[4] full disclosure rules should discourage illegitimate sources of income; confidential advice when facing ethical dilemmas should be made available; and norms against the misuse of power on the personal level, such as demands for sexual favors, should be strictly enforced.

At the same time, corrupting practices directed at governance must be forbidden, including global norms against corporations offering kickbacks, already prohibited under United States law by the Foreign Corrupt Practices Act of 1978 and by an OECD convention. More drastic measures include international sanctions against clearly corrupt rulers, determined global action against drug cartels and similar cancers, and codes of ethics to guide senior politicians and government officials throughout the world.

Self-policing may help, as illustrated by Transnational International (TI), founded in 1993 to persuade companies to stop paying bribes and persuade officials to stop accepting them. But governments do pay bribes to other countries and break their own rules in order to encourage exports, as revealed in the UK by Lord Justice Scott's enquiry into Britain's role in arming Iraq. Strict regulations, vigorously enforced, are therefore clearly essential, with criminal sanctions against senior politicians who transgress them.

Certainly, all assistance, other than humanitarian, should be denied to states the heads of which flagrantly enrich themselves at the public expense. Similarly, countries that try to rid themselves of corruption should be given assistance, if necessary by putting military forces at their disposal and offering to judge persons who cannot be fairly and safely prosecuted in their own country.

But much more is needed, all the more so because of the cultural sources of root corruption. First of all, the present tendency to be cynical, apathetic or indulgent about the virtues, vices and character of rulers and senior governance elites must be reversed. The idea that elected politicians and appointed senior officials must be superior in virtues and moral character should become a central tenet of democracy. Without putting virtues and vices in the main deliberation and action agenda of improving governance, and thus squarely facing root corruption, all the other measures will be of limited benefit at best.

The qualities demanded of senior politicians and governance elites should be radically revised, with emphasis on virtues and character. These requirements should become a basic canon of democratic theory and political culture. Recruitment, election, promotion, incentives, development, mentoring and oversight of senior politicians and other parts of the senior governance elites should be redesigned accordingly.

It will take time to move ahead in this direction, but small steps are also worthwhile and may prepare the ground for more determined action later. In one matter, however, delay is too dangerous: evil rulers must be removed from power, by international action if necessary.

It is not impossible to arrive at a preliminary definition of evil rulers, though many gray areas remain and application to concrete cases requires a quasi-judicial procedure. Evil heads of governments are those who engage in atrocities, genocide and 'ethnic cleansing', support international atrocities, develop weapons of mass killing despite having undertaken not to do so, and start clearly aggressive wars. With time broader definitions of 'criminal' rulers can be developed, including for instance willfully causing serious damage to the global commons. But this is a task for the future.

Rulers accused of being 'evil' should have an opportunity to defend themselves before an independent quasi-judicial body, but delays should not be tolerated. International action, including military interventions, against rulers who engage in 'evil' is a must, and also constitutes an essential core element of evolving *raison d'humanité*.

Inevitably, careers similar to that of Alcibiades are sure to be repeated in many diverse contexts, being inherent in the 'ambition to rule' (Forde, 1989). We should not pin too much hope on efforts to reintroduce virtues and character as requirements from senior governance elites, or on governance reforms with this aim. However, it is essential to have an explicit vision of governance as a moral endeavor to serve as a basis for realistic attempts to raise the moral standards of governance and stop its working for evil, and to increasingly evaluate and try to improve senior politicians in terms of character, vices and virtues.

An important step is to make senior politicians personally responsible for the action and inaction of their governments (Bovens, 1997), building on the trial of war criminals after World War II but going much further. This includes more than putting them before an international tribunal for atrocities, without recognizing claims to immunity; it has implications for the idea of 'just war' and armed interventions, with leaders being much more of a morally justifiable target than their soldiers and populations.

A vexed question is that of the handling of former leaders who have acted in criminal and even barbaric ways after regime transitions. Amnesty policies in some Central and Latin American countries, and the operations of the Truth and Reconciliation Commission and the Independent Amnesty Committee in the Republic of South Africa illustrate promising approaches. The 'Pinochet effect' is a step in the right direction, though the damages of discouraging bad rulers from giving up their power must be taken into account. However, from the perspective of 'root corruption' expressions of contrition and shame and admissions of guilt are more important in building up norms for future rulers to follow. To take a paradigmatic example without presuming to judge a particular person: in a more ethical political culture, following his admissions (McNamara, 1995), Robert S. McNamara would have sought the modern equivalent of a monastery in which to spend the rest of his days to repent.

A draft *Code of Ethics for Senior Politicians* will serve to conclude this chapter:

1. *Regard your position in governance as a trust and a mission that is 'sacred'. Better to lose your position or resign than to forsake your integrity by subordinating your duties to personal considerations.*
2. *'Weaving the future' for the better, for your country as well as humanity as a whole, is your priority mission, together with taking care of the present and near future. To them you should devote yourself wholeheartedly, within the rule of law.*
3. *Accept responsibility for your actions and their consequences, avoiding the ease of blaming others, such as the mass media.*
4. *Beware of substituting image manipulation for your substantive tasks.*
5. *Be alert to the 'occupational diseases' of rulers, such as growing distance from reality, exaggerated self-confidence, narcissism, susceptibility to flattery, and much else. 'Bind' yourself against them, by among other means, developing self-skepticism, trying to 'exit yourself', and subjecting your reasoning and choices to frank critique.*
6. *However clever and knowledgeable you are, the tasks of governance require much more. Devote strenuous efforts to learning and reflection, and surround yourself with high-quality advisers whom you should encourage to remonstrate with you.*
7. *Serving as an educator of the public is one of your main responsibilities, with special attention to taking a long-range and global view and to advancing* raison d'humanité. *Tell the truth to the best of your knowledge, even when your followers and electors do not like to hear it.*

8. *Your private life should serve as an example.*

9. *Restrain your sexual and material appetites and practise some asceticism, to avoid any misuses of your power, strengthen your self-control, and concentrate all your energy on your mission.*

10. *Reveal in public all information that may be relevant to your performance, including on age, health, income and special personal problems. Resign when you feel inadequate, or your personal physicians tell you that your capacities are waning.*

11. *Do not accept any income or benefits, directly or indirectly, other than those formally allocated to you. After retirement, avoid large payments for activities related to your former positions and declare all such earnings publicly.*

12. *Accept the grooming of successors as one of your main tasks. Help your successor through the transition, even if he or she is anathema to you.*

13. *Regularly examine your conscience.[5] Evaluate yourself, your choices and deeds, devoting hours of solitude to contemplating the morality and effectiveness of your thinking and behavior. Be frank and also cruel to yourself in looking closely into a 'soul-mirror'.*

14. *Keep records of major decisions and activities and your related consideration, reasoning and feelings – in order to accept responsibility, help with self-evaluation, give account, and later to write memoirs that will have a historical value and provide lessons of experience for others to do better.*

NOTES

1. In a study of British MPs in the 1990s (Mancuso, 1995) only a quarter of the sample claimed to be determined to allow neither private interests nor their role as constituency representatives to influence their performance. Various revelations indicate that the situation is bad and worsening – and this in a country with an outstanding democratic tradition. Little wonder the British are trying to develop codes of ethics for politicians (HMSO, 1995), though I doubt their impact without more fundamental changes in the motivation of politicians and in political culture.

2. For two illustrations out of many, this time from Islamic thinking on governance, see Hajib, 1983 (written in 1069), and Meisami (translator and editor), 1991 (written in the mid-twelfth century).

3. To stay with Islamic moral and political thinking, Sachedina, 1988, is an exceptional modern discussion of the 'Just Ruler', as are, in a secular Western context, some parts of Hodgkinson, 1983. An important discussion, though overly reliant on self-interest as a panacea, is Goodin, 1992.

4. See International Monetary Fund, 1997. But, as usual, this study too deals with secondary issues rather than the crucial one of the character of top level politicians. Even in terms of limited approaches to remuneration, most proposals are rather lame. My own recommendation is to pay a president or prime minister a net salary of, say, one or two million US dollars a year and grant him a similar pension. However, he should then be liable for maximum punishment if found guilty of corrupt practices and be limited in the income he can make after retirement from having been a head of state, such as by publishing memoirs, advising other countries and so on.

5. I am taking the idea from *The Spiritual Exercises of St. Ignatius* (Puhl, 1951, pp. 32 ff.), though in a quite different context.

Empowering the People with Public Affairs Enlightenment

Before moving into the substance of this chapter, let me outline my main concern as what I call 'public affairs enlightenment'. This term indicates enlightenment on matters directly salient to understanding major public affairs and essential for arriving at a well-founded, or at least not completely erroneous, opinion about them.

Public affairs enlightenment depends on the overall levels of enlightenment of the public, an increasing level of the second being essential for building up the first, while the border between the two is vague and changing all the time. But I will focus on public affairs enlightenment, leaving it to the reader to consider derived implications for overall enlightenment of the public. Doing otherwise would lead me into cultural theories and civilizational contemplation far beyond the main subject of this book, though closely connected with it.

It is a basic norm of democracy to regard all political power as stemming from the people. Non-democratic states also accept this idea, or at least pay lip service to it. In principle, therefore, empowering the people by increasing their control over governance and their roles in governance should be a central dimension of governance redesign.

Leaving aside normative approaches, there are many empirical indicators that 'the people' are quite capable of participating in governance and having an impact for the better. For instance:

- Grass-roots organizations and social communities often reveal considerable capacities to engage in successful economic activities (Soto, 1989), to build up authority from below (Regan Jr. and Williams, 1992), and to agree on 'local justice' (Elster, 1993).
- Various studies demonstrate good capacities on the part citizen groups play in the discussion and comprehension of complex public affairs issues (Sniderman, Brody and Tetlock, 1991; Gamson, 1993), including taking long-range views (Lewin, 1991).
- Some of the most promising features of present circumstances, such as the near-certainty that democracies will not wage war against one another in

the foreseeable future, are largely the results of the feelings and opinions of the citizen body (Russet, 1993).

However, there are also strong indications that people today, even in the most educated societies, are ill equipped to exercise power over complex policy issues:

- The vast majority of voters appear to be frighteningly ignorant of major facts, issues and problems, whether global or national. Tacit processes and common-sense understanding partly make up for these failings, as does interest in local affairs – hence the reasonableness of many results of elections and referenda. But these factors cannot be relied upon when complex and partly abstract issues beyond personal experience are at stake.
- Television currently does little to provide in-depth coverage of major policy issues (Zaller, 1992; O'Neill, 1993; Page, 1995). Furthermore, global perspectives are largely absent from the television programs that most people (including local opinion leaders) watch, the radio programs they listen to and the newspapers they read.
- Although mass psychology is unpopular nowadays, its main findings should not be ignored (Davies, 1980; Brantlinger, 1983; Moscovici, 1985; and different but also relevant Canetti, 1960 and Gasset, 1985). All of them suggest that tense situations, such as are prevalent during global transformations, do not bring out the best in human collective behavior, causing disorientation and trauma. Television changes the nature of classical masses from mobs in the streets into a huge number of individuals and small groups glued to the same images on a screen. The implications are not yet clear, but are not necessarily for the better.
- It seems well proven that the human mind is prone to some prevalent types of reasoning and thinking errors, such as distortions and wrong deductions when facing uncertainty (Kahnemann, Slovic and Tversky, 1982), unless it is trained to follow explicit procedures. This results in many misperceptions, inconsistencies, 'motivated irrationalities' (Pears, 1984), logical mistakes, and so on, such as are reflected in cultural attitudes to risk (Wildavsky, 1988; Breyer, 1993). These failings render 'public intuition' largely unreliable in judging complex issues.
- The same applies to systemic relationships, the understanding of which is essential for comprehending most policy areas (Jervis, 1997; Gharajedaghi, 1999) but very difficult to achieve.
- Growing apathy towards politics (Eliasoph, 1998) further adds to the factors reducing capacities of 'the people' to exercise power for the better.

Such findings and many similar ones, as well as mixed experiences with participatory and deliberative democracy in the Israeli Kibbutzim (collective settlements),¹ in no way negate the valid judgment often demonstrated by the public. Equally, they cast no doubt on the ability and right of 'the people' to choose the values by which to live and die. Nor do they pose any definite boundary beyond which public understanding of complex issues may be unattainable, given efforts to enlighten them (Kegan, 1994; Hunt, 1995; Lupia and McCubbins, 1998). Neither do they indicate that the growing apathy towards politics in some countries is irreversible, especially as it seems to be caused by negative but partly changeable characteristics of contemporary politics.

Nonetheless, the weaknesses of public views and opinion shaping processes do suggest that many efforts and redesigns are needed to 'approximate a rational society' (Sprangens Jr, 1990, esp. ch. 7), including raising standards of interest, levels of knowledge and qualities of thinking.

Overall, taking into account the demands imposed on democracy by the complexities of global transformations (Zolo, 1992), there is very good cause for what Romano Guardini called *Sorge um den Menschen* – worrying about people (Guardini, 1988 and 1989), including their empowerment in politics. *Unless the people improve their understanding of complex public affairs, democracy will therefore either become more of a fiction, or democracies will increasingly fail in their more demanding tasks, including 'weaving the future'. Upgrading the understanding of complex public affairs by larger parts of populations is therefore essential for empowering them for the better rather than the worse.*

To balance these conclusions it should be noted that governance elites are prone to equivalent and partly overlapping incapacities. Also, the concept of 'the people' must be disaggregated, with many distinctions to be made, such as between highly educated strata and very backward ones.

However, this does not invalidate our main conclusion about enlightening the people as a whole as essential for empowerment. But also required are measures focusing on specific parts of 'the people" with special attention to upgrading the understanding and faculties of governance elites. The first of these tasks involves going into details specific to particular societies and situations, which is beyond the scope of this book. The second is central to our concerns and is also a prerequisite for the public affairs enlightenment of the people as a whole, and will be taken up in the next chapter.

Empirical findings demonstrate both that public affairs enlightenment of the people is a very neglected area, and that there is great potential for doing much more. Elementary measures to increase public affairs enlightenment, which are relatively easy to implement, are grossly neglected. Thus, in no country, to the best of my knowledge after extensive investigation, are all university students required to take courses on major public issues, or even offered such an option. And, though schools in many countries have some courses in 'civic education', 'citizenship' and the like, most of these are very shallow and many are chauvinistic, causing more schooled ignorance than educated enlightenment. Therefore, *a relatively easy essential first step in public affairs enlightenment is to introduce new types of citizenship courses in high schools and pluralistic workshops in public affairs obligatory for all university students.*

The mass media present more difficult problems, oriented as they are to audience ratings and catering to the mass market. But some public television stations do manage to present complex issues in comprehensible and interesting ways, showing that the potential exists for doing so.

In some views the cybersphere will meet this need, providing easy access to information and reasoning. The potential exists, but the reality is quite different. Access to the cybersphere in most countries is limited to parts, however expanding, of the population. Using the cybersphere to become more public affairs enlightened depends on already being quite knowledgeable and wishing to become more so, which holds true at present for only small parts of the public. Moreover, the present contents of the cybersphere are far from meeting public affairs enlightenment needs.

As most of the mass media and much of cybersphere are demand-driven, we run into another vicious circle: in the absence of effective demand, the owners and shapers of mass media and the cybersphere will not devote much resources to making them more effective as instruments of public affairs enlightenment. But without the mass media and the cybersphere contributing much to public affairs enlightenment, no such enlightenment will come about and no effective demand for such enlightenment will emerge.

It is not impossible for governance units and for rulers to serve as agents of change and to help in advancing public affairs enlightenment, as illustrated periodically by the German *Bundeszentrale für politische Bildung* (Federal Center for Political Education). However, as a rule governments cannot be relied upon to take charge of public affairs enlightenment, due to the unacceptably high likelihood of such activities being used for political marketing. The supplying of public affairs enlightenment should therefore be the responsibility of pluralistic public institutions rather than governance bodies, as illustrated by independent public television in some countries (Task Force on the Future of Public Television, 1993). *To counterbalance the anti-enlightenment effects of the mass media and a cybersphere driven by audience ratings and marketing considerations, governance should support multiple bodies engaging in public affairs enlightenment, in ways assuring pluralism.*

This also applies to the development of better formats for presenting complex analyses to the general public in intelligible ways, in the mass media and in cyberspace.

Public affairs enlightenment includes other facets than cognitive ones, such as emotions, attitudes, values and feelings. Thus, feelings of solidarity with humanity as a whole may well be regarded as a part of public affairs enlightenment essential for advancing *raison d'humanité*. However, the role of governance with respect to the emotional and moral facets should be limited to clearly justified areas, such as 'anti-hate' measures. Otherwise, dangers of misuse are likely to multiply. Emotional enlightenment is more a matter for spiritual leaders and civil society, though neither can be relied upon to meet this need. Intellectual and educational elites on one hand, and rulers on the other, therefore have crucial roles to fulfill in all facets of public affairs enlightenment, as discussed in the next two chapters.

Let me turn to another avenue for empowering people by enlightenment, in the form of elections. Elections constitute the main process in representative democracies through which the people directly exercise their power, by deciding who shall represent them and who shall rule on their behalf and by calling senior politicians to account (Przeworksi, 1999). However, this process is being perverted by contemporary electoral dynamics, in which candidates rather than parties or programs are central, with electoral campaigning blinding people to the real qualities of candidates and thus dispossessing them of the real power to choose.

As political marketing becomes more professional and election results are increasingly influenced by television, rational and half-rational candidates have little choice other than to adjust to the rules of the game of a new type of 'beauty contest'. Candidates who appear more attractive on television and present a more appealing semblance of a 'program', usually in the form of striking slogans, have a better chance of winning, quite independent of their moral or intellectual merits or demerits, and of the real meanings of their declared policy postures. Dramatic stage-managed confrontations between candidates on television, and theatrical meetings with 'the people' – with handshaking, kissing of babies and the like – make elections even more of a circus, while implicit promises to various interest groups and money-providers are largely hidden from public scrutiny. The people therefore have hardly any chance to glance behind the mask and assess the candidates' true worth.

It may well be that politicians are caught in a web of delusions spun by self-anointed 'political marketing experts'. My own view is that a serious candidate who adopts what can in shorthand be called a 'De Gaullean' posture of credible gravity (for a concise profile, see Debray, 1994) would defeat his 'political marketing' competitors. This is just one example out of many of the false world pictures that condition contemporary politics. These are self-reinforcing but also provide opportunities for iconoclastic world-picture-changing behavior – and may even make many of the proposed redesigns more feasible than meets the eye.

Whether my optimism on the possibilities for the iconoclastic transformation of parts of politics is correct or not, if elections are to be a meaningful way of expressing deliberate and at least somewhat informed choice, the disguises behind which candidates hide must be lifted. They should therefore be forced to reveal more of their real character.

Voters should have access to as much information as possible about leading candidates, and also have opportunities to observe them in situations where their true character and opinions break through the manufactured facades.[2] Efforts to limit the financial resources at candidates' disposal for election campaigning are an attempt to move in this direction. But however desirable this may be for other reasons (such as reducing the role of wealth and the trends towards corruption in modern politics), quite different measures are required to reveal more of the candidates' real qualities to voters. *Leading election candidates should therefore be required to supply information on their life history, wealth, military service, health, and so on. An independent body of 'candidate examiners' should be entitled to demand further information. Any substantive disinformation should be treated as a serious criminal offense. Also, leading candidates should be subjected to a number of public hearings on television, each lasting one to two hours, during which their knowledge, opinions, proposed policies, and so on should be explored through questioning by teams selected by the candidate examiners.*

The effectiveness of these recommendations hinges on the novel institution of 'candidate examiners'. Their main function would be to help the public to get a more authentic view of the main candidates, undistorted by political marketing. They might be named 'Candidate Tribunes', recalling the *Tribuni Plebis* of the Roman Republic but in a modernized form, or a 'Candidate Court', to lend to this body the prestige of the courts and emphasize its quasi-judicial function and status. But the name does not really matter.

The members, between five and fifteen persons, would be drawn from two main sources. First, public figures of the highest standing, such as judges, respected academics, spiritual leaders and widely accepted senior statesmen and stateswomen and second, some 'representatives of the public' to be chosen by a lottery combined with challenge procedures.

The specific details – the type of personal information, the manner of appointment of candidate examiners, the nature of the public hearing, and so on – would depend on the circumstances and preferences of different countries. But some steps in this direction are essential to counter the camouflaging of candidates behind carefully constructed masks, and to change the nature of the political circus so that voters can make a more informed choice.

In the future, if and when reliable personality tests (and, perhaps, genetic information – though this is a Pandora's Box) become available, leading candidates might be required to undergo tests of this kind, with the results to be published. Certain extreme personality types might then be barred from becoming candidates. But one should to be careful in this area because of the fine line between the 'genius' and the 'psychopath' (Lange-Eichbaum and Kurth, 1967; Simenton, 1984).

A radical rejoinder to all that has been proposed claims that all elections distort the voters' wishes and that direct democracy is thus to be preferred. This is all the more pertinent as traditional arguments that direct democracy is not possible in mass societies are no longer valid, with modern information technologies making feasible direct, democratic, continuous decision processes (Slaton and Becker, 2000).

To take a short cut through the massive literature and available evidence, my evaluation of this position can be summarized as follows:

- Direct democracy can work reasonably well in small communities, where the voters have personal experience of most issues, provided that this is combined with suitable deliberative processes and professional explanation of complex choices.
- Experience with frequent referenda on complex issues involving large numbers of voters is uneven. Thus, when referenda deal with global transformations, such as on joining the European Union, the voters tend to be too conservative and reject necessary innovations – but opinions on this matter differ.
- On the other hand, infrequent referenda on crucial national choices which are vigorously debated and go beyond the usual political agenda have proved an effective means of achieving consensual decisions, with results that, if not always wise, can be lived with and revised if necessary. Indeed, such referenda may permit breakthroughs which otherwise cannot be legitimized, as illustrated by the 1998 referendum on the Irish Peace Agreement.
- Also justified are referenda on issues of outstanding symbolic importance, quite apart from their substantive significance. This is the case, for instance, with the approval of constitutions.
- The dangers of ruling by plebiscite are serious, including the subversion of democracy by demagogic appeal of rulers to the masses. Sometimes this may be necessary for reforming corrupt political systems, but it is a medicine of which an overdose can be fatal to democracy; the recent history of Venezuela illustrates both its usefulness and dangers. Strict limits on the frequent use of plebiscites should therefore be imposed, without excluding their occasional use in special cases.
- Various experiments with 'deliberative democracy' are promising (Williams, 1982; Fishkin, 1991; Hirst, 1993), providing important ways for increasing public affairs enlightenment as a basis for local direct democracy, among other things. The literature includes additional interesting proposals that should be experimented with, such as Bertand de Jouvenel's idea of holding referenda on alternative realistic visions (Jouvenel, 1967).

Taking these considerations into account, the following recommendations emerge: *on crucial national choices where no decision can be arrived at by normal political processes, referenda should be held at the instigation of the legislature or a democratically elected ruler. However, rule by plebiscite should be limited in duration and to special situations. In local bodies and communities direct and deliberative democracy should be advanced, including experiments with electronic voting, accompanied by steps to increase public understanding of the issues involved. Experimentation with advisory referenda at a national level are also advisable, subject to intensive public education tied to them and stimulated by them. However, further expansion of direct democracy must wait for order-of-magnitude increases in public affairs enlightenment. Even then, the maximum advisable scope for direct democracy is quite limited in the foreseeable future.*

An important related issue is the right or power of a small but very committed minority in effect to force its opinions on the majority. To take a concrete example, let us assume that a country resumes whaling by domestic democratic choice and in compliance with international agreements. What legitimate ways of protest and resistance are open to those who regard whaling as endangering the survival of an important species, and to those who regard whaling as a moral and even mortal sin?

Vigorous efforts to gain support for such a position in the political arena, as well as non-disruptive protests, are acceptable ways for a minority to try to sensitize a majority to an issue, and perhaps ultimately to become a majority. But what about a group of true believers that feels morally committed to use force against whaling ships?

Any coherent view of empowering the people, and of democracy as a whole, must condemn a minority willing to use force against actions that have been legally sanctioned by democratic decisions. But this presupposes true democracy, and excepts genocide and similar atrocities even if approved by a democratic majority, against which forceful resistance is a moral imperative. This leaves open the case of differences of opinion on 'atrocities' and even genocide, if, for instance, some groups regard the elimination of a species of animals as a kind of 'genocide'. I would therefore suggest that violence is permitted and even mandated against 'atrocities' and 'evil', even if democratically approved, within the meanings of these terms accepted by an overall consensus of humanity.

This still leaves many situations undetermined, but it is better to leave open questions than close the door to strong resistance against 'evil', even when its definition is not fully agreed.

However much one may respect the moral motives of activists, nevertheless, if they try to impose their views on the majority by force they have to be restrained by superior counterforce, so as to maintain the democratic power of the people. An exception is resistance to 'evil', even when approved by a majority, which is a moral duty justifying violent countermeasures. However, in terms of democratic values, this is legitimate only in cases recognized as 'evil' by overall consensus of humanity.

This leaves unsolved the problems posed by acts regarded by a minority as 'evil' but accepted as just by a large majority, such as slavery during most of human history and experiments with animals essential for advancing life-saving medical knowledge nowadays. The minority may be committed by its own morality to act against such 'evil', while the democratic majority is entitled and also obliged to take measures against efforts of a minority to impose its values, if the minority persists in trying to do so after the majority has offered a reasonable compromise if this is feasible. The possibility that later generations may justify the minority and condemn the majority is irrelevant in terms of democratic theory other than calling for caution in 'absolutizing' moral judgments and democratic choices, however important the issue is in terms of moral philosophy, theology and historic judgment.

It may be possible to invent or reinvent various means of upgrading public affairs enlightenment. A thought-provoking historical example is that of Greek tragedy, which permitted and encouraged collective confrontation with fundamental issues (Euben, 1986, 1990) and provided a 'publicly shared communal mode, either for representing political conflict or for subjecting politics to philosophical interrogation' (Euben, 1990, p. 50). Clearly, public affairs enlightenment needs much creativity. However, new mass-influencing instruments may also operate in an anti-enlightenment direction. Thus, despite many optimistic views (see D. Morris, 1999) I think it is too early to judge what will be the mix between the positive and negative impacts of the cybersphere and its explosive expansion.

Until some breakthrough comes about in the public affairs enlightenment of the people, a very troubling two-sided question must be faced, which challenge some popular assumptions about democracy. *Should people be given more power even without becoming more public affairs enlightened, either in the hope that power will breed such ccapacities, despite the absence of any empirical evidence to support this assumption, or because empowerment is intrinsically right, regardless of the consequences? Or should the actual power of the people in regard to complex and global issues be limited, for instance by giving more authority to non-democratic units within a mixed model of democracy?*

My own tendency is to prefer constraining of the power of the people if there is a danger that they may misjudge critical issues and endanger the future, while making maximum efforts to upgrade their public affairs enlightenment. However, this recommendation assumes that other problem-coping actors will do better than non-enlightened populations, which is not at all certain: sightless elites may do even worse. I now turn to such concerns about the role and qualities of governance elites.

NOTES

1. Nearly all discussion on participatory and deliberative democracy ignores what is probably the most extensive modern experience with direct democracy. This is the role of frequent general meetings of all members in the Israeli Kibbutz and the many deliberative committees, where all important and many unimportant decisions are discussed and made, or at least ratified. My evaluation of this experience is mixed. The record is not too good on economic policies and on emotive personal issues. However, as a whole, participatory and deliberative democracy in the Israeli Kibbutz works and there is much to learn from it. At present the system is undergoing reform, prompted by economic and demographic crises, and including the limiting of direct and deliberative democracy in economic and management matters, while leaving them in full force in community matters.

2. This is also important because the manner in which elections are conducted strongly influences people's decisions about whether or not to enter politics and be active in public affairs. Current election and campaigning practices probably put off personality types that have a good chance of becoming moral and competent senior politicians.

I2

Refashioning Governance Elites

In a book review, Arthur Schlesinger Jr criticized the view that governance elites are not necessary (or that the need for them should be repressed or ignored) because they are anti-democratic and anti-egalitarian:

> All government known to history has been government by minorities, and it is in the interests of everyone, most especially the poor and power-less, to have the governing minority composed of able, intelligent, respon-sive, and decent persons with a large view of the general welfare. There is a vast difference between an elite of conscience and an elite of privilege – the difference that Thomas Jefferson drew between the 'natural aristocracy' founded on 'virtue and talents' and the 'artificial aristocracy founded on wealth and birth', adding that the natural aristocracy is 'the most precious gift of nature' for the government of society.
>
> (Schlesinger Jr, 1993)

His argument is solidly founded on the fact that the quality, motives and character of its senior personnel, including politicians, civil servants and other governance professionals, largely determine the actual performance of governance. This is not to deny that behavior and performance are also shaped by structures (March and Olsen, 1989; Weaver and Rockman, 1993). But Thucydides was right to emphasize the dependence of good governance on outstanding individuals, as against the effort of Hobbes to eliminate this factor (L. M. Johnson, 1993).

The higher the tier of governance and the fewer the number of persons who reach it, the greater the importance of the personal characteristics of the incumbents, as compared with structure. This is particularly true at the highest levels, where a small group directs governance as a whole, within many constraints but also with a considerable amount of freedom.

If the world were in a stable phase of development, small elites in charge of high politics and national as well as transnational policies would matter much less. However, the situation is very different at a time of global trans-formations in which national and supranational governance elites make many of the future-influencing choices, actively or by default. The quality of the higher governance elite is therefore of the utmost importance.

This would be a banal statement but for current fashions which tend to downgrade the importance of governance elites, both compared to civil society actors and 'the people' as a whole, and compared to other types of elites such as entrepreneurs and media barons. The crucial importance of senior governance elites is therefore in need of explicit assertion and underlining, all the more so as its recognition is a *sine qua non* for deliberate efforts to improve that elite – a necessity widely ignored or regarded as utopian.

Before proceeding, a serious caveat should be introduced. Human history and the contemporary scene alike provide little evidence on which trust in governance elites can be based. But there is equally little evidence on which to base trust in populations and 'the people', or in business leaders and various private elites.

Therefore, when asked if I really believe that governance elites can deliver what is required from them, I must confess that I am skeptical. But one must avoid the logical mistake of concluding from the glaring weaknesses of governance elites that other elites or populations at large can be relied upon more. When asked if public opinions, grass-roots activists, non-governmental organizations, popular deliberative forums, market leaders, mass media owners and so on can be relied upon to play a major role in weaving the future for the better, one should be no less skeptical.

The question must therefore be reformulated to ask what should receive priority: the upgrading of governance elites or the upgrading of 'the people', civil society and of private elites. Here my answer is a double one: first, there is little hope for upgrading the people and empowering them through enlightenment, and of upgrading non-governmental actors, unless governance elites are first radically improved.

The second answer is that it is relatively less impossible to upgrade small elites than populations at large. Moreover, because of their crucial importance, governance elites should receive priority in such an endeavor, though other elites too should be sensitive to their public roles and responsibilities.[1] The recommendations presented in this and other chapters should serve to make at least a prima facie case for this proposition.

However, one should remain very apprehensive about the dangers of putting too much trust in governance elites. I therefore place moral imperatives and empowerment of the people first, before taking up the refashioning of governance elites. Upgrading of governance elites must start with encouraging and enforcing virtues; and it must be accompanied by increasing empowerment of the people through public affairs enlightenment.

However, with all these and additional reservations and caveats, my conclusion is still that *unless senior governance elites are significantly improved there is little hope of upgrading capacities to govern and 'weave the future' for the better.*

The term 'elite' should be used with care. The dangers of it acquiring a narrow, inequitable and even racist meaning must be recognized and guarded against. However, avoiding the idea of governance elites carries the risk of making mediocrity into a virtue and of protecting the inept (Goode, 1967). This can have serious consequences for humankind by hindering the recognition, development and achievement of the extraordinary qualities required in the higher levels of governance. To counteract such errors I use the term 'senior governance elite' deliberately, without making an effort to camouflage the real issue behind less emotive terms such as 'senior governance staff'. *The need for outstanding senior governance elites should be frankly recognized, together with the consequent requirements to draw 'unusual' persons of extraordinary merit into high governance positions, constantly to monitor and improve their qualities, and to motivate and remunerate them accordingly.*

It is not easy to establish how many people are in fact included in higher governance elites, especially when trying to limit the number to those who exert real influence, rather than merely holders of high-sounding titles and bubble blowers. Several factors make a difference, such as the size of the country, the amount of social differentiation, and the political culture and constitutional arrangements. Accordingly, countries with a differentiated social structure, egalitarian political culture and decentralized governance tend to have larger elites than less differentiated societies with hierarchical cultures and centralized governance.

Taking into account such differences, my guesstimate – based on such studies as are available, as well as personal experience with high governance staffs — is that the number of persons belonging to higher governance elites probably ranges from 100 to 1,000 per country. Since most of the 200 or so (*The Economist*, 1993, p. 52) countries of the world are quite small, a maximum of about 50,000 persons probably constitutes the senior governance elites of humankind at any point in time, including multi-national, supra-national and global governance institutions.

The top governance elites – the people directly responsible for making or shaping the most crucial decisions – are at most one-tenth of the total senior elite – that is, a maximum of 5,000 persons. If we focus on those whose decisions significantly affect humankind as a whole, 1,000 is probably more of an exaggeration than an underestimation.

To continue with somewhat speculative number games, let us consider not only governance but also other elites with a major influence on the future, such as spiritual leaders, creative scientists, leaders of grass-roots and other movements, outstanding entrepreneurs and top executives of large corporations, prominent cultural figures, mass media stars, and so on. As a guesstimate, this group might be one order of magnitude larger than the senior governance elites. *For humankind as a whole a total of about 10,000 persons domi-*

nates the shaping of the future, in so far as it depends on human beings. A much smaller number of heads of major states, major inventors, cultural heroes, outstanding entre-preneurs, and so on, concentrate in their hands most of the future-shaping power. It is perilous to ignore this fact that a minuscule part of humanity holds in its hands decisive influence over the future, however unpleasant this is in terms of human and humane values. On the contrary, this fact should be clearly recognized so as to guide efforts to upgrade the qualities of this 'Global Super-Elite' as essential for assuring a thriving future for humanity and its constituent groups.

This conclusion is tempered by the impacts of grass-roots initiatives and social movements, and by the selection of some of the most important deci-sion-makers by many individuals. Moreover, senior and top governance elites operate within political, social, cultural, economic and scientific infrastruc-tures, institutions, processes and settings that significantly constrain their freedom of movement and shape their actions, both objectively and subjec-tively. These constraints, while in part inherited from the past, are often shaped by the general public and its various parts. The people thus impose strict limits on politics as the art of the possible – especially in democracies, but also in undemocratic regimes.

Nonetheless, the future-shaping power of a very tiny elite is a sobering and somber fact,[2] putting human aspirations for equality, self-determination and genuine democracy into the universe of utopias. All the more dangerous is neglect of the improvement of the quality of top-level decision-makers and decision influencers.

The Latin statement 'An nescis, mi fili, quantilla prudentia mundus regatur' (don't you know, my son, with how little discretion and knowledge the world is governed), which apparently goes back to Pope Julian III (1550–1555),[3] expresses up-to-date realities. This is rather obvious, unless one suffers from a kind of ideological or cultural *agnosia* – 'mind blindness' or 'psychic blind-ness' – in which the brain does not identify what the eyes clearly see (Kosslyn and Koenig, 1992, p.111ff).[4] One might expect intense concern with the question of how to ensure that senior and top governance elites (as well as other elites, but that is another subject) are of suitable moral and intellectual quality, as proposed in Chapter Ten. Yet shockingly, though not surprisingly, such is not the case. Institutional mechanisms to oversee and curb decision-makers rightly receive considerable attention; the quality of civil servants is regarded with some concern: but the improvement of politicians is hardly discussed seriously, neither in practical politics, nor in public discourse or political philosophy – despite obvious and increasingly serious problems with their qualities.

Not that there is widespread satisfaction with politicians – rather the contrary. Trust in politicians is declining almost everywhere and must be expected to drop further as a result of the continuing failure of governance to meet expectations, further revelations of corruption, growing impacts of the mass media and much else besides. However, these feelings are not translated into a proper discussion of how to improve matters. Politicians are often elected and removed by protest votes, but without any serious effort being made to remedy the deep causes of their inadequacies. And when institutional changes are introduced, such as time limits on terms of office or changes in election rules, these are often based more on emotional reaction and wrong assumptions, than on a true understanding of underlying processes – with counter-productive results. This is like kicking a broken television set: it releases frustrations but will not make the television work, and often will increase the costs of repair or make it impossible to repair, sometimes giving the kicker a dangerous electric shock.

No reliance on market mechanisms, non-governmental organizations, civil society, grass-roots movements, participatory democracy and the like reduces the crucial importance of the quality of senior, and especially top-level, governance elites. *Far-reaching improvements in the qualities of top level political decision-makers are therefore the single most important task for governance redesign. Taboos surrounding this subject must be broken, so as to permit unconventional but practical measures to be introduced.*

On a more fundamental level, the question must be faced: Will we be smart enough? (I borrow the formulation from Hunt, 1995).

This question has two levels. The first throws up the fundamental issue of absolute limits on human capacities, as set by the structure and 'wiring' of our brains. It is quite reasonable to speculate that evolutionary processes developed (or creation provided) capacities and potentials which are adequate for survival in the natural environments which humanity has faced since its beginnings, but that shifts in human environments and in the predicaments of humanity, as paradoxically brought about by the human species itself, do pose survival requirements that perhaps surpass the maximum potential of the human mind, even when acting collectively. If this is the case then either humanity is doomed to self-destruction or, to be more optimistic, it will get 'frozen' on a plateau that humanity cannot surpass. Otherwise, catastrophes may simplify environments and make them fit human limits. Or perhaps, on the level of meta-capacities (that is, capacities to bring about new capacities not included in the earlier ones), some breakthrough will occur, such as genetic or pharmacological enhancement of human abilities bringing about self-transformation into *homo superior*.

For the purposes of this book, such speculations are interesting but not essential. Certainly, humanity has not reached the limits of its potential for management of both itself and its environment, there being much scope also for improving capacities to govern and build a better future. This is illustrated both by historical experiences of outstanding achievements and by the very proposals presented in this book, however doubtful in detail none of which presupposes a radical leap in the potentials of the human mind.

Here the second level of the question is reached – namely, whether there are enough human resources available to enable the significant upgrading of governance elites. My answer is in the affirmative. Much can be done to improve governance elites by enlarging and better utilizing societal human resources, by mobilizing larger parts of the best qualified into governance elites, and by developing the governance elites themselves.

My overall answer to the question of whether we will be smart enough is therefore that we can be much wiser, more virtuous and more knowledgeable in governance. The more fundamental issue of whether this will prove to be enough should be left open for an inconceivable future, our urgent job being to do the best we can to upgrade senior governance elites within the large and presently underutilized potential for doing so. Let me move step by step through various approaches for doing so.

But firstly, I must justify jumping over a step which may seem logically required – namely, specifying the required characteristics of members of senior governance elites. Clearly, highly moral character, intellectual excellence, knowledge, creativity, commitment to their missions and so on must distinguish them. Senior governance elites as a whole should also be open, pluralistic and representative. However, this is obvious and borders on the banal. More operational specifications are required, which I shall partly provide in this and the next chapter, leaving details to other of my writings (Dror, 1993, 1997a, 1997b and in preparation). I will also use, from time to time, the relative term 'the best' in meanings that will be clarified by the context, it being understood that this is a multi-dimensional and pluralistic concept (partly in line with Gardner, 1993, and further explored in Gardner, 1995), changing with time and circumstances, and partly open-ended in its contents.

The first and broadest approach to upgrading senior governance elites is to enlarge the recruitment base. In the longer run, this depends on the overall scope and quality of education, and the inclusion of women in the recruitment base is also important. This is not only a matter of gender equality, but also a way to improve the senior governance elite, both quantitatively and qualitatively: quantitatively, because discrimination against women reduces the number of good candidates; qualitatively, because the inclusion of more women in the senior governance elite adds important modes of thinking, imagination, sensing and judging that are more pronounced among women (Miller, 1976; Gilligan, 1982; Belenky *et al.*, 1986).

A second approach requires the motivation of a larger proportion of 'the best' to try to enter politics and governance, and ways for them then to advance to senior positions. Concerning the entry into politics, the problem is unfortunately all too obvious: only a very few of the most moral, intelligent and knowledgeable persons choose politics as a career; and if they do so, they often become disillusioned and leave very quickly or adjust to politics at the cost of their starting qualities.

If politics were not so important, this situation might not be so bad, as the 'best' could be making valuable contributions in spiritual leadership, science, the economy, culture and other endeavors which also shape the future, sometimes more so than politics. However, in view of the crucial importance of politics and its future-weaving tasks, the outlook caused by the low quality of many entrants into politics is bleak. *Strenuous efforts to improve the quality of persons entering into politics and reaching its higher echelons are therefore a top priority.*

Greater awareness of this need may help, by encouraging more of 'the best' to choose politics as their life's mission, by educators trying to motivate their outstanding students to go into politics, and by movements with high moral standards sending their 'best' into politics. Changing the electoral rules may also help, including, as already proposed, fuller exposure of the nature of candidates to public evaluation. In many countries it may also be a good idea to raise payments and pensions for politicians (and other senior governance elites), so as to attract better candidates.

But such relatively easy steps will not be enough, because the rejection of politics as a life mission, especially by many of 'the best', is often a result of its 'dirty' image and reality (Eliasoph, 1998).

In the better days of the Roman Republic and Empire, one of the acknowledged duties of senior politicians was to bring 'new blood' into politics by searching for fitting candidates and grooming them (Wiseman, 1971, esp. pp. 107–16). This tradition should be revived, in ways appropriate to democracy. Senior politicians should regard it as one of their responsibilities to seek out young candidates, test them, groom them and try eventually to democratically pass on power to them – instead of being afraid of competition and preferring to keep the spotlight on themselves, surrounded by inferior colleagues.

However, only when the image of politics as 'dirty', and the objective reasons for this perception (Jamieson, 1992), change, will morally superior individuals in sufficient numbers choose politics as a vocation, stay with it, and succeed without becoming corrupted.

We encounter here another vicious spiral: due to its 'dirty' image and reality, morally superior people do not enter politics, or else fail or compromise their morality if they do. Moreover, movements claiming high moral standards advise their members not to go into politics (or the movement and its leadership adjusts to the 'realities' and become corrupted, as happened in some countries to green movements once they joined governments). As a result, the situation further deteriorates and becomes harder to reverse.

Outstanding leaders sometimes appear who have both intelligence and integrity. They raise the standard of politics and motivate superior candidates to enter politics. But we cannot rely on a steady supply of such outstanding people, especially since in normal circumstances exceptional candidates will not reach the top in mass-media dominated democracies (Dogan, 1989). Radical action is therefore needed to avoid this slippery slope.

When my advanced students become overconfident, fooling themselves that they are ready to solve global problems, I remind them that it is much harder to become a senior politician than a professor, because the competition is much tougher and the constraints much harsher. But political competition favors attributes that are neither related to future-building capabilities nor necessary for good governance. This situation is further aggravated by the media circus that blights much of modern democratic politics. As a result, politicians are often and increasingly more involved in politicking than in developing policies. Furthermore, they do not work their way up the political ladder in ways which ensure constant learning and which test and hone the qualities necessary for higher positions; in some democracies, people can be elected directly to top positions without having gained relevant experience.

In undemocratic regimes the situation is usually worse: the way up is via intrigue, flattery, cliques and ruthlessness, with little preparation for the requirements of high-level governance and future-weaving. There are exceptions, however, such as Singapore.

As well put by King and Schneider:

> Reform of structures, procedures and attitudes will be of little avail unless men and women of the right quality and capacity are willing to serve and the citizens capable of appreciating these qualities are willing to vote for them. It is simply not good enough that access to leadership be achieved through skilful television performances and simplistic speeches aimed at manipulating the masses into enthusiastic support with empty promises and avoidance of realities (King and Schneider, 1991, p. 153).

Consensus-building processes may further aggravate the situation by advancing 'power-brokers' rather than policy leaders. This seems to be the case in Japan, even when public opinion and economic exigencies clearly require a different kind of senior politician. As explained in an item 'Bold Leaders Elude Japan' in the *International Herald Tribune*, 21 July 1998:

> 'It's terrible hard for (prime ministers and ministers) to manage the job they are given', said Kiichi Miyazawa, a former prime minister ... 'Their basic knowledge is inadequate, I would say, to carry out day-to-day duties as cabinet ministers' ... Their 'only preparation is years of political machinations'.

To continue in the same vein, most politicians, however intelligent, politically astute and well intending, arrive at senior and even top positions with characteristics fitting the description by John Ralston Saul: 'The single thing that modern managers and politicians cannot do properly is to manage ... They can administer detail, but they cannot manage civilization' (interview reported in the *International Herald Tribune*, 16 December 1992).

The implications for governance redesign are clear: *there should be less emphasis on image manipulation as the main route to political positions, and especially to the top; political mobilization and career structures should attract outstanding candidates; young politicians should pass through learning experiences and not jump directly from mass politics or party politicking into top posts, but exceptional 'high flyers' should advance rapidly.*

These principles should serve as guidance in all governance redesign, with special attention to electoral procedures, appointments to senior positions and so on. It is difficult, however, to translate these principles into concrete proposals fitting given situations and assuring desirable results. *One cannot rely, therefore, on a rapid improvement in the quality of candidates entering politics and reaching top positions. Intense efforts to enhance the quality of the politicians produced by existing selection and promotion processes are therefore required as a 'second best' approach.*

Having discussed virtues and vices in Chapter Ten, let me concentrate now on upgrading the cognitive capacities of politicians.

To engage well in 'weaving the future' (as distinct from other functions which are more 'political' in nature and which successful politicians usually know much more about), all senior governance elites, including in particular top politicians, need a great deal of competence in the following areas, among others:

- Information about and understanding of major environments and their dynamics, including their own society and culture, as well as regional and global predicaments and opportunities. They must be aware of long-range demographic trends, geo-economic shifts, domestic political changes, social and economic developments, and so on, as well as global processes. Indeed, 'globalization' of the knowledge and thinking of high-level politicians is essential if they are to be able to handle the growing number of tasks that are beyond the capacity of any single country and to increasingly take care of *raison d'humanité*.
- Literacy in science and technology, so as to be able to cope with this key factor shaping the future.
- Language skills, including a command of at least one, and preferably two, languages in addition to their mother tongue, with English being essential. In addition (and this is a much neglected requirement), it is important to be numerate as an essential tool for thinking and reasoning (Paulos, 1988, 1991).

- A good sense of history, and at least some familiarity with, and under-standing of, fundamental historical processes and the factors and struc-tures shaping them, so as to be capable of 'thinking-in-history', in the sense of combining cogitation in terms of history with a 'feel' for historic processes grounded in explicit and tacit knowledge.
- Good policy reflection abilities and habits, such as systems thinking and sophistication in 'fuzzy policy gambling', as discussed in Chapters Four-teen and Fifteen.
- An ability to apply moral reasoning to tragic choices involved in major deci-sions (a quite distinct matter from personal virtue).
- Knowledge of main policy domains.
- Societal and governmental macro-management skills.
- At least some literacy in the traditional disciplines relevant to governance, such as public law, economics, and political science.

Above and beyond such specific knowledge, senior politicians must be able and accustomed to build bridges between abstract knowledge and concrete issues, to be balanced in their thinking, and not to trust what first meets their eyes. In addition, they need certain traits of character, such as the capacity to be detached, to observe and reflect on themselves; the willingness to learn and the ability to change their mind; innovativeness; curiosity; and the skills and habits of self-improvement.

Given the quality of actual and potential politicians as given, upgrading their qualities along such lines requires unconventional, but quite feasible innovations. *Politicians on all levels should be provided with opportunities and incentives to acquire and develop appropriate knowledge and skills, with the help of new types of courses and workshops, sabbaticals, policy colleges, text-books and experience ladders.*

The gulf between the training of medical doctors and senior governance elites is striking. A medical doctor must undergo seven years of very difficult and intensive studies and supervised practice, and then at least two more years of specialization. After all that, most of us would not let him treat any seri-ous condition of ours before having accumulated years of experience. Fur-thermore, all studies of professionalism show that the development of high level skills requires years of intense learning and supervised practice (Ericsson and Smith, 1991). Yet nothing like that is required from senior politicians. Even senior civil servants, the explicitly professional component of governance, go through training that prepares them less adequately for the higher-order tasks of governance than a paramedic is trained for brain surgery.

Most contemporary senior governance staffs can fairly be compared to *Feldshers* (practical surgeons before the development of modern medicine who gained their knowledge mainly from apprenticeships and experience, Kossoy and Ohry, 1992), who were sometimes better than nothing, but who often caused more harm than good and could never bring about the modern advancements in medicine. Similarly, many contemporary senior politicians have significant knowledge, often 'practical' in nature, but are very inadequately prepared for the higher-order tasks of governance.

Can it be that the tasks of the senior governance elite are less demanding than are those of a medical doctor or of other professionals? Or is there less that can be taught to them? It seems unlikely. Nonetheless, the only country which tries to offer appropriate training for both future top politicians and civil servants is France, with its National School of Administration (ENA), which needs to be restructured and broadened but is much superior to what is available elsewhere. But it too suffers from the growing disinclination of 'the best' to choose a public career, with the number of persons who want to enter ENA declining.

Existing facilities, such as a variety of public policy schools, can and sometimes do help in preparing politicians and professionals for the senior governance elite in three major ways. First, they offer courses attracting students interested in politics, especially when the studies can be combined with a professional qualification that serves as a standard route into politics, such as law. Second, they provide training for students who want a career as policy professionals in governance. Third, they offer mid-career learning opportunities for politicians and governance professionals, assuming senior governance elites are granted sabbatical leave for study purposes.

Countries that have no good public policy graduate university programs should set them up. Such programs should also be established on a regional and global basis. But much more is needed than public policy schools in their present form. Thus, it may be advisable to establish a new type of 'School for Advanced Governance Studies' (Dror, 1993) with a five-year graduate program, after a masters degree, and including two years of internship combined with continuing studies, leading to a professional doctorate in governance studies.

At least one such institution should be set up on a global level and with an emphasis on global policy problems, and also to serve as a prototype and pilot model.

Every politician, civil servant and other member of a senior governance staff should be entitled to a sabbatical on a regular basis, and be induced to avail himself of it, on condition that the sabbatical is properly used for study and to gain relevant experience. A possible incentive for politicians might be to be assured of time on television to talk about their studies and their importance for their political tasks.

But it will take a while for such sabbaticals to be introduced and to bring about substantive improvements in performance. Shorter study periods are therefore essential, and for this purpose Policy Colleges should be established on national, multi-national and global levels.

The idea is based on experiences with public and business executive training programs, with defense colleges, and also some study activities in political parties. It involves a mixed group of governance and public elites spending four to six weeks together in residential facilities, studying selected major policy issues and approaches, with the help of information and methodology inputs, and individual and group mentoring.

The benefits of such an activity can be considerable, both in improving knowledge and understanding, and in building up consensus. Sometimes, too, innovative ideas may be produced. The concept is not difficult to implement, and the costs are low compared with the potential benefits. The absence of such learning centers for politicians is thus another symptom of the neglect of the need to upgrade politicians and of the taboos surrounding it.

The highest levels of governance, including heads of governments and senior ministers, present a special problem. Possible learning opportunities for them include short retreats and summit meetings, counseling and mentoring by senior advisers, and short seminars and workshops. Some of the Aspen Institute activities could be emulated, but much more is needed. Pioneering strategic exercises by the Office of the Chancellor of Switzerland for the cabinet and other policy makers and influential figures in policy illustrate innovative practice-tested possibilities (Carrel, 1999 and http:/www.sfa.admin.ch), as do experiences with modular study days, including some of my own workshops in strategic choice and policy planning for cabinets. These demonstrate that senior governance elites, including top-level politicians, can be induced to participate in suitably structured workshops over three to ten days and, in their own view, benefit a great deal from them.[5]

It is symptomatic of the neglect of study needs by governance elites, including the top echelons, that there are few serious texts written for politicians and senior civil servants (exceptions include Wriggins, 1969; Heineman Jr and Hessler, 1980; Hodgkinson, 1983; Dror, in preparation). This scarcity is striking in comparison with the proliferation of manuals for business executives and the long and honorable history of *Mirrors for Princes* and statecraft texts. The writing of serious books for high-level governance elites should therefore be encouraged. Variations on this proposal include distance-learning courses in relevant subjects and professional (as distinct from scholarly or popular) journals in statecraft for governance practitioners.

To acknowledge the obvious and to avoid misunderstandings, two reservations need to be stressed. First, moral character is more important than intellectual capacities. Since we cannot rely on the Platonic assumption that more knowledge makes humans more moral, no cognitive qualities should be permitted to excuse moral inadequacies. Second, no formal or de facto quasi-academic meritocracy (as depicted in the striking dystopia of Young, 1958) is aimed at or should be tolerated. 'Practical intelligence' (Sternberg and Wagner, 1986) is also essential. A rich and diverse experience of life is thus needed for the senior governance elites as much as structured knowledge, both as a foundation for empathizing with the people, and as a source of the tacit and personal knowledge (Polanyi, 1974) essential for governance. Accordingly, the provisioin of multiple experience opportunities is an additional road to upgrading the qualifications of senior governance elites, including politicians.

In short, *pre-career and mid-career learning opportunities for senior governance staff, including politicians, should be provided, including advanced governmental study schools, policy colleges, workshops, and modern versions of 'Mirrors for Rulers'. Sabbaticals and structured experience opportunities should be provided; but formal qualifications and studies should never serve as a substitute for the moral character and life experiences essential for those in senior governance positions.*

Most of what has been said also applies to senior civil servants and similar professional components of the senior governance elite – in many respects even more so than to politicians. Politicians can claim to be, and be regarded as, entitled to govern because they have been elected. Besides, it can be argued, they can always rely on civil servants and policy staffs for professional knowledge and advice. No such alibi can be allowed for civil servants. To be able to fulfill their crucial and partly autonomous functions in governance, and to be legitimately entitled to do so, they should possess advanced professional and personal qualifications, yet often do not.

The qualifications and qualities in nearly all higher civil services everywhere are grossly outdated compared with what might be achieved, and with what is required. The extent and forms of obsolescence vary from country to country: in many, the weaknesses arise from a mainly legal training, in others from an obsession with 'all-rounders', or from the 'governance of strangers' (Heclo, 1977). Recent fascination with the so-called 'new public management', however useful on the level of service delivery, further assures a lack of future-building qualifications. At the same time, there are promising models in the French ENA and in the selection and further training in Singapore, though these too need extensive redesign.

Whatever present failings or strengths may be, all of governance needs a new type of senior and top-level civil service, combining advanced governance professionalism (a concept that dissolves the very misleading dichotomy between 'generalists' and 'experts') with a greater capacity to innovate. This applies even more to the United Nations family, where the country quota system and other political constraints hinder the development of a highly professional global civil service, as is now widely recognized. Compared with such needs, all contemporary civil service systems and reforms (Bekke, Perry and Toonen, 1996) are inadequate.

It is not difficult to construct and implement innovative policies for the senior civil service if there is a strong political will to do so and an adequate understanding of needs (Dror, 1997a). In practice, however, civil service reforms encounter strong resistance from existing staffs and bring few political dividends. There is thus all the more need for top politicians to understand the need to build up a new type of senior civil service and strongly support necessary reforms.

Imaginative senior civil service policies leading to radical reforms are thus required, so as to ensure compact, well-qualified, open, pluralistic, representative and innovative professional staffs, adapted to changing functions of governance, and with special attention both to public service delivery and to future-building. Top level politicians should be involved in necessary reforms and support them vigorously.

It would lead us into too much detail to discuss here various other elements of the senior governance elite, such as scientists, lawyers, economists and the like. But at least one needed key professional group must be mentioned, because of its importance and novelty – namely, highly trained policy professionals (sometimes, in their early incarnations, called 'policy analysts' or 'policy planners'). They are essential for raising the quality of future-building in the central minds of governance. However, their required characteristics are directly related to the prerequisites of deep policy reflection. It is therefore more convenient to discuss policy professionals in Chapters Fourteen and Sixteen.

To conclude, it is necessary to return to the imperative that senior governance elites should possess a sense of vocation and mission (the classic discussion is by Max Weber, reprinted in Mommsen and Schluchter, 1992). Only such a sense can give a deep personal meaning to aspiring to join the senior governance elite and serving in it. Without it, there can be no intense commitment to tasks, no profound job-satisfaction, and no adequate motivation for developing one's virtues, fighting one's vices, developing one's character and engaging in constant learning (Goldman, 1988).

Such a sense of vocation and mission is not easy to 'engineer', depending as it largely does on cultural factors. But outstanding rulership can help to provide such a sense, both by giving a personal example and by instigating policies to build up the governance elite as a real 'elite', if necessary distinct in some of its characteristics from prevailing societal features. The next step in our inquiry must, therefore, take up issues of rulership.

NOTES

1. Training and development of all elites should include heavy doses of public affairs enlightenment, together with deliberation on their moral responsibilities for the *res publica*. Appropriate codes of ethics may also be of some help. Still, the difference between the main orientations and responsibilities of business, mass media and other non-public elites and those of governance elites is profound, since only the latter are charged with looking out for the common good as their main and overriding mission.

2. *Vanity Fair*, in its November 1997 issue, includes 65 men and women in 'A Portrait of World Power'. The list includes a number of media moguls, in addition to many politicians, while a list of 'Leaders of the Information Age' published in *Vanity Fair* in October 1997 includes no politicians. I leave it to the reader to ponder whether this is a result of the widespread underrating of the actual importance of top level politicians, or whether it reflects realities of weak politics with heads of important states not qualifying as 'leaders of the information age'.

3. See Bückmann, 1964, p. 607, where a Portuguese collection of proverbs from 1733 is quoted as the basis of the following story, and the probable source of the proverb. Portuguese monks expressed compassion for Pope Julian on his undertaking the burden of ruling the whole world, and this was his reply.

4. I am indebted to my son Itiel Dror, a cognitive psychologist, for drawing my attention to this neurological disease, which I use metaphorically.

5. See Dror, 1988a. Outlines of such workshops are available from the author on request.

13

On Rulership

Much of what is said in this book is brought into sharp focus when we zoom in on heads of government, be they prime ministers, presidents or otherwise designated. To make matters as clear as possible, I am using the term 'ruler', despite its seemingly undemocratic nature, because what we are speaking about is indeed 'rulership', however attenuated by contemporary ideologies, regimes and institutions.

Quite a number of issues relating to rulers have already been discussed, in relation to governance elites, electoral systems and more. However, it is in this chapter that the main, and perhaps shocking, points are made that the actual power of rulers is growing, even in democracies and that strong though constrained rulers, despite their dangers, are essential for capacities to govern and shape the future. Also, a number of additional ways to improve their performance are presented, with emphasis on enclaves of excellent staff work, with further elaboration to come in following chapters.

To continue with the statistics presented in the last chapter, when the crucial importance of rulers is taken into account the unavoidable conclusion, however unpalatable, is that about one to two hundred heads of major polities are pivotal in making critical choices. The qualities of their will, moral character and cognitive capacities are of paramount importance. One would therefore expect that ways to improve rulers would be central to the study of governance and political discourse; indeed, a large and expanding literature deals with presidents and prime ministers, especially of the major states. But comprehensive studies and theories of rulers and rulership over time and space are very scarce. The available improvement proposals are somewhat useful but very limited. Thus, the crucial need to upgrade the moral character of rulers is in the main ignored, as is the need for ways to improve their cognitive capacities. These oversights are all the more striking when compared with the unending stream of books dealing with business leaders and directed at them – but we have already discussed this very significant symptom of our times.

The brute facts are that the individuality of rulers within their institu-tionalized rulership and societal settings is very important in governance, and that their importance is increasing even in democracies. The growing stand-ing of rulers in democracies is not only an empirical fact, but a functional necessity. *The authority of heads of government should therefore be strengthened in demo-cracies where they are weak, subject to strict constrains (but weakened in non-democracies, where they are too strong).*

This view is iconoclastic in comparison with textbook knowledge and public discourse preferences, which tend to concentrate on the need to control and limit the powers of heads of government. Certainly, constraints and oversight are essential and often need upgrading; but the most urgent need is for improving the performance of rulers because of their actual and inescapable importance both in governance as a whole and in future-building in particular.

The importance of rulers raises serious issues. In terms of liberal and egalitarian norms it is very disappointing that a few individuals enjoy pre-dominant power; and in terms of performance it is very dangerous that the quality of government depends so much on a few individuals – all the more so since the very power enjoyed by them corrupts their minds. But all realis-tic approaches to improving governance must take full account of the crucial importance of rulers, as both a fact and a necessity.

To take a look at Western democracies, it is quite clear that rulers, together with a few other top-level politicians, become increasingly impor-tant. While they depend on voters and are subjected to oversight by courts, legislatures, the mass media, interest groups, civil society actors and others, and their actions are constrained by law and limited by colleagues and opposition, they are nevertheless becoming more pivotal in most of modern democratic politics. This conclusion also applies, *mutatis mutandis*, to other levels and forms of governance, including grass-roots movements, where a few individual leaders often play an extremely prominent role.

Leaving aside evolutionary explanations of the importance of rulers and the human needs for 'heroes' (Lash, 1995), 'great men' (Godelier, 1986) and so on, going back perhaps to the higher primates, and psychoanalytical conjectures, such as the importance of 'father figures', several factors are enhancing the status and functions of rulers in the present and foreseeable future. The mass media devote considerable attention to heads of government, thus making them constantly more powerful. Political cultures around the world are mes-merized by the United States, where the main emphasis is on the President; the growing number and importance of summit meetings strengthens the role of heads of state, as well as raising their public visibility; and mass psychological processes related to traumas, widespread anomie in Durkheim's sense (Mestrovic, 1991), 'fear of freedom' (Fromm, 1960) and other human predica-ments accentuated by global transformations, such as globalization, combine to make rulers important in the psycho-dynamics of individuals and societies.

Not only are these and other factors augmenting the actual standing of rulers, but strong democratic rulership is often essential in order to enable governance to carry out its tasks. Thus a strong 'center of governance' is necessary in order to insure a certain coherence of policies and actions as departments compete for feudal control over their 'latifundia'. Powerful top politicians are essential for innovations to break through 'the tyranny of the status quo' (Friedman and Friedman, 1984) and serve as leverage factors and agents of change, as well illustrated in the early history of the European Union (Roussel, 1995) and various international episodes (Sheffer, 1993). When clear-cut but hazardous choices are faced, strong executive leadership focusing on rulers is of great importance. The psychological functions of rulers are necessary for containing and relieving traumas, and the didactic roles of rulers can play an important part in moral education.

There is therefore a need in many countries to strengthen democratic rulership, but the dangers of doing so must not be downplayed. Strong rulership is like a kind of *pharmakon*, in the Greek sense: 'both poison and the antidote to poison, both sickness and cure ... any substance capable of doing an extraordinary good or evil action according to the circumstances [and] dosage' (Euben, 1990, p. 102, note 21). Humanity, in its present state of immaturity and transformation, needs strong rulership in increasing amounts, but much care must be taken in handling, and managing the dosage.

Care must therefore be taken not to let powerful checks and balances block strong democratic rulership too much. When writing constitutions, countries must therefore not allow bad memories of dictatorship to distort their view of what the future requires, including strong but constrained rulership.

This need is very pressing in the United Nations, as the core structure of global governance (Urquhart and Childers, 1990, 1996). As elaborated in other chapters, *the authority of the Secretary-General of the United Nations should be strengthened so as to have greater executive power to initiate and implement policies, even in the face of reluctance on the part of some of the major powers.*

As already mentioned, Tacitus clearly diagnosed the susceptibility of rulers to professional diseases – the more serious of which can best be called, as already explained, 'rulerscraze'.[1] The mass media further aggravate such dangers by providing the extra temptations of narcissism and a fixation on blowing of bubbles to a degree unprecedented in democracies. [2]

For example, only very primitive notions of democracy neglect the crucial educational and opinion-shaping functions of leaders, presuming that they are merely passive instruments for executing popular desires. Only very cynical and shortsighted views limit such influences to electoral image-manipulation and political marketing. Senior politicians unavoidably provide emotional guidance, intentionally or unintentionally and this role increases in times of global upheavals (Madsen and Snow, 1991, Gaucher, 1997), and it can work for good or ill. Emotional demagogy can become a substitute for deliberative governance (Tulis, 1987), even serving as an instrument for evil (as we have seen more than once in the twentieth century), or it can serve high moral purposes. Strict safeguards are therefore essential. But to ignore and underutilize the potential educational influence of rulers for the better makes essential tasks, such as the strengthening of human solidarity, impossible.

To further concretize the dilemmas faced in trying to balance the need for strong rulership with the necessity to avoid its dangers and maintain constraints, let me move through a number of scenarios and possible ways to deal with them.

In countries where relations between the prime minister or president and the elected legislature produce many deadlocks, because of dependency on fragile coalitions or an absence of disciplined parties, it may be advisable to authorize the prime minister or president to call for new elections. However, in presidential regimes the legislature should be entitled to remove a president with a special majority, but without the necessity for 'impeachment'.

Applying this proposal, as a thought experiment, to the USA, however unfeasible in the foreseeable future, what may need consideration is a constitutional amendment permitting the President to call new extraordinary elections for the two Houses of Congress and for the Presidency, subject to limiting this possibility by, say, making it available only two years after he has been elected, and subject to a veto by two thirds of both Houses. By the same token, a two-thirds majority of both Houses should be able to remove a President and call new extraordinary elections for the Presidency and both Houses, without any impeachment procedure.

To move on to another dilemma: the dangers of weakening a president or prime minister by subjecting him to court cases makes it desirable to limit cases that can be brought against him while in office to very serious criminal charges. The importance of the tasks of a ruler require the freeing of his mind as much as possible from personal worries, even at the cost of other values such as the legal rights of claimants and equality before the law. Also, the necessity to encourage frank consultation and debate with his advisers requires that discourse between a ruler and his main advisors be made immune to legal inquiries and the demands of freedom of information.

These examples are sure to be controversial, but the importance of rulers for capacities to govern requires serious attention to protecting the quality of their performance, even at the cost of other values.

Strong rulership, however necessary, is not a cause for self-congratulation. Rather, the dependence of modern governance on the qualities of individual rulers and a handful of their senior colleagues and advisors, with all its attendant risks, is a sign of serious human shortcomings.

The strengthening of the position of rulers without reliable constrains is therefore to be avoided; but not less important are vigorous efforts to upgrade their quality in positive ways. Proposals to improve rulers through redesigning electoral processes, drawing better candidates into politics and providing learning opportunities have already been discussed. Structural ways of improving rulership as part of the central mind of government will be taken up in later chapters. At present, I will concentrate on another approach to improving rulership which is in many respects the most important one – namely, restructuring advisory systems. However, before doing so, let me reiterate that nothing can compensate for serious personality faults. The personal qualities of a ruler are more important than any advisory or other quality augmentation system, with the useful operations of the latter depending largely on the former. *The improvement of the process of election and selection of rulers, and efforts to better their moral, volitional, emotional and cognitive qualities should have top priority.*

Nevertheless, institutional arrangements can be of much help. In many ways much of the machinery of governance both supports and restrains heads of government, but this is far from adequate: rulers need high-quality professional staff to help them think through the main policy choices from a coherent and long-range perspective, and they need male and female counselors who can say politely but clearly, 'no' and discipline themselves against idiosyncratic behavior and error, as in the narrative of Ulysses and the Sirens, in which 'binding' one's own weaknesses and temptations is presented as the ultimate wisdom of outstanding leaders (Elster, 1984, 2000; Schelling, 1984). A crucial function of advisers is to debate with rulers, as Confucian political philosophy and governance morality preached and as was sometimes actually practiced during the long history of Chinese statecraft (Wright and Twitchett, 1962; Hucker, 1966).

The idea of professional advisers and mentors for heads of government is an old one (Goldhamer, 1978), as tried out by Plato in undertaking to advise and 'educate' Dionysius II, the ruler of Syracuse. Many modern attempts with advisory units have fared little better, as demonstrated by the demise of the Central Policy Review Staff in the United Kingdom (Blackstone and Plowden, 1988). My own studies of 42 offices of heads of government, covering industrialized as well as Latin American, Asian and some East European and African ones, lead to the unequivocal conclusion that less than 10 percent of the heads of governments are supported by staffs with appropriate professional qualifications, able to take a coherent and long-term view of critical policy issues and debate with the rulers.

There are many reasons for this unsatisfactory state of affairs, including: domination of policy by politics; main concern with image-building rather than future-building; opposition by departments to independent prime-ministerial staffs; and, in some countries, political as well as public resistance to visible expressions of the power of heads of governance implicit in the creation of a 'Prime-Ministerial Department'.

However, it is my conclusion that the main explanation lies in rulers' reluctance to work with qualified professionals. Many top politicians are very sure of themselves, often increasingly so the longer they remain in office. As a result, they usually want glorified *aides de camp* to execute their 'brilliant' ideas, not strong staffs who will say to them 'wait a moment' or even 'Madam, you are wrong'. At the same time, many rulers are afraid of exposing their ignorance by working with high-quality staffs. Most rulers are anxious, with good reason, about frank position papers leaking and causing a lot of political trouble – although those responsible for the leaks are usually their political colleagues rather than the policy professionals. Moreover, many top politicians are much more interested in assuring their personal position and their party's success, and would rather avoid staffs who point out the damage to national interests caused by giving priority to such considerations and to 'eye-catching ideas'. Moreover, most rulers do not really want or feel the need to 'bind' themselves in any way, but this is an inherent part of working with serious staffs.

However, experience shows that many of these difficulties can be alleviated. Suitable professional policy staffs for heads of government can be built up as 'enclaves of professional excellence' if there is a will on behalf of the rulers to do so, or such units can be institutionalized and legitimized so as to serve even rulers not too eager to have them. Creating such units is therefore one of the main recommended redesigns, assuming that suitable professionals are available or can be readied, as discussed in Chapter Twelve.

Accordingly, *professional policy staffs should be set up as enclaves of excellence close to rulers and other top decision-makers, to help the latter make long-range, integrative strategic choices, and to serve as discreet mentors, while working hard to counter-balance propensities to error.*

One of the principal roles of the proposed units is to help their clients to engage in deeper policy reflection, as well as to 'educate' them in other ways, thus making a contribution to the perennial problem of the link between knowledge and power. But this is very difficult unless the time budgets of senior decision-makers change radically.

Empirical study of the use of time by heads of governments that I have been involved in matches the findings of comparable studies on the time budgets of senior politicians and corporate chief executive officers. Most senior decision-makers are horrified when they see how their time is wasted. The way they actually use their time is often very different from their impression of what they are doing, and even more different from what they think they should be doing. In the vast majority of cases, there is little time for reflecting on policy. Meeting follows meeting, telephones intrude without interruption, pseudo-emergencies consume whatever time has been allocated for longer discussions, rituals take up a lot of energy as well as time, and so on. There are exceptions, such as weekend cabinet retreats as practiced under some Prime Ministers in the UK, and personal retreats like those of David Ben-Gurion. But, as a rule, rulers lack time for thinking. Unless this misallocation of time and energy changes, there is little hope for improving the performance of rulers, and their benefits from their staff, however excellent, will be very limited.

If followed, quite simple techniques such as constant monitoring of time use (which is easy with computerized time management), and institutionalization of policy retreats, may sometimes help with very important choices. This is an important point for governance redesign as a whole – upgrading capacities to govern does not always require grand reforms and dramatic change, though these are needed too. With enough knowledge and imagination it is often possible to make significant contributions to capacities to govern even by relatively simple redesigns which are easy to implement without significant political or other costs. Better time budgeting is one of these, as are the improvement of briefing methods, well-considered use of information technologies, decision process management, and much else. However, these are well-established techniques which need not occupy us here, other than noting their importance and pointing out that they are often underutilized within the higher echelons of political power.

Main decision processes and work habits should therefore be improved, with emphasis on better use of time, scheduling of opportunities for thinking, correction of group deliberation dynamics, better briefing methods and information inputs, and decision implementation monitoring. This is a task that can be undertaken by good management consultants applying tried and tested improvement techniques. It thus illustrates practical ways to improve important decision processes when more radical redesigns, as proposed in this book, are hard to implement. The failure of most governments to utilize these relatively simple improvement methods indicates the primitive nature of core components of governance, with dire consequences for capacities to govern.

If we could explore the deeper recesses of rulers' minds, my conjecture is that many of the rituals surrounding presidents and prime ministers in most democracies would be found to have a harmful effect on their performance, though meeting important social and political functions (Lapham, 1993). Not only do they waste scarce time and energy, but they also cause positive damage by feeding narcissism and megalomania, and increasing their distance from reality. It may therefore help to have symbolic heads of state, including constitutional monarchs when this fits with established traditions (Akzin, 1962; Bogdanor, 1995), who reign but do not rule, to take over most of the ritualistic and symbolic functions. Rulers are then free to concentrate on essential tasks, and will hopefully be wiser in their use of time and less convinced of their own importance.

There may be other benefits in having a constitutional monarchy. As the example of Spain shows, kings and queens can fill important social and political roles, being above politics but able to intervene during crises. They can also help to maintain national identity in non-chauvinist ways (Longford, 1993; Maclean, 1993). But their usefulness depends on them and their families behaving in exemplary ways.

In countries not used to monarchies, a good alternative may be to have a symbolic Head of State, such as a President who acts mainly as a figurehead but has reserve powers in case of emergency. Electing such symbolic heads of state for long terms of office – say, eight years with provisions for recall if necessary – may help to strengthen their useful functions while keeping them out of politics. Such an innovation may be especially valuable in countries that lack democratic political traditions, by providing some stability and thus improving the chances for building democratic institutions and political cultures. However, care must be taken not to have such heads of state interfere in politics, as this may cause serious damage.

The potential contributions of monarchies to freeing rulers for their main tasks, while stabilizing politics and fulfilling important symbolic and psychological functions, should therefore be recognized. In republican traditions, a similar role can be played by institutionalizing heads of state with symbolic functions and reserve powers, with long terms of office subject to recall and strict safeguards against them interfering with party politics.

However, this is a different matter from a division of functions between a president who has overall authority as regards the direction of policy while also fulfilling many symbolic functions, and a prime minister in charge of running the government on a day-to-day basis. There are some potential advantages to such a structure (Blondel, 1980, pp. 264–6) if the two rulers cooperate. However, as some experience in France shows, such a double-rulership architecture can also cause much trouble. Redesign along these lines must therefore be evaluated in the context of specific social and political settings.

NOTES

1. The German term *Caesarenwahnsinn* is much more expressive. See, for instance, Hentig, 1924.
2. This is well illustrated by the recommendations in Morris, 2000. Let me add a personal experience that further elucidates the dangers. I was very impressed by the profile of the President emerging from the Kennedy Tapes documenting the Cuban Missile Crisis (May and Zelikow, 1997). However, when telling a good friend of mine, who was a very senior US official who knew the actors in the crisis well, how impressed I was, his response was: 'Yehezkel, what happened to you? After all your experiences with heads of governments you suddenly become naive. The President knew he was being taped and was speaking to future historians.'

14

Deepening Policy Reflection

The German historian Christian Meier described the main problem facing Julius Caesar after he became the all-mighty ruler of Rome as one of 'powerlessness of the all-powerful' (Meier, 1980), because he had no idea what to do with all his power. Governments and rulers find themselves increasingly in a similar situation in the face of shifting problem spaces and imagination-surpassing possibilities. Even when they have power to act, they often do not know what to do, because past options are increasingly and obviously useless, and no new and better ones are available. And even when they think that they know what to do, they are often wrong in trying to apply old remedies to new issues. It is enough to recall genetic engineering, globalization, the growing gap between the poor and the rich, both within and between countries, and the proliferation of weapons of mass killing and the means to deliver them at a distance, in order to demonstrate an abundance of problems for which no ready solutions are available. This is a major predicament of governance which is sure to exacerbate during the twenty-first century.

Therefore, a major challenge to governance redesign is to improve policy thinking so as to yield options that supply adequate probabilities of desired outcomes without a plethora of undesirable and unexpected side-effects. This brings us to the crucial processes of policy reflection in governance, as rooted in society's overall capacities for coping with problems.

Here we reach one of the two core processes involved in capacities to govern and weave the future, the other one being value judgment (with decision implementation to be added, although this is a lower-level process not dealt with in this book, as already explained). Values, such as are provided and shaped by political philosophy, spiritual leaders and prophets, intellectuals, the preferences of the people, and the judgment of rulers, provide the goals to be striven for by improved capacities to govern. Deep policy reflection, in addition to helping with value deliberation and goal elaboration, is the core process through which choices are made. Most of the other aspects of capacities to govern and their improvement discussed in this book, such as staffing, structure and the like, are instruments for improving value judgment and policy reflection.

Hence the importance of this and the next chapters, and therefore their somewhat different and more 'methodological' content, designed to fit the nature of cognitive processes.

Most studies on governmental decision-making, and many writings by insiders, show that actual policy reflection in governance is usually poor in quality,[1] both compared to what is needed and to what is possible. One should take into account that academic studies focus more on glaring failures, while memoires by insiders often exaggerate the successes of the author by contrasting them with the failures of others and of the system. Moreover, history presents a mixed picture of dismal failures and amazing successes.

However, efforts to view major governmental processes as if they were similar to markets and therefore taken to be more 'intelligent' than they seem to be (Lindblom, 1965, 1968), are plainly wrong. The clear overall finding is that thinking within governance tends to be poor. It is often shallow and prone to inertia, with misplaced reliance on 'common sense' for coping with 'uncommon' problems. It frequently rushes forward with its eyes fixed on rear-view mirrors, reading new situations as more of what has gone before, and relying on the ideas of yesterday for treating the radically different issues of tomorrow. A pronounced weakness is to concentrate on surface symptoms instead of fundamental issues, and to prefer piecemeal and short-term views to comprehensive and long-term perspectives. Increasingly malignant, as already discussed repeatedly, is the preoccupation with image and pseudo-realities, and so on.

Typical of this is what Rudolph Klein called 'cognitive parsimony', which prevents complex issues from being properly comprehended and handled. In his words:

> How do we, as political animals, make out as 'information processing' machines? How do we make political judgments? The evidence is conflicting, but, on the whole, seems to suggest that the answer is 'not very well'. We react to the plethora of information generated by the media, and the mass of conflicting signals generated by political debate, by acting as 'cognitive misers'. Whether as politicians taking decisions about affairs of State, or as voters making up our minds about whom to support, we tend to rely on symbolic cues, to cut through complexity and to search for certainty. We prefer simple decision rules and explanations to weighing up arguments pulling us in different directions. In short, we are constantly searching for short cuts which will reduce the burden of information processing (Klein, 1994).

Exaggeration must be avoided. There are many cases of good decisions and also outstanding statecraft based on excellent reflection. Thus, the situation can best be characterized as 'mixed'. However, as already clarified,

because of the increasingly complex nature of policy areas and the growing costs of mis-
takes, 'mixed quality' governmental thinking and choosing processes, which may have
served in the past, are increasingly inadequate and may well become catastrophic in their
results. Hence the need for radically improved governance choice processes – including what
I call, as a kind of shorthand, 'deep policy reflection'.

If we could rely on non-governance processes to do the job, it would be less necessary to take up the arduous and in some ways even impossible task of improving governance reflection; best of all would be processes that can aggregate weak components into overall good outcomes. The paradigmatic example is the pure model of a market, where limited and often narrow choices by individual enterprises add up to the high-quality cognitive capacities of the market system as a whole. Efforts to transfer governance tasks to market processes, or to try and make governments work partly according to market processes, are therefore fully justified in terms of efficiency and effectiveness, when possible.

However, democratic norms require that governance should make critical future-shaping choices, or at least closely monitor and when necessary intervene in them. In terms of effectiveness many of the higher-order tasks of governance cannot be transferred to market and quasi-market processes, being distinct in their dynamics. Similarly, the processes of civil society, however important, should not and cannot release governance from critical future-shaping tasks. Upgrading capacities to govern and 'weave the future' therefore requires radical changes in policy reflection within governance.

To explore the idea of 'deep policy reflection' and indicate some ways to improve it, I will outline seventeen of its principles, to be followed in the next chapter by a frame of thinking on the essence of policy reflection.[2]

(1) Reflection in terms of 'rise and decline' and long-term evolutionary processes

The framework of rise and decline and long-term evolutionary processes brings out the full ambitions and difficulties of the required deep policy reflection.

Policy thinking should take account of historical and theoretical conjectures concerning the rise and decline of nations, civilizations and humanity as a whole, and consider the factors shaping the long-range impacts of revolutions, the successes and failures of development, the breakdown of societies, and the fate of other 'great enterprises' (I borrow this concept from Wakeman Jr, 1985).

Our knowledge of the variables shaping the fate of nations and societies is rudimentary, and even less is known about the way humankind evolves while interacting with its environments. An interesting body of literature dealing with various aspects is available (see, for example, Olson Jr, 1982; Hawrylyshyn, 1980; Kennedy, 1987; Unger, 1987b), as is a large number of monographic studies, not to mention the illuminating speculations of Edward

Gibbon, Oswald Spengler, and Arnold J. Toynbee. But knowledge in this field consists at best of partial explanations, of mainly weak conjectures, and often of no more than informed speculations.

Also at issue is the value relativism of such concepts as 'rise and decline'; the same two historical processes can be seen as the rise of the USA and the amazing successes of Zionism, or as the decline and catastrophe of Native Americans and the Palestinians.

Nevertheless, posing salient questions and trying to penetrate some of the causes of rise or decline, and of thriving or destruction, is both possible and necessary for making policy reflection relevant to the really critical issues of 'weaving the future' of humankind and its major component parts. This is true even though the main variables shaping rise and decline are multiple, partly unknown and even unknowable with present epistemological capacities, changing, and partly specific to their period.

(2) Focus on long-term 'weaving of the future'

Policy reflection should concentrate on strategic choices making a significant difference for the future, to the point of setting and changing long-term trajectories. This contrasts with 'muddling through' and a myopic preoccupation with immediate pressures and considerations, glorified by misuse of the term 'pragmatism' (in ways having nothing to do with its philosophic meanings, as developed by Charles S. Pierce, John Dewey and others).

A related matter is the need to think in terms of 'historic projects' and large-scale interventions in history, aiming at putting societies on a different and preferably better track. Revolutions belong to this category, but they pose special problems that require separate treatment (Dror, 1988b, pp. 95–7).

(3) Thinking in terms of evolutionary potential

Evolutionary potential within decision-relevant time horizons, both of specific societies and of humanity as a whole, is an important consideration. This potential is obviously both good and bad, and the task of governance is not only to reduce the negative and enhance the positive possibilities within given conditions, but also often to raise society to higher evolutionary potentials.

The basic logic of this dimension is to map the main potentials in all their uncertainty and open-endedness, then to identify the main variables that determine the path which history will take within its potential – or even in changing it. The investigation and development of such variables should enable some of them to be 'reset', and thus serve as policy instruments. These policy instruments will be the elements out of which options can be synthesized.

However, there is often need for a more innovative approach. When all of the evolutionary potential is unacceptable, or when no policy instruments exist which may lead to the realization of more favorable possibilities within the given evolutionary potential, 'break out' options which lead to a new and better evolutionary potential[3] need to be sought and invented.

(4) Estimates of situations and dynamics, processes and mutation possibilities

Governmental choice and action are predicated on images of the world. Consequently, improvements in 'reality maps' are essential – all the more so in an epoch of rapid change, when mental maps become rapidly obsolete.

This involves two interacting levels. One is more abstract, and deals with rules, symbols, concepts, schema and theories to be applied in constructing more valid and dynamic estimations of reality; the other deals with substantive estimates of major trends, processes, dynamics and possibilities, with special attention to non-linear processes and possible mutations.

The persistence of security intelligence failures, despite intense efforts to overcome them, raises serious doubts as to how to achieve substantive improvements in estimations. However, the tendency of policy-makers to produce and cling to incorrect images of reality (Vertzberger, 1990) makes it all the more important to improve estimations and their use in critical choices. More emphasis on opportunities as compared with threats and dangers is urgently needed, and is also achievable (for some preliminary ideas, see Carmel, 1999).

This applies fully to the global scale, where there is an urgent need for much improved intelligence capacity. The plan to set up a surveillance system for the Amazon based on modern technologies illustrates some of these possibilities, but better global policy-making requires much more, such as the early identification of evil rulers.

(5) Thinking in historical terms without being bound by the past

The 'weaving of the future' is based on the premise that the future is not fully determined by the past (Unger, 1987a; Hawthorn, 1991; McCall, 1994), but rather is a product of dynamic processes and interactions which are a combination of necessity, contingency, chance and choice. Freely chosen human activities (without going here into the philosophical issues surrounding 'free will'), including governance action, can therefore make a meaningful impact on evolving realities, including radically shaping some aspects of the future.

Nonetheless, the past affects and limits future possibilities. It also provides the raw material for studying and trying to understand societal processes and mapping our present position. If policy reflection is to help in future-building, a historical perspective is therefore essential.

But there are dangers in being captivated by history and historical thinking, especially in an age of transformations. To do so may result in a failure to recognize that the present and future differ from the past in important respects. This can produce a nostalgic attachment to images with no real

THE CAPACITY TO GOVERN

relevance for the future. It also reinforces policy inertia and incrementalism, and suppresses creative thinking about the future. Therefore, historical thinking is valuable but must not act as a mental strait-jacket.

(6) Emphasis on 'futuribles', grand designs, and realistic visions

There is a related tendency towards narrow interpretations of what might be feasible. To avoid this trap and stimulate creative thinking on possibilities and future evolutionary potentials, policy reflection should emphasize *futuribles, grand designs*, and *realistic visions*.

Bertrand de Jouvenel coined the term *futuribles* to explore, describe and 'invent' possible futures (Jouvenel, 1967) – and this is essential for deep policy reflection. Long-term grand designs, realistic visions – and also 'realistic nightmares' – may often be helpful in providing better links between long-range goals and values and immediate decisions and are, therefore, an important part of deep policy reflection.

Realistic visions are also valuable in mobilizing support for painful interim policies, which people may bear more willingly if they believe that the future will be better thanks to present sacrifices. On a subconscious cultural level, too, prospects of a better future fulfill essential functions by reducing despair and helping to overcome traumas and disorientation.

To move a step beyond policy reflection to its cultural infrastructure, utopian visions for the future of humankind are needed. These provide contemplative and idealistic foundations for advancing *raison d'humanité* and help to build up human solidarity, in addition to serving as a grounding for realistic visions. For example, utopias have played a significant role in Zionism (Elboim-Dror, 1993) and in other movements (Naville-Sington and Sington, 1993), as well as in the history of ideas – which, in turn, strongly influence politics and policies, even if often indirectly so.

A mixture of realistic and utopian visions is also required in order to set goals that 'stretch' governance beyond what seems possible, as Gary Hamel and C.K. Prahalad argue in the context of business (Hamel and Prahalad, 1993, further developed in Hamel and Prahalad, 1994, chs 4 and 6). This is why policy reflection should be related to societal 'dreaming', though a distinction between them must be maintained.

(7) Identifying, developing and focusing on critical choices

The effort to influence trajectories into the future within given or mutated evolutionary potentials requires the identification of critical choices – that is choices likely to have a significant impact on the future. When harsh realities are faced or anticipated, but no critical choice can be identified that permits coping with them, then an effort to develop critical choice opportunities must be made.

This requires either the creative development of new options which open up critical choices, the instigation of crises, or otherwise 'throwing surprises at history', or in other ways relaxing constrains and opening up new options.

(8) Emphasis on creativity

Governmental organizations tend towards incrementalism and other non-innovative approaches to decision-making. But this is inadequate in the face of novel problems, shifting situations and new knowledge. Imaginative thinking is required, coupled with iconoclasm in respect to accepted policy orthodoxy.

Many processes and actors outside governance are much more innovative and creative, such as markets, some grass-roots movements, free-floating intellectuals and university academics, 'think tanks' (which, in effect, are policy research-and-development units), and spiritual leaders. Governance, and in particular central governments, should therefore rely on the creativity and innovativeness of other structures and facilitate them. This is no substitute, however, for building up creativity in governance.

Governmental policy reflection involves two main sub-processes: generating options and screening options. Creating new options is more challenging and open-ended, whereas screening them is a more mundane task, however methodologically difficult. To devise new options requires inventiveness, which ultimately depends on the creativity of individuals and involves processes that are poorly understood, while the organizational and societal factors that encourage or repress creativity are only partly known, Thus, what seems to be involved is in part 'fantasy' – the ability to imagine and play with nonexistent possibilities (Nussbaum, 1995b, ch. 2) and to engage in counterfactual thinking (Tedlock and Belkin, 1996).

Because many predicaments and opportunities are unprecedented, devising new options should often take priority over the better screening of existing, or easily synthesized, ones. Some relatively simple steps can broaden the range of available options, such as better study of history and of comparative experiences. Since these sources of options will often be inadequate, it is essential to be innovative and to create new options, including radically novel ones (in the sense of categoric newness or 'newness of kind' discussed in Hausman, 1984).

However, because creativity is largely a 'black box' the internal processes of which are unknown, this requirement is distinct from most other deep policy reflection dimensions, depending on suitable mixes of creative people, creativity-encouraging organizational cultures and societal creativity as a whole.

(9) Iconoclasm, learning, and changing one's mind

To permit innovations – not only by generating new policies but also by getting them adopted and implemented despite stubborn rigidities and resistances – existing policy traditions must be critically re-evaluated; and, if necessary, policy paradigms and orthodoxies should be overturned.

However, undermining accepted canons can do more harm than good if the main results are trauma, despair, loss of nerve, maze behavior and similar counter-productive responses. What is needed instead is a capacity to change one's mind: that is, to admit – as individuals, organizations, governance and societies – that a major policy is wrong or no longer appropriate, and then to adopt a new one. A striking and quite unusual illustration is the statement in May 1993 by the President of the Republic of South Africa that apartheid was a mistake.

Coping with global predicaments and opportunities will require both a considerable willingness to acknowledge historic errors and recognition of the obsolescence of policies which proved themselves successful in the past.

Closely related to this is an exceptional capacity to learn, captured in the term *metanoia*, meaning a shift of mind (Senge, 1990, esp. pp. 13–14). In the apt words of Donald N. Michael, we must learn to plan and plan to learn (Michael, 1997). This apparently mundane principle requires far-reaching changes in the behavior, structure and – most important and most difficult of all – culture of governance. Within central minds of governance it requires special evaluation and learning structures; and in policy reflection it requires mental elasticity and a certain kind of 'courage' (Walton, 1986).

(10) Concern with resources

As a counter-balance to utopian visions and unrealistic image-oriented programs, often mainly to impress public opinion, action-directed policy reflection must take full account of resource considerations: allocating resources according to explicit orders of priority, husbanding scarce resources, and making efforts to produce additional resources both in the short and long run. A much improved capacity to budget (Schick, 1990) is therefore an essential component of deep policy reflection; but it should be a long-term one, beyond short-term monetary considerations, a myopic obsession with macroeconomics, bureaucratic politics and the purchasing of political support.

(11) Sensitivity to power, but distinct from politics

A conceptual distinction between politics and policy, however much inter-related and overlapping they may be, is essential for deep policy reflection. Many languages use the same word for both, so new terms may have to be invented.

Policy thinking must be sophisticated about politics and sensitive to issues of power. This implies a good understanding of the realities of power and politics, within a dynamic view that does justice to the changing nature of politics, its cultural bases, and its dependence on accidental features, individual top decision-makers and unpredictable exogenous events. At the same time, there must be a border between power-oriented political advice and policy reflection. Governance needs both,[4] but they should be kept distinct though in contact.

These suggestions apply also to global policy reflection, but here they run into formidable barriers. The United Nations especially is super-saturated with inter-state and also intra-state politics, making policy thinking on major global issues that tries to distance itself from daily politics either impossible or irrelevant. Only significant reform of the United Nations can reduce this fundamental defect.

(12) Concern with implementation

The details of implementation belong to the fields of public administration and public management and are fully treated in the standard literature. Therefore, as already mentioned, I do not give them the attention they deserve. However, from the perspective of capacities to govern a number of points must be noted, which have important implications for policy reflection.

Implementation probabilities, dependent on power, human and economic resources, administrative capabilities and so on, are a major consideration and constraint, and therefore must be given much attention. However, too narrow a view of them is devastating for policy entrepreneurship, innovativeness and creativity. Circumstances are sure to change, strength of will is an important factor and resources can sometimes be imported. An 'open' rather than 'closed' look at 'feasibility' is therefore recommended, giving priority to statecraft as making the advisable possible over the narrow view of politics as the art of the possible. This is all the more true in an epoch of rapid change, where what seemed impossible yesterday often becomes very possible the day after tomorrow.

However, the opposite error of expanding the image of the possible beyond realistic evolutionary potentials must also be avoided. Finding a balance between excessively narrow and excessively utopian views of the possible is therefore a main challenge for policy reflection.

An understanding of implementability should be added as being partly open to deliberate expansion, for example by increasing administrative and managerial capacities and restructuring politics to facilitate democratic power concentration. Policy reflection should take into account such possibilities and develop strategies for doing so, with details to be handled by other units in charge of administrative reforms, government machinery and so on.

(13) Managing and utilizing crises

To balance an impression one may get of policy reflection as wholly systematic, it is important to emphasize the 'wild', cascading and mutating nature of major policy spaces.

In its purest form this is expressed in the need to pay a great deal of attention to crisis decision-making, which is increasingly important as the last resort in the face of surprise events inevitably generated by global and local upheavals.

As classical Chinese statecraft well recognizes, many crises also constitute opportunities (Godet, 1985), because they break down rigidities, open up possibilities that do not normally exist, and force upon governance innovations which are rejected out-of-hand under ordinary circumstances.

Let us consider a hypothetical situation to illustrate this point within a global context. Let us assume that suddenly it is discovered that an unstable country has acquired a few nuclear bombs and is planning to use them to 'solve once and for all', as their top-secret internal policy memorandum says, a long-festering conflict with a neighboring country. This would constitute a major global crisis that could be managed in two ways, one limited and one broad. The limited approach would be to disarm the country in question, or deter it, or resolve the particular conflict, thus containing one specific crisis. The broader approach would be to use the crisis as an opportunity to establish and enforce a strict global regime arresting and reversing the proliferation of nuclear weapons.

However, in order to turn crises into opportunities, there must be extensive reflection beforehand on relevant problem areas, so that unavoidable improvisations are based on well-considered ideas (but not detailed 'contingency plans', which seldom fit actual crises and can result in rigid thinking unless very sophisticated). High-quality policy reflection must therefore integrate crisis management and utilization into long-range policy reflection.

(14) Grounded in moral reasoning, value analysis and goal-search

Value judgment and goal-search together constitute the most fundamental bases of problem perception, choice and action. The approach of improving other capacities of governance while leaving value judgment and goal-search as they are is, therefore, not only inadequate but positively dangerous, leading to efficient and more effective policies advancing more rapidly in a wrong direction. A paradigmatic example mentioned above is better planning and improved logistics for starting a war that is both immoral and disastrous for what would be recognized as the long-range goals of the country if more thought had been devoted to them.

However, value judgment and goal postulation are a prerogative and duty of 'legitimate value judges', as they are themselves normatively defined by basic norms grounding all polities (Kelsen, 1961). Democratic values postulate that the people and their representatives are the supreme value judges and goal setters for public action, subject to legal values as determined by judges and, in increasingly accepted views, to overriding human or transcendental norms.

Policy reflection thus faces the challenge of helping the legitimate value judges and goal setters to improve their reasoning, without usurping their judgment. No wonder that nearly all the literature in policy analysis, policy planning, decision improvement and the like shies away from considering the improvement of value judgment.

Deep policy reflection must take up this challenge, and it can be done in three main ways. First, by better analysis of values salient to a decision, with the help of the methods of moral reasoning, improved political philosophy and the idea of *raison d'humanité* and other value innovations.

Second, by helping the legitimate value judges, namely in democracies the senior politicians, to understand better the required moral judgments, such as by explicating the need to make a choice between values that cannot all be realized, the necessity to take into account time preferences, and the need to decide prudently what mix of uncertainties to prefer.

A third way to help is to allocate better the authority and responsibility to make value judgments, as illustrated by Helsinki Committees put in charge of very difficult value judgments concerning medical experiments. Many of the radically novel problem areas emerging from biotechnology, gene mapping and so on may well require new value deliberation forums, though politics and governance cannot absolve itself from overall responsibility for such future-shaping issues. Deeper policy reflection will propose such bodies and interact with them, while helping governance to make the value judgments which are necessarily theirs, whether they like it or not.

Overall, much attention to helping professionally with value judgment and goal setting is one of the main features differentiating deep policy reflection from shallow 'policy analysis', 'decision theory' and the like.

(15) Better interaction with societal thinking and research

Radically new alternatives, counter-factual assumptions, hermeneutic contemplation, value invention, social critique, pure theories, and the like are products of individual thinkers and free-floating intellectuals, academics and professionals, ideologues, grass-roots activists, prophets, social dreamers, entrepreneurs, special interest groups, universities and think tanks – not of governance units. However, they are essential for high-quality governance thinking, all the more in an epoch of change where 'wild' innovations may prove to be more 'practical' than the best thinking in established institutions. It is thus a major task of deep policy reflection to facilitate such societal contemplation, learn from it, apply its results to governance and maximally benefit from it for innovative future-building capacities.

Governance should not only seek insights, ideas and approaches throughout societies and humankind, but also should actively encourage societal creativity in ways not interfering with its substance. This is important not only in order to assure more and better inputs into governance thinking, but for societal learning as a whole, while moving towards 'governance through social learning' (Paquet, 1999). Although democracies have a crucial advantage here, their societal creativity in policy thinking also needs to be stimulated, and their abilities to govern enhanced by being able to discriminate between good and bad ideas, especially when the latter are presented more vociferously than the former.

(16) Acknowledging and coping with complexity

All that has been said can be partly summed up as the need to cope with what appears to the human mind as extreme complexity.

Complexity is recognized to some extent as a problem in policy thinking, to be handled with the help of techniques such as systems analysis in its various forms. But, chiefly, governance tends to be very poor at coping with growing complexities, because of the cognitive limitations of the human mind, the tendency of group discussions to over-simplify issues, the limitations of available modes and methods for comprehending complexity, and weaknesses in governance structures and staffing. Nevertheless, progress is possible, thanks to available and emerging knowledge (Rosenhead, 1989; Jervis, 1997), including some beginnings of a 'science of complexity' (Nicolis and Prigogine, 1989; Waldrop, 1992).

One of the main requirements for handling complexity involves perceiving, accepting and processing contradictions. This must be done by policy reflection, thinking partly in terms of dialectical processes and ironies of history. Related is the need to accept and utilize counter-intuitive dynamics, such as 'micromotives and macrobehavior' (Schelling, 1978), and to overcome the mental traps of culturally conditioned 'common sense', partly by giving more attention to counter-intuitive processes and counter-factual thinking.

An easier requirement, but one that is important and usually neglected in governance, is that of adopting multiple perspectives (Linstone *et al.*, 1984), so that major issues are considered from various points of view, in terms both of theories and models, and of types of actors.

The complexity of issues can only be comprehended, if at all, by complex policy reflection. This involves the use of a combination of different images, symbols, principles, frames, approaches, orientations, methods, methodologies and tools – applying the already-mentioned principle that coping well with complexity requires meta-complexity.

Paradoxically, a greater understanding of complexity may lead to a recognition of underlying realities that are in some respects essentially 'simple' (Slobidkin, 1992). An example is provided by the inappropriateness of the very idea of nation-states for African social and cultural structures as a fundamental and 'simple' cause of dismal failures of governance. One way of coping with complexity is therefore to search for relatively 'simple' underlying core factors and essences, though this is often impossible and care must always be taken to avoid over-simplification.

(17) Self-reflexiveness

To assure a constantly improving quality of policy reflection, governance must be self-conscious about its policy reflection processes and try all the time to improve them. This is all the more necessary as the state of the art in policy reflection – both in practice and in relevant theories – is unsatisfactory, bringing us back to the need to seek novel knowledge as a professional support and basis for a new statecraft, or more correctly 'humankind-craft'.

Self-reflexivity in policy reflection requires being able to reflect critically and creatively on policy reflection within what metaphorically can be called the 'metamind' (Lehrer, 1990) of governance. This leads us to the subject of 'central minds of governance' as the ecology of policy reflection, to be discussed in a following chapter.

There is much to be added on the dimensions of deep policy reflection, such as concern with institutional and legal dimensions. But a better way further to clarify the idea of deep policy reflection, and indicate some of its requirements, is to return to the need for a largely novel type of staff composed of highly trained policy professionals, as discussed in Chapter Twelve.

Crucial for raising the quality of policy reflection is the development of highly qualified policy professionals, sorely scarce at present. This requires restructured public policy schools, intense workshops and so on. Such policy professionals should serve as the core of units dedicated to deep policy reflection, near rulers, throughout central minds of governments, in political decision loci, in think-tanks and in society at large. All policy professionals must, inter alia, be well familiar with thinking in terms of global perspectives. But there is also a need for a sub-specialization of global policy professionals, in order to improve the cognitive capacities of global governance.

Another requirement of improving policy reflection is to develop and advance salient theoretical knowledge. Policy reflection can deepen only when abstract knowledge and general theories are available which permit better understanding of complex processes and systems. Moreover, policy recommendations can responsibly be based on such theories only when the latter are sufficiently validated to give such recommendations a higher chance of desired outcomes than of undesired ones. This applies also in disciplines that in the past served policy-making well, such as economics, with global shifts making many theories which were valid in the past increasingly inadequate and even misleading.

Advancing theoretical knowledge is not a task for governance, but it can do a great deal to facilitate the development of theories, empiric knowledge, insights and methods relevant to policy reflection and its improvement, by encouraging salient research and contemplation.

The nature of deep policy reflection and its internal and external difficulties are further brought out in the following chapter, where the essence of choice as 'fuzzy gambling' is clarified, with its implications for redesign of governance as a whole and for deepening policy reflection in particular.

NOTES

1. The following books may serve as an introduction to the vast literature on the subject: Tuchman, 1984; Hart, 1990; Butler, Adonis, and Travers, 1994; Murray, Knox, and Bernstein, 1994; Bovens and Hart, 1996; and Baron, 1998.
2. The proposed conception of policy reflection is much broader than 'policy analysis', moving more in the direction of what can be regarded as in between 'policy reasoning' and 'statecraft professionalism'. The main texts in policy analysis tend to focus on micro-issues, to lack uncertainty sophistication, ignore moral reasoning as an essential dimension and not to face the need for option creativity as often more important than 'analysis'. Most of the public policy university programs suffer from similar weaknesses. A great deal of relevant material is nonetheless included in better books in policy analysis, such as: Dery, 1984; Quade, 1989; Rosenhead, 1989; Zeckhauser, 1991; Weimer and Vining, 1992; W. Dunn, 1994; and the three volumes of Miser, 1995 and Miser and Quade, 1985 and 1988. My own approaches will be presented in Dror, in preparation a and b respectively.
3. Strictly speaking, the new evolutionary potential must have been implied in the original evolutionary potential, otherwise it would be 'impossible'.
4. Political thinking too needs much improvement, all the more so since many politicians lack real understanding of the changing nature of politics – with their experience in the past (as with all experience) becoming more of a trained incapacity than a source of practical wisdom. This is illustrated by the increasing subjugation of politics to what is perceived to be the public mood, with public opinion polls determining main policy declarations and policy choices. However, most of the polls are methodologically weak, relying on cheap methods to try to map shifting and complex public opinions. Thus, nearly all polls lack intensity scaling, in which respondents are asked not only what they think or believe, but how intensely they feel about their views. What is worse, most senior politicians underrate the possibilities of enlarging the domain of the politically possible through influencing public opinion in ways going far beyond fashionable 'political marketing'. This presupposes that senior politicians understand the changing dynamics of their societies – which often they do not.

   There is therefore an urgent need to deepen political (as distinct from 'policy') reflection as well, as an essential component of developing capacities to govern, but I leave this subject for another occasion (Dror, in preparation a, and Morris 1999b).

15

Qualifying in 'Fuzzy-Gambling'

In the face of pervasive uncertainty and inconceivability, as confronts all significant decisions and, in particular, options for 'weaving the future', decisions are in essence gambles in which the pay-off is not only largely unknown and even unknowable, but not predetermined. This has always been the case, but ongoing transformations are increasing such uncertainties by orders of magnitude, with crucial choice domains being dense with the inconceivable. Critical choices are therefore increasingly 'fuzzy'[1] gambles – that is gambles which cannot be reduced to probabilities, such as a dice game, or to event chains with fixed distribution rules and known categories of result, such as a horse race.

This has very disturbing implications, because what I designate as 'policy gambles' are, because of their fuzzy gambling essence, at variance with psychological, political and cultural needs and propensities, and therefore cannot be adequately handled intuitively. Matters are made worse because many decision-makers are uncertainty-illiterate, most professional planners rely on simplistic probability calculations, and there are political as well as cultural barriers to recognizing and accepting that critical choices are fuzzy gambles. To acquire the insights necessary for improving unavoidable policy gambling, it therefore is necessary to redesign the main facets of governance, as well as political culture and overall societal orientations and world-views.

At the very least, enclaves of excellence in central minds of governments must become policy gambling qualified, with senior politicians being uncertainty-sophisticated and policy reflection staffs acquiring policy gambling professionalism. Furthermore, policy gambling skills and knowledge may have to be exercised in enclaves of excellence partly insulated from inhibiting external influences, such as uncertainty-rejecting political cultures and traumatized societies intolerant of ambiguity.

The characterization of major future-building endeavors as fuzzy gambles has implications going far beyond the policy gamble sophistication and professionalism requirements among central minds of governments. It constitutes a basic predicament of all of human life, as reflected in the most human of all existential questions: Why me? (Gelven, 1991; Nussbaum, 1995a). Equally, it pervades modern moral discourse (Statman, 1993). Certainly, it makes all governance activities in pursuit of higher-order tasks fragile (in the sense of Nussbaum, 1986), and often tragic.

Leaving aside the psychological and philosophical implications, the nature of efforts to weave the future as fuzzy gambles, often for high stakes, is at the heart of the difficulties and requirements of upgrading capacities to govern and a core requirement of deep policy reflection. This chapter is therefore devoted to exploring it as a continuation of the preceding one.

To pose the challenge starkly: *although anathema to contemporary risk-averse political cultures, governments have no choice but to engage in fuzzy gambling with history for high stakes, though this overtaxes by order of magnitude their present capacities. This is of the essence of critical choices in the face of ubiquitous uncertainties, irreducible indeterminacy and substantial inconceivability. Upgrading fuzzy policy gambling qualifications is therefore crucial, although difficult emotionally, morally and cognitively, requiring innovative and exacting redesigns.*

The problematic of uncertainty has been fully recognized by decision-makers throughout history. Greek tragedy epitomized the difficulty (Nussbaum, 1986), while Thucydides fully discussed it (Edmunds, 1975), and Spanish classical statecraft literature focused on it (Fernandez-Santamaria, 1983). Interplay between 'fortune', 'opportunity' and 'virtue' was central to Machiavelli (Mansfield, 1996, *passim*).

But a brief look at the history of governance clearly demonstrates that only small improvements in handling the uncertainties involved in critical choice have transpired during the last three to four thousand years, where records are available. Some useful tools have been developed, such as cost-benefit-risk analysis (though hardly new, the principle familiar to Thucydides), scenario preparation (preceded by contingency thinking in antiquity), game theory (going back to war games, not later that the eighteenth century and perhaps much earlier), and systems approaches.

However, modern choice techniques, such as operations research and Bayes's theorem, only fit decision series with statistical regularity. Subjective probabilities and their uses are based on incorrect ontological assumptions. While approaches which potentially do match critical choice features, such as 'thinking-in-history' and some ideas in the cognitive sciences, are as yet underdeveloped. The overall result is that available knowledge is not adequate for upgrading fuzzy policy gambling.

In particular, the statistical handling of uncertainty is not only inadequate but also misleading, and often even dangerous. Probabilistic calculus was explicitly used by a major Dutch policy maker in the seventeenth century, later by a German policy adviser before and after the First World War, and more recently in Vietnam. However, all of these and most similar uses had dismal results, because of the rigidities of probabilistic calculus, which ignores and falsifies the 'fuzziness' of choice as rooted, as presently perceived, in ontological indeterminacy (Gigerenzer *et al.*, 1989).[2]

Contemporary political cultures add to these difficulties, being intolerant of uncertainty and trying to deny it or hedge against it in illusory and counter-productive ways, as illustrated in some widespread approaches to environmental concerns. Little wonder that the classical escape routes from uncertainty, such as astrology and other magic techniques, seem to be as widely used as ever, including by senior politicians and even some heads of states.[3]

Instead, central minds of governments should both explicitly understand and tacitly absorb advanced notions of uncertainty and inconceivability as bases for improved policy reflection and choice. This depends on conceptualizing much better the processes shaping the future in terms taking full account of uncertainty and inconceivability. *In order to comprehend and improve future-building as fuzzy gambling, historical processes should be conceptualized and understood as a dynamic compound of necessity, contingency, chance and choice.*

Given present and foreseeable dynamics the future is largely shaped by processes that are not deterministically 'necessary', but rather include many contingencies and 'chance' events, even amounting to inconceivable mutations. There is a great deal of hyper-turbulence, while 'cascades' abound, together with dramatic ruptures in continuity. This is the force-field within which choice operates, adding to uncertainty and inconceivability.

Such a cartography of processes shaping the future negates linear thinking, as well as most present modeling techniques and much probabilistic calculus. Even more so, it negates most human and organizational thinking habits. Branches of mathematics dealing with jumps and metamorphoses, such as catastrophe topology and chaos theory, can serve as heuristic tools – but not more than that.

Once more, exaggeration must be avoided. Many situations and processes are quite robust and relatively stable, providing solid foundations for policies. However, as illustrated dramatically by the *Shoah*, the sudden implosion of the Soviet Union, and by the AIDS epidemic, mutations which often transform policy-worlds are to be expected, while being in advance inconceivable in their particularities.[4]

Equipped with these insights, governments should not delude themselves that more study, larger investments in intelligence, or improvements in methodologies will necessarily reduce uncertainty. Sometimes this may happen, but in an epoch of hyper-turbulence the converse will frequently be the case, with better understanding of ongoing processes often revealing more uncertainty and inconceivability, resulting in human thinking clinging to a subjective illusion of certainty instead of accepting the facts of objective uncertainty and of 'knowing that we cannot know', that is recognizing unavoidable ignorance about many domains including crucial ones, such as future scientific breakthroughs.

This can have grave consequences. Decision psychology has identified many weaknesses of human intuition when facing uncertainty. Modern cultural barriers to admitting and consciously living with risks reinforce counter-productive delusions. Decision-makers may become more reckless when fully aware of the gambling nature of their critical choices, while doubts are cast on 'responsibility', 'accountability' and learning when results can no longer be regarded as reliable indicators of the quality of choice. The legitimation of governance may be further undermined if the fuzzy gambling nature of decisions is widely recognized. Choice may become paralyzed, allowing default options to take over, while intolerance of explicated uncertainty may swell an addiction to mystical decision supports.

An argument can therefore be made for repressing the realization that weaving the future necessarily involves so much fuzzy gambling. This view was strongly expressed to me both by academic colleagues and senior politicians when faced with the conceptualization of critical choices as fuzzy gambles. But I reject the suggestion that knowledge of the real nature of critical choices as involving a large measure of fuzzy gambling should be repressed, though it may be necessary temporarily to quarantine and compartmentalize it. Human advancement as a whole depends on the fuller understanding of reality and our place within it. Even if recognition of the fuzzy-gambling nature of critical choices would cause mental anguish without any beneficial consequences, as a matter of philosophical principle I therefore support, in the long run, the explanation and diffusion of that knowledge.

This preference of mine may be debatable, but a different line of argument clinches the issue. *The improvement of critical choices, made democratically, can be achieved only if their true nature as involving significant fuzzy gambling is fully and widely recognized. Popular public affairs enlightenment should therefore include strenuous efforts to make people more uncertainty-sophisticated, with efforts by rulers to explain the nature of their choices being an important component of this task.*

There is much to be said on the ways and means of making people more uncertainty-sophisticated, starting with appropriate teaching and interactive computer environments in schools. Computer games involving structured uncertainty, together with surprise events and sudden changes in situations, may help to 'rewire' human cognitive capacities at an earlier age, before thinking habits are frozen. At the same time, suitable television programs can help adults to acquire at least some understanding of uncertainty.

However, considerable time will pass, at best, before the people and main elites gain such understanding, while their emotional reactions to uncertainty and inconceivability may be even harder to improve. *In the foreseeable future the improvement of fuzzy policy gambling will therefore have to be the responsibility of small knowledge-elites, a limited number of moral philosophers and thinkers, select senior politicians, and a new breed of policy professionals. Full recognition of the fuzzy-gambling nature of critical choices, with all its implications, will de facto be limited to enclaves within the central minds of governments and civil society.*

Luckily, this does not require a new regime of secrecy and closed governance; the vast majority of the people, and most of the elites, will in any case not accept that fateful choices are often fuzzy gambles, even when they are told that this is so. However, to avoid additional traumatization and anxiety-driven counter-productive reactions, I cannot in good conscience recommend the public presentation by senior politicians of major decisions as fuzzy gambles before populations are ready for it, which at present they are not.

This is another illustration of democracy as a mixed regime in action, in this case by the confinement of certain kinds of understanding to select governance and civil society actors. This is legitimate, subject to overall democratic control. But it is undesirable and also dangerous, as it imposes on governance the hard choice between not knowing and not telling all that it knows. In view of the imperative to improve future-shaping choices, I prefer the second option. But this choice can be democratically justified only if two conditions are met: first, maximum efforts should be made to enlighten the people and make them uncertainty-literate, so that quarantining of the view of critical choices as fuzzy gambles is temporary; and second, maximum efforts should be made by the policy-reflection and decision-making enclaves within central minds of governments to improve critical choices, with full recognition of their true nature as unavoidably constituting fuzzy gambles with much as stake.

This brings us to ways to improve policy gambling, without 'de-gambling' it. Without going into technical aspects, let me mention some examples of doing so in ways already operational though under-utilized (Dror, 1988c; Dror, 1995; Stacey, 1992).

- The use of new concepts, terminology and symbols doing justice to various forms of uncertainty and inconceivability, instead of misleading classical probabilistic vocabulary and calculus.
- Working out the logical dimensions of fuzzy gambling – in particular the distinction between mapping various forms and degrees of uncertainty on one hand, and value preferences between various bundles of such uncertainties on the other (so-called 'lottery values', Raiffa, 1968).
- The design of display and presentation methods permitting the comprehension and processing of complex outlook mapping in ways fitting the cognitive capacities, habits and preferences of top decision makers, while at the same time upgrading the latter.[5]
- The development of protocols for handling the main types of fuzzy gambling situations, such as contingencies with very low probability and very high impact, surprise-prone domains, and 'butterfly effect' situations.[6]

- Changes in group decision processes and organizational behavior so as to reduce the repression of uncertainty.
- Reducing errors to which the mind is prone when facing uncertainty and inconceivability, by introducing deliberation frames and decision protocols that improve comprehension and processing.
- Devotion of much greater attention to crisis management and utilization, as mentioned in the previous chapter, as a last resort against the uncertainty that is of growing importance in an epoch of hyper-turbulence, including the basing of inescapable improvisations on deep policy reflection.

Further and more effective ways to cope with the fuzzy gambling nature of critical choices will hopefully be supplied by new theories and applied with the help of a novel breed of policy professionals and uncertainty-sophisticated senior politicians. However, such possibilities to improve fuzzy policy gambling are of little practical value unless their use in select components of the central minds of governments is assured, bringing us to the need to redesign the latter.

NOTES

1. My use of the term 'fuzzy' is different from its uses in fuzzy logic (P. McNeill and Freiberger, 1993), though there is some affinity.
2. In the seventeenth century John de Witt, in effect the Prime Minister of Holland, tried to use probabilistic calculus for major policy choices. His failures, ending in his lynching, clearly illustrate the dangers of calculating what seems to be predictable and quantifiable, while ignoring what is 'jumpy', non-linear and hard to conceive, and does not fit into simplistic 'subjective probabilities'. As summed up in a revealing biography of de Witt: 'He did not understand the starkly emotional nature of their love for "our Prince" and thought only of cool calculation of desired ends and best means' (Rowen, 1978, p. 88).
   Similarly, Kurt Riezler, who served as a senior advisor to top decision-makers in Germany around the First World War, tried to calculate probabilities for major outcomes, suffering complete failure, caused in part by the rigidities of simple probability calculus (W. Thompson, 1980). On Vietnam and its failures, again caused in part by concentrating on what could be quantified and considered probabilistically, see McNamara, 1995.
   These cases, to which many more could be added, do not negate the importance of efforts to 'tame chance' (Hacking, 1975, 1990) and the usefulness of probability calculus for simple issues, and its heuristic utility in complex issues too. But they bring out the need for much more multi-dimensional and open-ended methods for improving fuzzy gambling than those supplied by textbook probability calculus.
3. Senior decision-makers are instinctively right in rejecting misleading techniques, such as subjective probability, as a basis for their decisions, though usually unable to explain their reasons for doing so. The reliance of many decision experts on such methods, which cannot be validly applied to complex choice situations, may therefore explain and even justify the scarcity of professional policy reflection units near rulers. It is only

on the assumption of advancement in policy reflection knowledge, including on fuzzy policy gambling, that my recommendations to engage in deep policy reflection, to develop qualified policy professionals and to set up policy reflection units can be justified.

However, no lack of useful ways to improve fuzzy policy gambling can justify a reliance on astrology and other nonsensical pseudo-supports, however psychologically understandable.

4. The paradoxical certainty of such inconceivability is well demonstrated by Karl Popper, as recounted in a lecture I heard: There is near certainty that science and technology will provide radically new knowledge and techniques of fundamental significance for humanity. But present knowledge cannot know the content of innovative knowledge in the future. The logical conclusion is that we know that the future is in important respects beyond our present thinking – that is, 'unknowable' and in part 'inconceivable'. According to present world-views, this is not a limit of epistemology but inherent in ontology. However, this world-view too is provisional, and in principle open to paradigmatic revolutions (in the sense of Kuhn, 1970, 1977).

5. This leads into the urgent need for new types of what I call DSSR: that is, decision support systems for rulers – a subject of much practical importance, but very neglected. It is too technical for discussion in this book.

6. This concept is taken from chaos theory and applies to situations where a very small effect can have very large consequences – a 'random event' from a human perspective. The metaphor, or 'story' from which the concept stems, is one of a butterfly which by the movement of its wings over, say, Tokyo, causes a hurricane in Florida. This is a physical possibility, through a complex causal chain, but one of infinitely small probability that is beyond calculation.

16

Improving the Central Minds of Government

Processes are at the core of governance, but structures are also very important (March and Olsen, 1989; Weaver and Rockman, 1993). They establish the pathways within which processes operate and influence their characteristics (North, 1990), while in turn being shaped and reshaped by them. Structural reforms are therefore a main avenue to better governance, though they can also result in nominal or ritualistic changes that make no real difference, as illustrated by quite a number of 'reforms' in Latin America.

This chapter focuses on what I call 'Central Minds of Government'. One way of envisaging central minds of government is as a complex multi-processing network, along the lines of models developed in modern cognitive and computer science, and as 'thinking institutions' (Douglas, 1987) as well as goal-seeking systems (Ackoff and Emery, 1972). The metaphor of 'nerves of governance' (Deutsch, 1969) is relevant, as are various attempts to apply cybernetics to governance processes (Beer, 1966; Steinbruner, 1974), including illuminating distinctions between the 'brain' and the 'heart' of large organizations (Beer 1979, 1981).

The term 'central minds of government' can be understood in an inclusive or more restricted sense. In an inclusive sense, the central minds of governance include all the organs of governance which engage in cognitive processes related to major choices and future-shaping capacities. Included, therefore, are some legislative committees, constitutional and supreme courts dealing in fact with major policy decisions, the policy making tiers of central banks, and parallel bodies, both in multi-state and global institutions and at sub-state levels of governance.

The restricted sense refers to what can be seen as the 'core' of central minds of government, which includes the top decision-making levels and their staffs as well as other components that play a major role in critical choices, such as strategic intelligence units, think tanks and so on. Also included, if they exist at all, are what can be regarded as the 'meta-brain' – that is, units and processes managing, monitoring and improving the operations of the central mind of governance as a system.

In different countries additional bodies are included in the central mind of government, both in its inclusive and restricted senses. Thus, party headquarters may be central to policy making. Also, there is usually quite a difference between the institutions formally being part of the 'core' and those who exert substantial de facto influence on critical choices, often without important actors and well-reputed observers knowing the real facts. These issues do not undermine the main redesign proposals, but they are important for applying the recommendations to specific countries and governments.

Much of this chapter, as well as other parts of the book, applies to the central mind of government in the inclusive sense. However, in line with my overall selective-radicalism redesign strategy of focusing on the components and processes most critical for capacities to govern, I pay special attention to the core parts of the central mind of government. Accordingly, this chapter adds selected redesign proposals to those that have already been presented, such as the pivotal recommendation to set advisory staffs, crisis teams and policy reflection units near rulers, presented in earlier chapters.

Central minds of government must be helped to think in terms of *raison d'humanité* via special high-level units dedicated to this task, among other ways. Such units should enhance governmental understanding of issues concerning humankind, while serving as a kind of lobby for a global perspective within the 'brain' (and 'heart') of governance. In countries ready for such a step, 'global impact statements' – similar to the environmental impact statements required in a growing number of countries – should be prepared for major policies under the auspices of the proposed unit.

Global and local non-governmental organizations too should independently undertake the preparation of global impact statements on major policy proposals, but they cannot adequately assure the taking into account of global perspectives and *raison d'humanité* in critical choices. This requires in-house units within the core central mind of government.

Similar units and processes are also needed in legislatures, providing additional openings for non-governmental organizations to represent and advance global points of view.

This redesign also applies to global governance. At present various international agencies and bodies operate quite separately from one another, making choices and proposals which may be well considered within narrow perspectives but lack an integrated global, long range view. Therefore, the office of the Secretary-General of the United Nations should be reconstituted to serve as a 'core central mind of global governance' with the help of suitable staff, deep policy reflection and think tank units.[1]

Units in charge of global perspectives should be set up in central governments, preferably in the office of the head of government. Global impact statements should become an integral part of considering major policies, to be prepared within governance, and by non-governmental organizations. Legislatures should set up committees to consider global perspectives. The Secretary-General of the United Nations should strengthen capacities to take a global, long-term and integrated view of major issues, with the help of suitable staffs and deep policy reflection units.

A partly related domain in which central minds of government need much improvement is strategic intelligence and foresignt. This need has been touched upon when discussing estimates of potential, situations and processes as a policy reflection dimension in Chapter Fourteen, but now some institutional aspects must be taken up, starting with global governance.

The intelligence needs of 'humankindcraft' (see Codevilla, 1992) go far beyond security matters, though these will continue to be acute. Dynamic global estimations covering major policy domains within an integrated systems perspective are required, based on careful data collection and processing. Also required are mappings of evolutionary potentials, explorations of alternative futures, and preparations of scenarios – all taking full account of uncertainty and inconceivability. These staff documents should serve as a basis for deep global policy reflection, as well as 'alerts' for crisis prevention and management.

Quite a number of bodies collect important global data and process it, often well. The World Bank, the World Resources Institute, various UN bodies such as UNDP, OECD, the Worldwatch Institute, the International Institute of Strategic Studies, International Alert, Amnesty International, The International Crisis Group — these are only a few of the many bodies doing so, sometimes with real originality (as illustrated by the UNDP Human Development Reports). To these must be added the mountains of books and reports by research institutes and scholars which provide many important estimates of the circumstances and prospects of humankind and planet Earth.

However, it is this very proliferation of material that results in six main weaknesses of these estimations and outlooks (which are often shared by national outlooks):

(1) The quantity and variety of material make it almost impossible to integrate it into a coherent overall outlook.
(2) The quality of the material varies tremendously, and often advocacy and speculation are mingled with balanced and well-founded evaluations.
(3) Despite the mountains of data and opinions, many areas in which estimations are urgently needed suffer from neglect, such as global trends in mass psychology and trauma.
(4) Many of the studies avoid longer-term outlooks which, however laden with uncertainty and inconceivability, are essential for setting global trajectories; and when they do attempt long-range predictions, the methods are very often naive in their handling of uncertainty and inconceivability.

(5) Attention focuses on 'situations' rather than structures, processes and dynamics, and more on threats than opportunities (a distinguished exception being Kirdar, 1992).

(6) The link is often very weak between available global estimates and decision-making on global issues.

To try and overcome such deficiencies, a new Global Estimation and Outlook Institute may be essential. The proposed institute would have no authority over the estimation activities of other organizations, and should work with and through networks. But it should suggest subjects to the Secretary-General for his consideration, and as inputs into global policy reflection units. The Institute should also be empowered to suggest agenda items for UN organs, in order to overcome the propensity of political bodies to ignore slowly evolving but serious problems until their symptoms are highly visible, when it may be too late. As well put by *The Economist* on the destruction of biodiversity: 'A problem that is daunting but gradual, and complex to boot, is likely to induce worry and hopelessness, but little action' (*The Economist*, 10 April 1993, p. 15).

A Global Estimation and Outlook Institute should therefore be set up, to integrate available estimates of global situations, develop better methods for assessing global dynamic prospects, encourage additional data collection and processing on global issues, and engage in global outlook studies in neglected areas. The results of its work should be widely disseminated, but classified studies should also be prepared and suitably distributed. The Institute should be independent, with an assured multi-year budget, and should be headed by a professional international board. It should draw the attention of the Secretary-General of the United Nations and heads of other global bodies to issues that demand action. It should work closely with UN and other global policy reflection bodies and think tanks, and the board should be entitled to suggest items to be included on the agenda of the United Nations and other global governance bodies.

Not only does global governance need better estimations and outlooks, but so do nearly all countries. The above recommendation thus applies in principle to all central minds of government, with suitable adjustments.

More specifically, *in central minds of government integrative and long term estimations and outlooks should be prepared. These should be based on advanced professionalism, including uncertainty and inconceivability sophistication. The interface between estimations and outlooks on one hand and critical choice processes on the other need improvement, so as to assure that the first are fully taken into account in the second. To advance in these directions, it is advisable in many countries to appoint a national estimation advisor near the head of government. He should be independent from all intelligence and estimation units and from other policy and political advisors and staffs, and his task would be to assure preparation, presentation and utilization of integrated and long-term net estimations of salient dynamics, and to alert the ruler and his staffs to emerging threats and opportunities.*

Let me add, on the basis of personal knowledge in a number of countries, that even highly reputed estimation units need much improvement, as does their interface with actual decision-making. Details depend on specific situations and needs, but *the dependence of policy reflection and of critical choice on images of realities and their dynamics make improvement of estimation units essential for the improvement of central minds of governance as a whole.*

A further major need is for the establishment and improvement of 'think tank' institutions, as essential organisations for the pursuit of interdisciplinary pluralistic policy creativity, policy contemplation, policy research and policy development.

Apart from various distant ancestors, such as some aspects of the Hanlin Academy in China (Lui, 1981) and of Solomon's House of Wisdom as proposed in *The New Atlantis* by Francis Bacon, the modern form of such organizations started with the Brookings Institution and the RAND Corporation in the USA. Various types of think tank are common in the USA and have spread to other countries in various forms. But the operations of most of them leave much to be desired when measured against the needs of 'weaving the future'.

Think tanks[2] can take two main forms, with some variants and mixes. Most think tanks are of the RAND Corporation type, where the emphasis is on interdisciplinary teamwork on major policy issues by an adequate number of high-quality professionals and experienced individuals, with sufficient lead-time and massive investment of time and effort. The other type is more like an Institute for Advanced Study, where outstanding individuals work on policy issues mainly on their own, with some research assistants and other support, either on a permanent basis or for a year or two. Parts of the Brookings Institution and the Woodrow Wilson Center are examples of this. Both types are useful, but RAND Corporation type think tanks have the advantages of a team of experienced interdisciplinary professionals trying to achieve deep and comprehensive understanding of complex policy domains (for a different view of think tanks, see Stone, 1996). However, it should also be borne in mind that individuals working on their own often achieve breakthroughs beyond the achievements of any think tank – but such creativity, however essential, cannot be 'engineered' and is not guaranteed to appear when most needed.

Contemporary think tanks often work on critical problems, but they rarely work on long-range and trajectory-setting broad policy issues. Their methodologies are often biased either in quantitative or qualitative directions, very seldom combining, for instance, thinking in historical terms with mathematical modeling. Hardly any are able to engage in moral reasoning as a professional contribution to policy making. Many think tanks, with important exceptions, tend to advocate particular points of view. The vast majority face great difficulties when they try to combine access to governance with freedom in their thinking, including iconoclasm on policy orthodoxies. Financial dependency further aggravates this problem. Moreover, think tanks seldom have opportunities to contribute directly to major policy choices handled in the top echelons of governance.[3]

The difficulties of getting think tanks to make more significant contributions to major governance decisions are fully apparent in the USA, where there are plenty of excellent think tanks yet many grave policy errors are made. A certain, though unknown and probably unknowable, number of policy errors is unavoidable because of the inherent fragility of policy reflection and policy making and their 'fuzzy gambling' nature. Nevertheless, it is striking that, despite having more such organizations than any other country, policy making is not obviously superior in the USA.

The explanation for this contradiction lies partly in the weaknesses of the think tanks listed above, including their poor access to the Presidential Office. To these are added particular problems of the central mind of the federal government, such as the absence of a senior civil service elite (despite the Civil Service Reform Act of 1978). The way the White House is staffed tends to be detrimental to policy. For example, the lack of continuity of staff and the absence of reasonable transition arrangements between Presidents is an obstacle to cumulative learning. Particularly pernicious for coherent policy-making and setting of long-term strategies are the priorities often given to political and electoral considerations, and the standoffs between the White House and Congress, which elevate political and bargaining considerations much above policy needs. The stalemates end in compromises that often do more damage to policy than is justified in terms of building democratic consensus.

In parts of East Asia, some think tanks seem to operate well, with adjustments to local political cultures and needs (Ostry, 1991; Struyk, Ueno and Suzuki, 1993), as illustrated by the Centre for Policy Research in New Delhi. But in many countries, including some highly developed ones, there exist no real think tanks: without think tanks it is very difficult to achieve the levels of long-term and comprehensive deep policy reflection needed for 'weaving the future' for the better. Yet many political systems and political cultures lack the prerequisites for maintaining think tanks, for letting them operate freely enough to perform well, and for feeding the results of their studies into policy-making processes on crucial issues.

A 'supply-side' approach to improving policy reflection may be justified, even in the absence of an obvious demand for it, on the assumption that latent demand exists and will manifest itself, as readily available policy ideas are increasingly perceived to be inadequate. In many countries the social and political preconditions may become more favorable to successful think tank performance, for instance as some policy debates become less ideological. Furthermore, potentially useful redesigns have to be tried out even if success is not guaranteed in advance. *Think tanks should therefore be set up, improved, fostered and utilized in policy-making on critical and long-term issues, even in the face of a lack of demand or of resistance.*

This recommendation applies fully to global governance. Some think tanks work on global issues, such as the International Institute for Applied Systems Analysis (IIASA); the United Nations Institute for Training and Research (UNITAR) at least as originally conceived; a network of UN University bodies; and the United Nations University Institute for Advanced Study. But much more is needed (still very relevant, though in need of updating, is Platt, 1981). *A full scale, high quality, independent global think tank should therefore be urgently set up, with an assured multi-year budget, to be headed by an international board of globally recognized personalities with broad knowledge and experience. It should study in depth major global issues, on its own initiative and as requested by the Secretary-General of the UN. The results of its work should be widely disseminated, unless classified with the approval of the Board.*

Bismarck said that only a fool learns from his own mistakes and not from the mistakes of others. By this criterion, most governance behaves like a prize fool most of the time, not even learning from its own mistakes. It is enough to mention the shocking fact that virtually no legislature systematically monitors the results of legislation so as to improve it by learning (the so-called 'sun-set legislation' efforts in the USA have largely failed). This proves that governance is not keen to learn, to put it mildly.

There are many reasons for this deficiency (Argyris, 1992, esp. part one; Leeuw, Rist and Sonnichsen, 1993). One is the nature of political and bureaucratic competition, which deters people from admitting serious mistakes. In order to preserve a positive self-image, all outcomes are pronounced, and also subjectively regarded as, either a success (by so-called 'post-decisional dissonance reduction') or else ruined by unpredictable and uncontrollable factors. Also, many governance decisions really aim at implicit or hidden goals, or at no goals at all other than demonstrating that something is being done – eliminating any learning possibilities.

Nonetheless, a lot of policy learning does take place by governance bodies, but it is mainly tactical in nature and avoids re-evaluation of policy paradigms. More fundamental policy learning does to some extent take place in academic studies and independent research institutes, by interest groups monitoring the effects of policies, individual policy thinkers, and in parts of the mass media. The results of outside learning filter through to governance, illustrating the importance of diffuse policy contemplation in society for raising standards of capacities to govern. However, much more and better learning on fundamental policies is essential within governance itself. This requires substantial redesigns. *Special learning processes and units should be established in main governance bodies. Independent think tanks and 'policy evaluation institutes' should systematically study the outcomes of major policies and suggest lessons to be drawn. Non-governmental organizations should be encouraged to monitor and evaluate the results of key governance activities. Finally, legislatures should assure systematic inde-*

pendent evaluation of the results of major legislative activity. Above all, a 'culture of learning' should pervade governance, at least in the more critical components of central minds of governments.

Most of the reform proposals presented in this chapter so far strengthen central minds of governments and, especially, their core components. This is necessary if they are to cope with their higher-order tasks. However, such reforms must be balanced by improvements in other layers of governance, especially legislatures and political oppositions. The United States Senate and the party-based Political Academies in Austria, which are financed from the public purse, offer valuable models, as do Party Institutes in Brazil whose policy research functions were strengthened by legislation of 1997 allocating additional funds. But details depend a great deal on the specifics of different countries, all the more since various party political considerations are sure to be involved.

However, whatever the situation, *legislatures should be better equipped with professional staff to monitor and consider policy, and oppositions should be given the means to carry out improved policy reflection.*

George F. Kennan, summing up the distilled wisdom of many years as a policy-thinker in governance, reached the following conclusion:

> ... the federal government requires ... the presence at its side of a permanent, nonpolitical advisory body – one that permits the tapping of the greatest sources of wisdom and experience that the private citizenry of the country can provide ... meeting of this need would require an institutional innovation of a wholly unusual nature, quite devoid of precedent in the national experience (Kennan, 1993, p. 236).

He goes on to propose setting up what he calls a 'Council of State' – a select body of persons of outstanding distinction who are not politically active in any way. This body, supported by a small but first-rate staff, would study issues 'of major long-term importance for the fortune of the country' (*ibid.* pp. 236ff.).

Similar proposals have been made by other scholars and practitioners, such as the recommendation by Lester W. Milbrath to set up a 'Council for Long-Range Societal Guidance' (Milbrath, 1989, pp. 288ff.) and Bertrand de Jouvenel's proposal to set up a 'Surmising Forum' (Jouvenel, 1967, ch. 20). Without going into detail or comparing such proposals with analogous bodies that exist in a number of countries, such as in some respects the Dutch Scientific Council for Government Policy, I would argue that these proposals point in the right direction. Governance needs a non-elected and carefully selected pluralistic body which could be described as a 'Council of Knowledge and Experience', though it should not be called by any such provocative and hubristic name. In addition to making significant contributions to policy reflection and decision making in central minds of governments, such bodies can help in building consensus and upgrading public discourse, and they can make significant contributions to public affairs enlightenment of the people.

Consultative councils enjoying constitutional status, and composed of outstanding individuals, should therefore be set up to engage in policy deliberation on long-term critical issues, presenting evaluations, analysis, options and recommendations to governance and the public at large.

In the foreseeable future, no such body can enjoy constitutional status on a global level, in the absence of a global constitutional regime, and the United Nations' structure is too political to set up such a body. Instead, *the Secretary-General should set up a Consultative Global Policy Council to formally advise him on major global issues, which should enjoy global stature thanks to the selection of outstanding personalities to serve on it.*

My next and final recommendation in this chapter takes up the daunting ethical issues governance will face in the twenty-first century, such as those concerning genetic engineering. Legitimate value judges, such as democratically elected governments, must always make, or at least endorse, the binding decisions. But their legitimacy and moral stature are inadequate for coping with unprecedented moral dilemmas and for building consensus and enforcing decisions based on their value judgments. Advisory deliberative and in part also decision-making moral forums which are trustworthy are essential.

However, to apply an important distinction elaborated by Vincent Descombes (Descombes, 1993, ch. 2), these forums are not responsible for making moral pronouncements from outside the arena of public action, but instead must consider the political and social ramifications and, inter alia, advise governmental and other decision-makers. Forums of this kind can also help with other important tasks, such as working out codes of ethics for governance elites.

These forums should therefore include persons with experience in politics and governance, as well as moral philosophers, while also broadly reflecting pluralistic values of populations at large. The already mentioned experience of the Helsinki Committees on problems of medical ethics is relevant here (P. McNeill, 1993), but the approach must be expanded and adapted.

Ethical reasoning and moral advice are urgently needed on a global level, all the more so because many value-laden issues cannot be handled effectively by national policies. It is up to religious leaders, spiritual personalities, and independent groups to engage in global moral deliberation. But setting up a Global Ethics Deliberation Advisory Forum may help, at least by raising issues and upgrading the standards of global policy discourse. Elaborating the alternative meanings and implications of *raison d'humanité* in the context of concrete policy issues is a main task for a Global Ethics Deliberation Advisory Forum, with care taken to recognize a variety of various value assumptions, beliefs and philosophies.

Experiments include a decision taken in 1999 to set up an institute on global ethics in Wittenberg, Germany, but more is needed. *'Ethical Deliberation Forums' should be set up, consisting of spiritual leaders, religious personalities, moral philosophers, poets, judges and other non-political public figures, together with people with considerable political and governance experience. The membership should be representative of pluralistic values. Their remit should be to consider and advise on the moral dimensions of major policy issues, with due consideration given to* raison d'humanité. *This recommendation applies also to global governance, with a 'Global Ethics Deliberation Advisory Forum' to be set up by the Secretary-General of the United Nations.*

This chapter started by emphasizing the importance of institutions. Let me conclude it by re-emphasizing the importance of the quality of the human beings who serve within central minds of governments. Better institutional arrangements may attract better people, help them develop, motivate them to do their best, and aggregate the work of good incumbents into very good overall outputs. But no structure can compensate for politicians, civil servants or advisers who are mediocre; nor reduce the damage done by those who are corrupt. Moreover, good structures are only an instrument, which can be used for the better and for the worse. Improving the structures while having evil rulers will enable them to do ill more efficiently, effectively and in highly sophisticated ways.

Therefore, no structural reforms should serve as a substitute for improving the morality, cognitive abilities, emotional propensities and will of the higher governance elite. This applies all the more so to the core of the central mind of government, where relatively few persons are in charge of critical choices.

Concomitantly, improving central minds of governments requires new types of knowledge and professionals, as illustrated by the need for highly qualified policy professionals. Without repeating here what has already been said or going further into the details of such a profession, its training and career patterns (Dror, 1997b), the development of a new breed of policy professionals to staff major policy units and to advise rulers is essential for improving the central minds of governments. But this is only one illustration out of many of the interdependence and potentially symbiotic relation between different redesign proposals in general, and between structures and personnel in particular.

NOTES

1. Some beginnings have been made, as reflected in the work of strategic units working for the Secretary-General and in various statements by him. The proposals by a panel of experts on UN peacekeeping, submitted in August 2000, recommend the creation of an information-gathering and analysis staff to create databases and operate as a

policy-planning staff (reported in Crossette, 2000). However, more is required. There is a striking neglect of this need in the Report of the Commission on Global Governance (Commission on Global Governance, Report of the, 1995).

2. The term 'think tank' is frequently used in other senses, referring to ad hoc study teams, policy advisory staffs and so on. There is some overlap and various structures can fulfill think tank functions, as illustrated by public commissions in Sweden and some university research institutes. However, I reserve the term for permanent policy-oriented study and reflection organizations with a full-time professional staff reaching a critical mass of, say, at least 15 or 25.

3. These evaluations are based on a comparative study by the author, in part summarized in Dror, 1984. A follow-up study showed no significant improvements, but rather some aggravation of weaknesses because of the negative influence of pressure-dominated multi-media mass democracy on the demands for comprehensive and long-term policy studies.

17

Restructuring Governance Architecture

Thus far, our main concern has been with individual governance systems. However, inter-governance relations – including divisions of labor, authority, jurisdiction, power and responsibility, and different modes of cooperative and conflictive interactions – are no less important, and often more so. Central to the subject are new and higher levels of political organization, including multi-country governance, as most fully developed in the European Union, and global governance in the making – the strengthening of which may well be one of the most important redesigns.

Traditional notions of intra-state centralization and decentralization, concentration and deconcentration, devolution and authority, are quite inadequate for handling the evolving architecture of inter-governance relations, based as they are on outdated doctrines of state supremacy. Similarly, standard concepts of inter-state relations, in terms of alliances, agreements, treaties, consensual norm-making and so on, are inadequate for current and future circumstances, based as they are on the assumptions of the supremacy of nation-states and the powerlessness of global governance.

Governance architecture is in need of creative restructuring based on the invention of new norms and constitutional principles. An enlightening metaphor is supplied by the transition from the Roman Republic to the Principate. Similarly to the inadequacy of then existing polities for coping with the changing world of the Roman Empire, presently known polities are inadequate for coping with the transformations of the twenty-first century. Hence the need for inventions in governance, of which the restructuring of governance architecture is a main one.

Inter-governance relations should not be considered exclusively in terms of hierarchical structures, where the main issue is that of the relations between higher and lower levels. Instead, 'variable geometry' (*The Economist*, 11 November 1995, pp. 51–3) concepts should be applied, with inter-governance relations being multi-dimensional.

Furthermore, current, expected and recommended changes are multi-directional requiring dialectical thinking. Globalization is thus accompanied by localism, with the slogan 'global village' being both partly true but also largely misleading. Strengthening of the European Union goes hand in hand with the growing autonomy of provincial polities going back to pre-modern-state traditions, as in Spain and the UK. And side by side with multi-state integration, some states break up, such as the Soviet Union, Czechoslovakia, Yugoslavia and perhaps with time Canada, not to speak of the 'non-states' of parts of Africa.

Churches, social movements, global networks of activists, world-wide informal colleges, transnational corporations, and mass media networks are examples of non-governmental actors that should be added to the spinning kaleidoscope. These are becoming more prominent, both interacting with states and other polities, and operating independently outside the authority of states and present global governance, thus adding further complexity to the dynamics of inter-governance relations.

To enrich the picture even more, a variety of independent agencies (such as grants committees, broadcasting authorities, and health management authorities) fulfill governance functions, in complex relationship with traditional governmental structures. Relations between traditional branches of governance, such as courts and the executive, are also undergoing quite radical changes in some countries, such as in Israel, adding to the fuzziness of the emerging picture.

To broaden the subject further, the growing strength of private power, as discussed in Chapters Four and Eighteen, should be mentioned. It is not misleading to speak of 'private governance' when large multinational corporations, global mass media empires, and local as well as global pressure and interest groups and NGOs (Ridley and Wilson, 1996; Willetts, 1996) are taken into account.

In short, inter-governance relations are undergoing quantitative and qualitative change, sometimes radically so. Theories and conceptualizations often lag behind, making understanding of new realities and problems even more difficult.

Changes in the nature of 'space', together with the emergence of new dimensions such as cyberspace, are probably the single most important factor influencing all of inter-governance architecture.[1] Classical ideas on 'area and power', 'the territorial imperative' and similar notions, including many aspects of 'borders', are partly obsolete and partly gaining new meanings. Thus, to return to some of the processes discussed in Chapter Four:

- An increasing number of important issues can only be handled on a large geographical scale, often a global one, including: the environment, financial flows, drug cartels, and regulation of the uses of new technologies.
- Borders and distance become less important, with information flows taking place in other spaces and the movement of materials and humans being rapid, cheap and difficult to control.

- Global and cosmopolitan actors, communities and processes develop rapidly, being beyond the control, and often beyond the understanding, of any territorial governance structure.
- At the same time, 'tribal' reactions to globalization are widespread, satisfying important psychological needs but often taking malignant forms.

Many additional space-related changes are taking place. Thus, the global reach of weapons of mass killing possessed by small actors and minor states changes the basic nature of 'security'. The increasing density of human uses of space evolving together with the growing number of human beings is of paramount significance. The exploration of space may change human self-perception and perhaps, in the longer run, provide new bases beyond this planet for human existence.

As space and its perceptions are fundamental to all social structures (as among the other higher primates), the shifts mentioned above have profound implications for governance as a whole and inter-governance architecture in particular. However, no single-factor deterministic model is proposed. Many other variables are important in reshaping inter-governance relations, such as changes in the meanings and significance of 'patriotism'. Nonetheless, shifts in the meanings of space serve as a good introduction to the consideration of inter-governance architecture.

However, despite all the changes in the nature and significance of 'space', the size of a country and the magnitude of its population, its location, the nature of its territory, and its natural and human-made resources continue to be of the utmost importance. Governing very large countries such as India and Brazil is thus in very significant respects very different from governing a small country such as Switzerland or Uruguay; while governing a country with a very large population, such as Indonesia or China, is very different from governing a state with a small or medium-sized population, even if very large in territory, such as Australia and Canada.

Many inter-governance relations thus depend a great deal on size of territory and population, together with other factors such as cultural homogeneity or heterogeneity (compare China and India, for instance). This should be kept in mind when considering the applicability of the analysis and recommendations in this chapter.

To start with states, four main tendencies are paramount for inter-governance architecture.

Firstly, states are an increasingly inadequate basis for handling major policy spaces (Elkins, 1955; Morris, 1998; Creveld, 1999). Hence the development of encompassing polities with larger spaces, as illustrated by North American and Latin American common markets, and moving even towards political integration, as in the European Union. Global governance is sure to become more important, in one way or another, for dealing with problems which are global in scale and which cannot be tackled otherwise.

Secondly, megacities with many millions of inhabitants are becoming very important as main spaces within which many critical service-delivery problems must be handled. Relatively small cities and communities too can and should do more to tackle some aspects of problems such as unemployment, drugs, and the environment, while regional governance becomes increasingly important in meeting cultural and ethnic aspirations and providing a sense of belonging, handling many problems that can be coped with locally. Regional factors therefore continue to be of the utmost importance for competitiveness (Porter, 1990). Relations between state and regional governments thus become increasingly consequential with growing potential for closer cooperation (as illustrated by Australia, discussed in Painter, 1998) as well as conflict, even including terrorism, as in Spain.

Thirdly, states nonetheless continue to be crucial. They have much power to influence the long-term future of their countries, such as in education and infrastructure, while continuing to influence short-term processes, for example in the economic sphere.

Fourthly, the main higher tasks of state governments are at the same time increasingly fulfilled through their participation in multi-state and global governance, and through the sharing of collective choices. This is the case also with sub-state governance, as illustrated by the Council of Regions established in the European Union by the Maastricht Treaty. Paradoxically, the more important state governments are in fulfilling roles within the governance of multi-state, continental and global governance structures the more they reduce their own autonomous action domain, while enhancing their position as partners in higher-level governance.

In short, the nature of the state is changing as the balance alters between territorial sovereignty, power and ability to act (for another perspective, see Jackson and James, 1993). The movement is from sovereignty towards what can be called the 'partnership state'. All states have always been engaged in a mix of cooperative, competitive and conflictive relations with other states. Competition – even conflict – will continue (Cerney, 1990). But collective action is becoming more important and should be further strengthened – whether willingly or by various forms of pressure and even compulsion. The term *partnership state* is therefore proposed to express the fact that states can now, more than ever, function effectively in a growing number of domains only in close partnership with other governance units. Indeed, state action is becoming so dependent on partnership with other governance and non-governance actors that there is need for a shift in our paradigms of thinking about states and inter-governance relations. Similarly, capacities to govern depend increasinlgy on a good ability to function in cooperation with a variety of external governance structures, and participate in building them up.

However, building up partnership attitudes and capacities in no way assumes that power and its uses will become unimportant, though changes in the mix between cooperation and conflict in favor of the first are aimed at.

States, as well as all other levels of governance, depend increasingly on mutual co-operation. Abilities to facilitate and engage such cooperation, and become more of a partnership state, are therefore a crucial requirement of capacities to govern.

But this is only one chapter of the new governance narrative. Another chapter deals with the continuous critical importance of states and their capacities.

In the foreseeable future, states will continue to be the single most dominant form of polity. All the empirical evidence suggests that the state is not withering away. The European Union, too, which is the most developed of all supra-state polities, is controlled and directed by its member states even while separate executive, legislative and judicial institutions are becoming more powerful. In many countries, a growing number of central government functions is being devolved to regions, non-governmental organizations, markets and other non-governmental structures and processes, as well as to global institutions. But states continue to dominate many, though not all, lower-level governance units on one side and the multi-state and international landscapes on the other.

Studies of change in fundamental institutions (Dietl, 1993) leads to the supposition that significant transformations in a system as rooted in history as international society (Watson, 1992; H. Nolte, 1993) take long-lasting 'social time', to use Fernand Braudel's concept (Braudel, 1980).[2] This applies to the power of states as now constituted. Therefore, in the absence of a history-reshaping event, such as a large-scale war or a very serious global economic meltdown, it is hard to envisage a far-reaching reduction in the role of states during the first part of the twenty-first century. The most likely evolutionary path is for a small group of major powers, led by the USA as the only ultra-power, enforcing and controlling, de facto, a new global regime, with the United Nations playing an increasing role but not really dominating the global scenery.

The recommended working assumption for upgrading capacities to govern is therefore that states will continue to be the dominant type of governance actor, but with significant changes in their role within inter-governance architecture, and together with the strengthening of sub-state, super-state and global governance.

Given these working assumptions, let me proceed to a number of recommendations for restructuring inter-governance architecture.

Enough has been said to make the case for strengthening global governance, which will be discussed further in a following chapter. This should, however, go hand in hand with augmented local, community, metropolitan, and sub-state governance, and with increasingly meaningful global/local interaction. But the usual formulation of 'acting locally and thinking globally' needs to be expanded to include also the reverse, namely 'act globally and think locally': that is, the careful consideration of the effects of global decisions on humans in their local settings.

A major reform, necessary from the perspective both of states and of humankind, is to promote some kinds of continental supra-state governance, as exemplified by the European Union.

As states become too small for many essential activities, and the global level too large and heterogeneous, an additional intermediate level of continental supra-state government would meet both national and global needs. It might also help to create a new balance between the local and global levels of governance, overcoming the limitations of states without submerging self-identities in too diverse and distant global structures. But care must be taken not to move towards a new collision course between continental and also cultural-religious blocs: overlapping memberships and cross-cutting governance and societal structures should ensure that conflictive tendencies are offset.

Accordingly, *the European Union, for all its problems, illustrates a new and successful form of supra-state continental government. Comparable governance structures should be developed in other parts of the world, as a way of compensating for the inadequacies of the state, providing an optimal polity for coping with many policy spaces, and as a basic component of global governance. But care must be taken not to create conflictive blocs.*

Present trends and recommended redesigns alike complicate inter-governance relations. In particular, the continuing dominance of states, together with strong continental and global governance, on one hand, and strong regional, metropolitian and local governance on the other, pose vexing questions of division of labor and executive authority.

Part of the answer is implied by the metaphor of 'variable geometry', which indicates that different areas of action are handled by different configurations of governance, with diverse interrelations. However, some principle is needed to prevent a degeneration into chaos. 'Subsidiarity' can serve as such a principle, supplemented by 'enabling' and subject to 'override'.

The idea of subsidiarity, originated in the Company of Jesus, became an important principle of governance in the Catholic Church (Mosiek, 1979) and has been adopted as a principle in the European Union. It means that authority, tasks and functions should be located at the lowest level at which they can be performed well.

An additional recommended, and related, principle is 'enabling', with higher-level governance having a duty to help lower-level governance to increase its capacities and to exercise additional functions. Doing so should become a main task of higher-level governance.

As is clear from its Jesuit origin, if the principle of subsidiarity is correctly applied it recognizes the need for an overriding authority to prevent dangerous stalemates resulting from too much reliance on local action or on collegial consensus when higher-order values may require steps disliked by lower-level governance. However, the principle of subsidiarity suggested here includes a clear rule that the higher level must make a strong for the need to override, and that this must be open to appeal, including to quasi-judicial bodies.

Accordingly, *the restructuring of governance architecture in line with the subsidiarity principle is recommended. This involves increasing the scope of authority and activity of lower levels of governance to the limits of their ability. It also includes a duty on the part of higher levels of governance to enable and help lower levels of governance to undertake expanding functions. However, overriding authority by higher-level governance is essential, subject to appeal and quasi-judicial review.*

Since local, metropolitan and regional governance, as well as the governance of various emerging forms of autonomous regions and other 'meso' levels (Sharpe, 1993), is likely to take on expanding functions, attention must be paid to improving their capacities to govern. Let me illustrate possibilities to do so in highly developed countries with three recommendations that emerge from a comparative study of the Bertelsmann Foundation (Bertelsmann Foundation, 1993), and then add two reservations.

1. The division of labor between politicians and local government management professionals needs strengthening, with the politicians concentrating on policy-making, setting standards, appointing senior staff, and monitoring, but leaving management to professionals.
2. Functional elections to bodies in charge of specific activities, such as education, should supplement general elections of local government. But the bodies set up by general elections should have overriding authority.
3. Citizens should be directly involved in deciding levels of services and their financing, in order to make them aware of costs and reduce impossible demands on governance, among other reasons.

My first reservation is that, although much may be hoped for from local and regional governance, not too much should be expected. Most of local life and governance has little to do with the dream of intimate communities, which is probably a chimera.[3] The harsher problems of local governance are those of the growing number of mega-cities, with no remedies in sight, especially in the Third World (Angelotti, 1993; Oberal, 1993). Moreover, with increasing mobility and modern communications reducing social distances and changing conceptions of space as a whole, as already discussed, the psychological and economic strength of the 'territorial imperative' may weaken, with far-reaching implications for the personal and social meanings of local and regional governance.

It is therefore unlikely that local governance will significantly ease the tasks of central governments and contribute much to handling global problems, even though local governance can and should undertake additional functions. Autonomous regions can do more, as they approach the sub-state level, but the limitations on the capacities of states apply to them even more.

My second reservation relates to the dangers of allocating too much power to local and regional governance in ways that tend to undermine broader interests. Thus, granting local or regional bodies too much of a veto power over nationally necessary policies, or even worse permitting them to disrupt national economic and financial policies, must be prevented by carefully limiting their authority. Brazil provides numerous examples of the dangers of giving sub-states too much autonomy in fiscal matters, leading to budgetary recklessness.

Significant changes in governance architecture may produce paralysis unless inter-governance relations are largely based on cooperation, mutual trust and a strong sense of shared interests, helped by strong higher-level leadership. The principal actors must know much more about one another, be capable of a great deal of learning, have elastic structures and satisfy additional requirements of cooperation (Bicchieri, 1993). 'Conviviality' in the sense of free, autonomous and creative intercourse, as proposed by Ivan Illich (Illich, 1973), is not only morally preferable but also indispensable for synergies to occur among the many configurations of governance sharing the challenges of global transformations. A shared sense of governance professionalism can also make important contributions, and is indispensable for smooth interaction in the face of pluralism, power conflicts, divergent pressures and often contradictory interests.

However, the possibility and desirability (Rescher, 1993, chs 8 and 9) of reaching consensus should not be overstated. In many instances agreement may remain out of reach, or the costs of compromise may be too high. At the same time, it may prove impossible or undesirable to impose authority from above. There must therefore be considerable reliance on rule-based decision-making (Schauer, 1991) for inter-governance relations, and for governance as a whole, to operate properly – especially in a period of transformations and with the emergence of new levels and forms of governance.

It will be increasingly necessary to apply the rule of law to inter-governance relations, with the help of suitably qualified constitutional courts. The European Court of Justice (Volcansek, 1992, to be contrasted with Amman, Jr, 1992) illustrate suitable changes in the 'law's empire' (Dworking, 1986). But more may be needed, such as inclusion of persons knowledgeable in governance among the judges of constitutional – whether called so or not – courts. Also, to overcome the conservatism of law, it is necessary to authorize high-level political bodies to override judicial decisions. But this should be done only exceptionally and by a special procedure so as to protect the independence and integrity of the court system.

I will return to these needs, with the discussion the role of courts in oversight, in Chapter Twenty.

The Tokyo Declaration, adopted by the April 1993 World Conference on Metropolitan Governance, includes the following statement: 'It is clear that we need new forms of metropolitan governance'. However, no really promising ideas on what such new forms may be came to light during the conference. This shows that finding or, more correctly, inventing promising ideas on making governance fit changing conditions is difficult. This applies with particular seriousness to global governance and its roles within a restructured global architecture. Hardly less difficult are the problems posed by relations between public and private power. To these the next two chapters are devoted.

NOTES

1. It is interesting to apply the terms 'topography' and 'imaginary landscapes', as well as the triad 'the imaginary, the symbolic and the real,' together with additional postmodern concepts (J. Miller, 1995; Apollon, 1996).

2. It is a great pity that Braudel was unable to finish the last two volumes of his planned four-volume history of the identity of France, dealing with government and external relations, which would surely have made a great contribution to our subject. (For the two published volumes, fully elaborating his approach, see Braudel, 1988 and Braudel, 1990. His theories of history are presented in Braudel, 1980.)

3. Although he over-estimates the potentials of communal ways of life, Selznick, 1992, is important. Similarly stimulating, but dubious, are comparable ideas in Gershuny, 1978, (Bell, 1993; Phillips, 1993). More applicable, perhaps, is Etzioni, 1993, but I have many doubts about communitarianism (Etzioni, 1996) as a possible way of life in the twenty-first century. However, should communitarianism really take off, finding workable forms of polity and the governance to fit it will be difficult.

18

Governing Private Power

Relations between governance and private power are in nature, though not in terminology, a part of governance architecture in a broad sense. Private bodies exercise expanding public power and, therefore, constitute a part of 'governance' in the functional, as opposed to legal, sense. The restructuring of relations between governance, in the strict sense, and private power is therefore a very important domain for restructuring governance architecture in a broad sense.

It is all the more important because of a pronounced antinomy between basic norms of democracy and societal necessity, on one hand, and pervasive views and actual developments, on the other. The basic norms of democracy, like nearly all political ideologies, as already pointed out, postulate that it is up to the political system and governance to be in charge of decisions shaping collective futures. This also applies when in some domains it is preferable, in terms of efficiency and of other values to leave many decisions to other actors and processes, subject to oversight and overriding by governance.

In terms of necessity, the required refocusing of governance on future-building cannot take place unless governance has the authority, ability and will to govern, however indirectly and 'softly', private powers which strongly influences the future.

However, current developments are moving in the opposite direction, with private power enjoying increasing autonomy in its relations with governance and often governing governance, rather than being governed by it (Wood, 1995). And with these trends being legitimized in terms of 'private rights' of one type or another.

This antinomy contributes much to growing incapacity to govern and engage in the higher-order tasks of governance. Therefore, the balance must be redressed, with governance being strengthened in its relations with private power, this being a main dimension of what I call the revitalization, and also resuscitation, of politics.

However, there are baffling problems of keeping some kind of balance between the 'failures' of public and of private governance (Wolf Jr, 1996). Even when value considerations suggest that on certain issues public governance may be preferable to private power, if public governance is judged unable to act effectively, wisely and with self-restraint, it may be better on balance to leave them to private governance.

Nonetheless, the proposed principle is to strengthen and assure the dominance of public power over private power, both as a matter of democratic values and as essential for 'weaving the future' for the better. Leaving the division of power between public and private power to a kind of competition over 'who fails a little less' is a road to failure all round. But strengthening the public governance of private power requires reducing 'governance failures', and a great deal of autonomy of private power should be maintained and also facilitated, both to permit it to operate efficiently and to fulfill important social functions, and to respect basic values of freedom and private rights. *As far as is necessary for fulfilling crucial governance tasks, public power should therefore dominate private power. This presupposes significant upgrading of capacities to govern within an overall revitalization of politics. However, detailed interventions should be kept at a minimum, so as to maintain freedoms and to maximise the benefits of autonomous markets, free scientific research, unrestrained mass media, and the autonomy of other non-governmental and private actors and processes.*

Let me translate this principle into redesigns with regard to three most important and highly problematic domains: governance of private economic power and of markets; governance of mass media and cybersphere; and governance of science and technology.

GOVERNANCE OF PRIVATE ECONOMIC POWER AND MARKETS

The public governance of private economic power and markets is a hotly debated issue, but a number of points stand out and permit some tentative conclusions:

- Public governance cannot engage in the detailed management of markets and hope to preserve their efficient operation, because a complex economy cannot be run on a command basis. In theory, this may change if and when much more powerful models and tools become available, or real artificial intelligence becomes practical. But such speculations are irrelevant for contemporary governance reform, though we should keep in mind that new knowledge and technologies may perhaps provide radically different ways to manage very complex systems, such as the economy.[1]
- Furthermore, detailed governance of markets by the state endangers the values of the autonomy of civil society and human rights, including property rights; it escalates corruption, and raises the spectre of totalitarianism, including pseudo-democratic authoritarianism.
- However, without a considerable amount of intervention by public governance in markets, private economic power will damage the market system

itself, for example by price-fixing and cartels. Unprotected consumers are at a disadvantage, even if enlightened – as they often are not, to judge by the gross under-utilization of information sources such as consumer reports and the massive consumer susceptibility to advertisements appealing to stupidity (Moorthy and Hawkins, 1998). Much harm is done when important public interests are neglected, such as environmental considerations, or equity values are negated, such as those on income distribution and equal opportunities for women and minorities. Many decisions, which should be made in terms of values and effectiveness alike, by elected governance, are in fact made by markets, often for the better but often for the worse (Schmookler, 1993).[2]

- As global experience shows, economic development itself may often depend on high-quality intervention by public governance (OECD, 1999), partly through various forms of cooperation between public governance and private economic governance. There are also associated dangers illustrated by the economic theories and governmental roles pioneered during East Asian industrialization (Wade, 1990; a different interpretation is offered in World Bank, 1993). The economic meltdown in some South-East Asian countries in 1998 can also be explained in part as a failure by governments in not adequately controlling short-term capital flows and currency speculations, not protecting themselves adequately against global speculative transactions, and being corrupt in their dealings with private economic power.

- Special problems are posed when governments try to introduce a market economy after a long period of having a command economy, such as in Russia and China. Tendencies towards the continuation of self-subverting features of what has been called an 'economy of favors' (Ledeneva, 1998) and the changing relations between economic oligarchs and political rulers illustrate hard-to-avoid dangers. Without presuming to deal here with these complex issues, on which opinions differ widely, clearly such transformations require very powerful and highly capable governments,[3] perhaps even emergency regimes as discussed in Chapter Twenty-One. Also to be noted is the apparent correlation between political regimes and the outputs of private economic power as it interacts with public governance. Thus, a study by Partha Dasgupta indicates that in democracies private power, in combination with governance action, tends to work in ways that reduce destitution (Dasgupta, 1993). But determined governance without a free-market system can at early phases of development be quite effective in reducing poverty, as illustrated in China (Bramall, 1993).

- There are serious difficulties with economic growth in Western Europe and East Asia, as well as the grave problems associated with transition to a Western-style market economy in East European and former Soviet-bloc countries. These add to the need to find a new balance between public and private power in managing economies and markets.

- This conclusion is reinforced by the growth in private economic power on a global scale. Powerful global actors operate outside the effective control of any presently existing public governance. At the same time, they cannot be assumed to satisfy value requirements and promote economic prosperity for the majority of humanity, if left to their own devices.
- However, despite such misgivings, markets largely dominated by private economic power are superior to public governance in managing economies and assuring economic growth. This is also true on the micro-level of individual enterprises, where a market orientation and the profit motive act as a better basis for achieving a superior economic performance than public ownership. An important, even if temporary, exception is very committed, 'true believer' organizations (in the sense of Hoffer, 1951). These can be of profound importance. *Establishing and maintaining 'true believer organizations' to engage in essential tasks requiring radical innovation is thus recommended when market processes, civil society and regular governance structures are inadequate.*
- As well as markets and often more so, various social forms of collective action can be very successful in 'governing the commons' (Ostrom 1990) much better than governments. But many large-scale 'commons' cannot be handled in this way, because narrow localism and single-value action groups often override the overall needs of society.
- Whatever the interface between public and private power, governments need high-quality capacities to regulate private economic power without damaging the economy. No market mechanism or other non-governmental economic structure can adequately compensate for lack of such capacities in governments. Many success stories (for some examples, see Bruno, 1993) testify that such governance capacities are achievable, but many more failures prove that this is very difficult.
- All that has been said must be subjected to the need to contain plutocracy, with private and corporate money enjoying undue public power because of the growing importance of money in political competition (for a theoretical economic treatment, see Ferguson, 1995).

These comments are fragmentary and neglect a large range of historical and comparative experiences and many sophisticated theories (though perhaps too artificial, in the sense of Simon, 1981). Still, some significant redesign proposals seem to emerge from the wealth of material underlying these observations. *The main features of governance must be adapted to the demanding tasks of exerting better control and guidance over private economic power and markets, yet without excessive intervention. Political leadership must therefore be strong enough to stand up to private economic interests; electoral chances should depend less on funds controlled by private economic power; policy reflection should in part focus on critical choices related to steering economies; all senior governance staffs should be well acquainted with the main theories of macro- and microeconomic political economy, and institutional economics, as well as criticism of them; and governance units in charge of economic affairs should include some high-level staff members with much experience in running economic organizations and operating in the market.*

Additional avenues to strengthening public governance over private power, such as restructuring the governance of large corporations,[4] can be helpful in reducing abuses of private power without hindering market processes. However, rather than going into the various specific possibilities, such as modes of self-regulation, let me conclude this sub-chapter by returning to the major issue posed by transnational and global economic power which operate beyond the oversight of any single country, and even outside present global jurisdictions. Expanding capacities to control and steer such economic power without ruining its many and often irreplaceable benefits is essential. Interestingly – and this is probably no accident – despite the multiplicity of global commissions, none has been set up to study the need to regulate global economic power. Furthermore, global commissions that could have taken up this subject have tended to avoid it. Revelations in August 2000 on efforts by the cigarette industry to subvert global governance processes further illustrate the seriousness off the issues posed by private global economic power.

Global governance capacities to oversee, regulate and steer private transnational economic power should therefore be urgently improved. However, this requires superb global governance bodies. In their absence, ill-advised interventions that damage market processes should be avoided, while trying to build up suitable faculties of global governance. Efforts by private interests to prevent global governance from developing these abilities should be unmasked and defeated. A highly qualified and independent Global Commission should be set up to study these issues and work out proposals for coping with them.

GOVERNANCE OF MASS-MEDIA AND CYBERSPHERE

The mass media, and especially television, are an increasingly powerful force in politics and in society, with cybersphere and its multiple uses adding a whole new universe. Specific influences are in debate, such as on the behavior of children, but there are no doubts about their growing impact. They exert direct influence on various issues and competitions, change the nature of democracy, transform parts of the economy, and – most insidious of all, though largely unintended – they reshape cultures.[5] Therefore, the controllers and producers of the mass media and cybersphere are very powerful and becoming more so.

Often a large number of producers, advertisers, commentators, owners and participants control their contents. This is especially the case in cybersphere. However, much mass-media power is concentrated in a few hands, creating 'rulers' more powerful than many elected heads of governments. These two types of power, one diffused and the other concentrated, pose quite different problems. But the whole field is very fluid, with new technologies changing its 'power maps', as illustrated by cybersphere redistributing and in part annihilating economic power in the field of copyrighted music.

Given present and foreseeable mass media and cybersphere technologies, three main issues posed to governance can be distinguished, as differently expressed in various mass-media and cybersphere domains: market-driven quality; misuses of the cybersphere; and very powerful actors.

Market-driven quality

Most television programs, and many printed publications, are consumer-driven, with ratings and sales being the dominant consideration in shaping contents. This also applies to many server providers in cybersphere, but much less so because of the many educational institutions active there. Here, the main dangers are that mass tastes will lower cultural standards and also encourage programs that are positively harmful, for example by stimulating violent behavior.

It may well be that 'root-treatment' is necessary, with public education having to be much more active in raising the cultural tastes of populations – and thus lead towards a demand-driven upgrading of mass media. Large-scale public television may help. In addition, some rules can be, and sometimes are, self-imposed or governance-imposed on the mass media. Efforts to make producers more professional, and also conscious of their cultural and social responsibilities are also needed. But, all in all, suggested treatments (Keller, 1990, Task Force on the Future of Public Television, 1993) are inadequate.

However, to avoid endangering democratic values and freedom of the mass media and of cybersphere, and so as not to intervene too much with market processes, a minimalist governance approach may be best. *Governance should concentrate on reducing clearly damaging effects of the mass media, increasing pluralism and supporting public mass media. The education system and other activities directed at social learning as a whole should devote efforts to improving cultural tastes so as to increase demand for high-quality mass-media products.*

Misuses of cybersphere

Even more difficult issues are posed by cybersphere as a new communicative universe. The main one is how to balance private rights and the very positive effects of free interactive uses on one hand, with the dangers of misuses on the other.

Responses depend on estimating more optimistically or pessimistically the potentials for uses and misuses, and on the relative weight given to private rights as against taking care of the public interest. My sensitivities to the potentials for evil lead me to give priority to controlling misuses. *Uses of cybersphere to encourage 'hate' should be strictly prevented, minimal censorship should be imposed, and surveillance of cybersphere, as far as is essential for preventing criminal and 'hate'-promotion uses should be given priority over rights to privacy.*

Very powerful actors

As mentioned, mass-media monopolies and oligopolies create private power concentrations damaging public interests. Preventing such monopolies can help. However, as mass-media power concentrations often operate globally, global governance must enter the arena. Debates about protecting national cultures, trade in television programs and movies, music copyright issues and language policies add to the complexities of doing so. But *global action to prevent transnational mass-media power concentration is essential. Global regulation of television ownership should be kept to a minimum, but disclosure of full details of ownership should be compulsory, as should minimum standards of fairness and protected autonomy of professionals from owners' dictates. Large, global mass-media monopolies should be broken up. Global censorship of the mass media and cybersphere should be limited to preventing 'hate'-speech programs and messages encouraging crimes against humanity, but should be strictly enforced, and mass-media programs and cyber-sphere sites and nets dedicated to global 'humankind interest' should be facilitated.*

GOVERNANCE OF SCIENCE AND TECHNOLOGY

The governance of science and technology poses the most vexing and critical long-term and fundamental problems of all for the public governance of private power. As clearly perceived already by Friedrich Nietzsche, especially in *Beyond Good and Evil*, science poses super-radical challenges to humankind. As summed up by Robert Eden:

> He sees in modern science what its originators promised: the power to remake the human condition from top to bottom ... science makes the human condition more precarious and dangerous, compelling humanity to face situations that call for new virtues, a new conscience, and the destruction of old moral codes (Eden, 1983, p. 95, and ch. 3 as a whole).

Science and technology exert a radical influence on the future of humankind. Their advancement and utilization should not, therefore, be left to scientists, engineers, entrepreneurs and markets. However, governmental efforts to regulate science and technology and their uses may be ineffective and will often be counter-productive. The issue here is radically different from that of trying to control 'evil' in the mass media and the cybersphere, as it is often easy to identify 'evil' and reach broad agreement on it. In contrast, advances in science and technology can be used both for good and ill. But it is impossible to know in advance what the actual uses will be, and there are sure to be many disagreements on the meanings of 'good' and 'bad' uses – as illustrated by fundamental disagreements on the relatively simple issue of research on human embryonic stem cells.

These difficulties would be formidable even if governments were well equipped for understanding science and technology and their creators, and if senior governance elites were minimally literate in science and technology. But this is not the case: present governance elites are mainly ignorant of science and technology, with the exception of special units usually having little influence on main policies.

Outstanding science and technology policy think tanks can develop some guidelines for governance, as illustrated by some of the work of the Science Directorate at the Organization for Economic Cooperation and Development (OECD) in Paris (OECD, 1998; and, much more specific, the briefing documents for annual meetings of science ministers organized by the OECD). But even at their best, such efforts are limited.

The military significance of many science and technology activities adds to this complexity, as do economic competition and global differences of opinion on research freedom, free access to scientific information and so on. Further complications stem from the fact that a lot of scientific and technological research and development is done by individual researchers and at academic institutions that are, and need to be, independent.

Government decisions are very important for branches of science that require very large resources, such as space exploration and experimental particle physics. But large parts of science and technology do not need such investments, reducing the significance of budgeting (including government contracts) as an instrument of government regulation.

In view of these and other considerations rooted in the very nature of science and technology, the chances of arriving at useful regulation by governance, at least in especially important or risky areas, seem very faint. Science and technology may well be a domain where self-regulation is the only somewhat effective form of governance, though it too is subject to many limitations, and is often non-existent.

Taking all this into account as well as the dominant and largely justified freedom of science values and economic approaches to technology, my conclusion is that science and technology will remain largely outside the domain of governance, including global governance. Efforts to diffuse knowledge of science and technology and its uses, if necessary by overriding patent rights, are feasible and sometimes necessary, such as in the case of life-saving medicines. But the restraining of science and technology is very difficult and entails high costs in terms of values and lost benefits.

The implications of the inability of governance to significantly influence science and technology are grave. What is probably the single most important process shaping the future is largely beyond control by collective human choice. When some control is possible, such as by prohibiting the use of some technologies, such as human cloning, lost opportunities may more than offset avoided dangers.

This is an important warning against expecting too much from governance and from human capacities as a whole. But the problem at least needs to be recognized, and efforts should be directed at advancing salient govern-ance capacities. *Upgrading capacities to govern science and technology so as to facili-tate their advancement, while containing dangerous knowledge and misuses and mini-mising the dangers of catastrophic results, poses an ultimate challenge to governance redesign, with no promising ideas in sight. Related value issues are even more difficult than the problem of how to make overview effective without endangering creativity and freedom. Until promising options are invented and developed, governance interventions within science and technology, other than ongoing and expanded support based on well-considered science and technology policies, should be limited to facilitating the creation, utilization and diffusion of useful knowledge, and to controlling access to and use of dangerous techniques. But possible dangers should not be permitted to override the large possible benefits – with the exception of catastrophic possibilities that have a discernible probability, the prevention of which should of course receive priority. Preconditions for meet-ing even such minimal requirements include making senior governance elites literate in science and technology, facilitating self-regulation by scientists and technology developers and users, encouraging moral discourse on the value issues posed by science and technology, and devoting significant policy reflection resources to the issues of governing science and technology.*

Whatever may become possible in governing science and technology will depend on effective global governance, bringing us to the subject of the next chapter.

NOTES

1. The history of fractal geometry, where what once were regarded as complex random phenomena where found to fit a deterministic form of calculus, should teach us that future views of what appear to us as semi-chaotic hyper-complex processes cannot be predicted. For a science fiction version of capacities which could easily program an economy, and much more, see Asimov, 1993. This book, the last one that he wrote, sets forth the beginnings of the *Foundation* series, which deals with the confrontation between a detailed super-program of societal architecture on a cosmic scale and random mutations.

2. However, care must be taken to avoid irrational sources of hostility to markets (see Haag, 1979).

3. Belatedly, the World Bank recognized the importance of good governance for economic growth (International Bank for Reconstruction and the World Bank, 1997). This is also happening within other United Nations bodies, the World Economic Forum, OECD and so on, but – as already noted – in much too narrow a sense of 'good government', ignoring the need to refocus democracy on 'weaving the future' and building up appro-priate core capacities, among other issues.

4. The British Cadbury Report of May 1992 illustrates relevant suggestions. Needs include the increased power of shareholders, the appointment of non-executive directors, the restraint of remuneration of directors and managers, and their deter-mination by committees dominated by outsiders, and the strengthening of new versions of industrial democracy, without abandoning essential management pre-rogatives.

5. Even if exaggerated, a quote from an interview in August 2000 with the President of the Czech Republic Vaclav Havel, a renowned intellectual, in preparation for the annual conference of the World Bank and International Monetary Fund is relevant here:

> These commercials say a lot. A handsome man with a great tan and strong muscles is running on a beautiful beach with blue sky in the background. A beautiful girl is running toward him and they are happy ... The stupidity of this world, which is offered to us as human happiness, should be analyzed. If billions of people look at it and take it for granted even though they live completely different lives, it's a very serious thing that testifies about our civilization and its problems (Erlanger, 2000).

19

Making Global Governance More Resolute

Global governance has been discussed in several contexts. Redesigns aimed at raising the standards of global governance elites and of global policy reflection have been presented, together with proposals to strengthen the position of the Secretary-General of the United Nations, set up various advisory forums, broaden the jurisdictions of global courts, and more. But the fundamental problem of global governance is different. As pointed out time and time again, humanity faces opportunities, dangers and challenges that can only be dealt with adequately on a global scale. But present and expected global governance, and global systems as a whole, lack the ability to crystallise and concentrate the will and the power needed to cope with the opportunities, dangers and challenges. *Global governance is not sufficiently resolute, in the sense of being firm, determined, tough when necessary, and decisive.*

This deficiency is all the more pronounced when compared with the requirements of 'weaving the future' and advancing broad and long-term conceptions of *raison d'humanité*. Even a cursory look at the wealth of studies and surveys of global issues published around the millennium[1] reveals a plethora of matters which can only be handled by a global governance cluster which is powerful and resolute enough to enforce necessary measures.

As pointed out, a major difficulty facing humanity is the lack of good ideas as to what to do about major global issues. Much value innovation, option creativity and deep policy reflection on world issues are therefore needed. But a large part of the problem is the absence of will and power to do what clearly is preferable from a long-term human perspective. A hypothetical powerful Global Platonic Ruler and his Guardians would therefore know very well how to preserve forests and biodiversity (United Nations Environment Program, 1995), prevent nuclear proliferation (Allison *et al.*, 1996), enforce humanitarian law, eliminate drug production and trade (Stares, 1996), and so on. However, in the absence of resolute global governance some decisions as to what should be done have been adopted in international forums; but many useful policy proposals are not adopted, many of those formally approved are not implemented, and a lack of global resoluteness discourages the development of innovative policy proposals that, prima facie, might be regarded as unfeasible. *A most urgent need is to make global governance more resolute.*

However, those improvements of global resoluteness that are feasible are inadequate, while those improvements that are adequate are unfeasible within present paradigms. The quantum jump in the nature and potential of issues faced by humanity requires a quantum jump in capacities to govern, including the resoluteness of global governance. However, while incremental improvements are not difficult to achieve, bringing about a phase transition in global governance approximates to the impossible.

To explore and try to overcome this aporia, I shall move through four levels of analysis and redesign, different in their degrees of possibility and adequacy: the first level takes present realities as given and takes up upgrades of global governance which are not very difficult to achieve and that are useful, but quite inadequate; the second level postulates some very beautiful futures of global governance that would be adequate, but are impossible to realise in the foreseeable future; the third level develops a global governance system which in many respects is 'ugly' in accepting unjust power realities, but which is both feasible and adequate; the fourth level moves on to a model of a 'Global Leviathan' which is very unpleasant but well able to cope with global issues and quite likely to come about if the first three approaches fail and result in escalating disasters.

Starting with the first level of analysis, fortunately global resolve is not completely lacking. Even during the Cold War agreement was reached on quite a number of issues.[2] Moreover, with the end of super-power confrontation, it has become somewhat easier to exercise political will effectively within the United Nations, as evidenced by the significant expansion of United Nations peacekeeping and enforcement actions, and realistic proposals to strengthen them (Crossette, 2000).

Global governance achievements include, for instance: some activities of the World Bank and the International Monetary Fund; the UN Convention on the Law of the Sea (but see Mass-Borgese, 1998); the Convention on Stolen or Illegally Exported Cultural Objects; the Convention on the Prohibition of the Development, Production, Stockpiling and Use of Chemical Weapons and on their Destruction (with its unique sanction and enforcement provisions), as well as other arms limitation agreements; the International Covenants on Civil and Political Rights, together with agreements on other rights; and much more. Growing competition for a seat on the Security Council also testifies to the growing importance of the United Nations.

Cooperation between countries, prodded by non-governmental organizations and also by grass-roots movements, has produced additional impressive results, such as on protecting the ozone layer; collective action against Iraqi aggression constituted a new precedent of international cooperation under the auspices of the United Nations; the Secretary-General of the United Nations has started a number of important initiatives, such as the 'Global Compact' involving large corporations in coping with some major global problems; judicial initiatives have made rulers more responsible for evil deeds, as will an international criminal court being established; many proposals for improving the operations of the United Nations system are being considered, and so on.

Some argue that such progress in strengthening the United Nations and broadening global networks, together with enlightened leadership by the democracies headed by the USA, can be relied upon to cope adequately with the main global issues (Cleveland, 1993), without any stronger global governance structures (Rosenau and Czempiel, 1992; and, differently, Reinicke, 1998). However, realities speak differently, with inadequacies outweighing achievements by far. The insufficiency of global capacities, as maximally improved within present paradigms, are clear from the gross failures of the international community in handling major tragedies and even genocide, as in Yugoslavia and parts of Africa; in not doing enough to prevent nuclear proliferation on the one hand and 'small arms' trade on the other; the inadequacy of the steps being taken on the greenhouse effect and environmental deterioration. Nothing significant is being or can be done within the present global regime rules on reducing growing inequalities.

To take one additional, relatively benign, example: a study by the World Energy Council (World Energy Council, 1993) highlights what should be well known: either most of humanity will continue to live without basic amenities, or energy demands will increase dramatically, beyond what can be supplied without radically new energy sources. The result is an impasse, with potentially very grave consequences. Yet no serious policy deals with this issue, governments avoiding it because the problem is not yet exploding, life cycles of energy-producing systems are very long, and change requires huge investments and will cause tremendous political difficulties.

Overall, global governance as presently constituted, however improved within its basic rules, will lack the authority and power essential for coping adequately with critical future-shaping issues. Relying on an improved United Nations as presently constituted, global networks, and a hoped-for broad consensus to do the job, is a chimera. Hence the need for a new global regime.

Moving on to the second level, literature and discourse abound with proposals for global governance radically different from present and foreseeable realities. But this study is not concerned with the post-twenty-first-century futures of global governance. And the opportunities and dangers facing humanity and its components will not wait for the twenty-second century and beyond.

There is thus no solace in proposals to establish a global constitutional government (Clark and Sohm, 1966), in the attractive ideas of the World Orders Models Project (Falk, Johansen and Kim, 1993), in the various World Federation proposals (Glossop, 1993), or in the many inspiring proposals for a New World Order (Tamames, 1991). These are useful in providing a utopian base for the long-term future,[3] but they have no chance of being realized in the foreseeable future. The problem of how to improve global governance within the foreseeable future, so as to give a chance for longer-range visions therefore remains.

This brings me to the third level, which is radical but may become possible and meet the main requirements. It involves a new mix between strengthening the United Nations, enlarging global networks and building up global elites and, with time, developing a global civil society (which at present does not exist), and a structured and graduated hegemony by the most powerful countries. This leads to a triple-pillar structure, integrated within the United Nations system.

Pulling together already presented redesigns, and adding to them some new ones, let me illustrate the institutional implications of such a conception of global governance:

- The authority of the Secretary-General of the United Nations is strengthened, including the right to initiate specified actions on his own initiative and to appeal against decisions of the Executive Council (as proposed in the following) to the General Assembly. The policy reflection abilities of the United Nations are significantly augmented, the executive authority of the United Nations as a whole is broadened and deepened, the United Nations has its own sources of income, in addition to obligatory contributions by member states, various implementation instruments and forces are set up within the UN system, a new type of highly professional international civil service is built up. All this also applies with suitable adjustments to other UN bodies, subject to the overriding authority of the UN Secretary-General.
- An 'Executive Council' is set up at the United Nations, instead of the Security Council. It has three permanent members, namely the United States, the European Union and China, with the USA having three votes and the other permanent members two votes each. There are five more members, nominated by the permanent members for six years, confirmed by the General Assembly and having one vote each, including at least one from Latin America, one from Africa, and one from Asia. There is no veto power, decisions being taken either by a simple majority or a two-thirds majority of votes, depending on the seriousness of the issue. This Executive Council is the supreme global decision-making body, subject to limited delaying

powers by the General Assembly, advisory decisions by the General Assembly, and augmented authority of the Secretary General. It is in command of expanding international forces and authorised to enforce measures that it regards as necessary for the good of humanity without regard to state sovereignty.
• Global networks are strengthened, advisory bodies on global issues are set up, various kinds of 'people's assemblies' render advisory opinions, a global policy college and global public-interest mass media help develop global elites and advance towards a global civil society.
• Global courts deal with crimes against humanity and constitutional issues of global governance; but the enforcement of decisions against states requires a decision by the Executive Council.

The details do not matter. What is important is the principle of recognising power realities while integrating them into global governance. This approach can provide a global governance system that is 'ugly' in accepting 'unjust' realities of power, and being hierarchical, with the explicit rejection of the fictions of 'equality' and 'sovereignty' of states. But the proposed system can be realized after some limited calamities make the need for a stronger global regime obvious, and can serve adequately. It also has the advantage of serving with time as a bridge to more equitable global governance.

It should be added that, paradoxically, in order to reach a broader global consensus, there must be an awareness that if no agreement is reached global matters will be decided, action taken, and command decisions will be imposed. Thus, the very strength of the Executive Council may help to bring about more agreement on global issues.

If the third level approach cannot be realized or proves inadequate, a fourth level, with an even more radical quantum jump in global governance, may become the only path for humanity to take. This is the emergence of a 'Global Leviathan' in the form of a hyper-power or oligarchy of super-powers which establish a 'Global Principate', to use this Roman term once more as a metaphor, enforcing what is necessary, hopefully in enlightened and benign ways – but this cannot be guaranteed.

However, this is a measure of last resort, if less extreme ways to make global governance adequately resolute fail and harsh failures force humanity to give up many values as the lesser evil – hopefully, before catastrophes engulf it.

All possibilities to improve global governance within its present paradigms and make it more resolute should thus be exhausted, including reforming the United Nations, strengthening cooperation between major powers, expanding global networks, facilitating global governance elites, developing global civil society, and more. But such steps cannot meet the needs of global 'future weaving'. Therefore, a more radical approach to providing global governance with essential resoluteness is recommended, despite its costs. At its core is better integration of power realities into the United Nations structure, with an Executive Council composed of the three super-powers and a few additional members nominated by them, with differential voting rights, becoming the supreme authority, enforcing global measures as necessary. However distasteful, this recommendation is much preferable to the emergence of a Global Leviathan, if an approaching Behemoth or other catastrophes leave no other choice for assuring the survival of humanity.

The most troubling question is not posed by the 'distasteful' nature of the main proposal, but by the likelihood that it will not be adopted because of strong resistance by most states and lack of readiness to cooperate by the major powers. If so, the most optimistic realistic scenario is one of radical learning by humanity, as a result of bearable failures, however painful, leading to the adoption of the proposed redesign or some equivalent. Otherwise, catastrophe will make a Global Leviathan essential, and probably produce one, with all its values negations, pains and risks.[4]

One requirement applies to all levels of redesign and is most urgent: namely, stabilizing the financial basis of global governance. At present, most of the resources of the United Nations and other international bodies are supplied by payments of member states, according to a quota. However, this is inadequate and does not work well: countries do not pay their dues on time, and the sums available for important activities, such as peace-keeping, are insufficient for meeting basic needs.

Building up global governance requires resources. The total amounts needed are a very small proportion of global product, but they must be assured on a regular basis. To achieve this, some kind of tax base exclusively reserved for the UN system is needed, such as a tax on capital flows, commercial cybersphere users, economic users of the deep sea, and so on.

Many technical problems must be overcome, but the real barrier is lack of willingness by major countries to strengthen global governance bodies and make them more independent by having their own income sources. Humanity faces here another vicious circle: making global governance more resolute and otherwise improving its operations requires additional resources; but to get additional resources, global governance must be more powerful and enjoy more powerful support.

I am afraid this catch gives further support to pessimistic scenarios that global governance will be adequately improved only after disaster strikes. But the need is clear: *to fulfill essential functions global governance bodies need more resources. These should, at least in part, be independent from the readiness of member countries to pay their dues on time. Independent income sources for global governance should therefore be developed, including taxes on global economic activities and the uses of the global 'commons'.*

NOTES

1. To mention just a few of the more relevant ones: Annan, 2000; The World Bank, 2000; United Nations Development Programme, 2000a, 2000b; International Monetary Fund *et al.*, 2000; Glenn and Gordon, 2000; and many more. As the official documents of international organizations, they tend to be optimistic, even when presenting serious problems. For an ex*mple of a more realistic estimation, see the series of *Washington Post* articles on AIDS in Africa and its neglect by the international community, despite catastrophic consequences (Gellman, 2000; Jeter, 2000; Vick, 2000). As is to be expected, the needs and possibilities of long-term future-building for humanity as a whole is not taken up in any of these and similar publications, with the partial exception of Glenn and Gordon, 2000.

2. It is often forgotten that in earlier periods, too, the United Nations did engage in professional and successful peacekeeping activities from which much can be learned. Relevant here are the efforts of Ralph Bunche and Dag Hammarskjold, as discussed in Urquhart, 1993.

3. Of all the global governance utopias I know, the most striking one is still Wells, 1967 (first published 1905), with its emphasis on a global governance elite. Nietzsche, in his fragments included in the *Will to Power*, makes some striking observations, such as 'there is approaching unavoidably, slowly, terribly, as fate itself, the great task and question: how shall the earth as a whole be managed?' (my translation, Fragment No. 957–1885).

4. Such a Global Leviathan will be faced by a more extreme question posed by Nietzsche 'And *to what* should "the human" as a whole – not any longer a people, a race – be educated and chastised?' (*ibid.*, emphasis in original, translated by author). But this leads to issues not to be taken up in a Report to the Club of Rome and, hopefully, never to be faced by humanity – though I am far from sure about that.

20

Augmenting Oversight

A main line of thinking underlying the redesign proposals in this book is that governance, and higher levels of governments in particular, engage in 'weaving' the longer-term future, in addition to service delivery and taking care of the present and near future in other ways. In order to fulfill well their tasks of influencing the future trajectories of societies and humanity they need outstanding moral and cognitive faculties. They also need a lot of power; but this is dangerous. Augmenting oversight therefore becomes all the more important.

Many countries do have highly developed oversight structures and processes, both within governance itself and by outside bodies, with free mass media playing a crucial role. Still, there is much to be learned from the traditions of Chinese governance. In the Confucian state the censorial system (in the sense of evaluation of the performance of the other branches of governance, quite distinct from the modern sense of censorship of publications, movies, and so on) constituted one of the basic 'Houses' (Yuan) of government. As summed up by Charles O. Hucker:

> In general terms, censorship in Imperial China was a formal, systematic institutionalization within the government of three principal functions or roles: (1) the maintenance of surveillance over all government activities from outside the normal hierarchy of administrative responsibility; (2) the consequent impeachment, censure, or punishment of civil officials, military officers, and other governmental personnel for violations of prescribed or customary norms of conduct, private as well as public; and (3) the initiation or transmission of recommendations, and in some instances the direct issuance of orders, that current governmental policies, practices, or personnel be changed, the recommendations often including direct or indirect remonstrances about the conduct and decisions of the ruler himself ... The ultimate purpose of all ... activities was, in the Chinese phrase, 'to rectify administration' (Hucker, 1966, p. 2).

This description, which is somewhat idealized and often was not matched in practice, can serve as a model for the oversight of governance today. In particular, the independent authority to judge and punish transgressing officials, and the right and ability to remonstrate with top politicians, are important ideas missing in many contemporary formal oversight bodies.

There is no doubt of the need to establish and strengthen professional oversight, particularly as only professional organizations can engage in effective and penetrating oversight of large and complex organizations. This is the advantage of oversight organizations that are part of the governance system, but independent from the centers of political power. Such oversight units should be appointed by legislatures and in the UN by the General Assembly with a special majority, and should report to them. The General Accounting Office in the USA and the State Comptroller's Office in Israel are among the examples of suitable arrangements.

The redesign recommendation is as follows: *at all levels of governance oversight should be strengthened with the help of special independent and professional comptrollership organizations. This applies also to the United Nations and all other global governance bodies.*

One essential but usually neglected function of oversight bodies is to help speed up the demise of obsolete organizations, functions, units, procedures and structures. Introducing redesigns into governance will not work without getting rid of the many governance components which survive only because of the weaknesses of 'natural selection' and market processes in the public domain (Kaufman, 1985).

There is therefore need for an oversight function conducting a critical assessment of existing governance in order to identify and 'kill off' obsolete elements, making suitable proposals to top levels of governance and the public at large. Units engaging in 'obsolescence oversight' must be completely independent, so as not to be bound by clientelism[1] or otherwise hindered in their work.

Accordingly, *special attention should be paid to closing down obsolete governance functions and units. This requires setting up oversight bodies authorised to identify and recommend phasing out obsolete elements of governance. Such oversight needs strong political support and should be kept separate from routine oversight, staff cutbacks and other more ordinary oversight activities.*

Oversight bodies specializing in handling complaints by citizens (and other residents) are very important. They meet important democratic requirements while helping to assure responsiveness and accountability.

This is a well-recognized need with ombudsman and similar structures being highly developed in many countries. I therefore limit myself to mentioning handling complaints by citizens as an integral part of a comprehensive approach to oversight.

Legal oversight is of paramount importance, though its functions vary between countries, depending on their legal traditions. A double necessity must be taken into account so as to improve legal oversight without doing more harm than good. The first one is to prevent too much 'legalism' and 'going by the book' in government, as a protective stance against excessively active judicial oversight. Professionalism-based governance is needed for 'weaving the future' and must be protected against excessive formalism (Silberman, 1993).

Courts in charge of oversight over governance must therefore understand governance well. Special administrative and constitutional courts are needed which also include judges who bring with them much knowledge of governance, rather than only legal expertise, however excellent. This is all the more important in countries where legal training and careers are often rather narrow. A good case in point is the Supreme Court in the USA, whose decisions prevent adequate control of campaign financing (Dworking, 1996; see also Ottolenghi, 1998).

With the strengthening of global governance, legal oversight over the operations of the United Nations and its bodies needs reinforcement far beyond the present limited jurisdiction of the United Nations Administrative Tribunal. But introducing an overly legalistic culture must be avoided, together with full respect for the autonomy of professional discretion and the legitimacy of political considerations within the rule of law. Therefore, the establishment of a kind of constitutional court for global governance is recommended. This is all the more necessary in view of the redesigns strengthening the Secretary General of the United Nations and making global governance more powerful.

Accordingly, *the legal oversight of governance needs strengthening, on condition that it does not become too legalistic, nor press governance to become so, and respects professional discretion and legitimate political considerations. To do so while being able to penetrate deeply into governance behavior, constitutional and high administrative courts should include judges with much knowledge and experience in governance, in addition to experts in law and jurisprudence. These recommendations apply also to global governance. Setting up a United Nations Constitutional Court, including also judges with relevant global and governance knowledge, should strengthen legal oversight of the United Nations and other international bodies.*

Quite different issues are raised by the need for oversight over state and continental governments. In the longer run, the setting up of a Global Constitutional Court within an expanding global judicial system will become essential, and even practical. Also, all persons everywhere should, with time, have the right to appeal to some global judicial bodies against their governments. A good model is provided by the European Union court system, which has authority over member states and to which private individuals can appeal against actions by their governments and domestic courts.

However, setting up such a global judicial system cannot realistically be expected in the foreseeable future. Until then, a variety of independent bodies should fulfill oversight roles. Some of them should have quasi-judicial status, being on the periphery of the strengthened global court system. The decision to set up a United Nations High Commissioner for Human Rights with power to intervene when basic freedoms are suppressed, and the right to report violations to the General Assembly of the United Nations or the Human Rights Commission in Geneva, is an important step in the right direction. Independent bodies outside the United Nations system can fulfill many important oversight functions. Human Rights Watch, the Worldwatch Institute, Green Watch and Amnesty International illustrate very important functions carried out by such bodies which should be strengthened.

However, non-governmental bodies also need oversight, all the more so as some of them become fanatical, irresponsible and perhaps even corrupt (Weir and Hall, 1994). *Independent global oversight bodies concerned with human rights, ecological damage and the like, should therefore be supported. However, oversight of them should be strengthened, with possibilities to appeal against their findings and apply sanctions against unjustified accusations, recklessness, and corruption. The setting up of a voluntary 'Oversight Panel' at the initiative of such bodies is a suitable first step, to be followed by global courts getting jurisdiction over voluntary global actors.*

But more is needed. As global governance develops, global inspectorates and intelligence collection agencies should be set up, with free right of movement, data collection and interviewing in all countries, and maximum use of remote sensoring technologies. They would be in charge of overseeing compliance with global laws, agreements and norms, in matters such as human rights, environmental protection, arms limitation, and so on. The experiences of the International Atomic Energy Commission and the 'challenge' provisions in the treaty against chemical weapons provide many ideas and lessons for setting up such an inspectorate and intelligence agency, and making them work, as do the successes and failures of various arms control bodies imposed on Iraq. However, movement towards a really effective global oversight, inspection and intelligence system depends on global governance becoming more powerful, and being further strengthened by it.

Existing international and global oversight and inspection should therefore be strengthened. Steps should be taken towards the setting up of international independent inspectorates and intelligence agencies to oversee compliance by states with global rules, agreements, norms and decisions.

The mass media fulfill key roles in surveillance over governance. This function deserves global recognition and support, together with greater transparency in governance and an increase in the public right to know and to have access to most governance material. But the qualities of much of mass media discussion of public issues, and of much investigative reporting, leave a great deal to be desired. A main way to improve their quality, without impairing freedom of the mass media as a basic value and an essential condition of effective oversight, is to provide correspondents, editors and commentators with ethical guidance, together with opportunities to improve their understanding of governance. (Doing so will also encourage the mass media to fulfill a greater role in the enlightenment of the public in public affairs issues.)

Investigative work by the mass media should thus be encouraged and protected globally, with libel and privacy laws giving priority to the public right to be informed about the conduct of governance and senior governance elites, including their 'private' affairs. A code of ethics for correspondents, editors and commentators should be prepared, to be enforced by professional and independent bodies set up by the mass media themselves, subject to appeal to the courts. Mass media correspondents, editors and commentators should be provided with intensive learning opportunities on public and governance issues. As already recommended, interventions of owners in the professional discretion of mass media staff should be restrained, and corruption in reporting should be subjected to severe punishment of both the corrupter and the corrupted.

The recommendations presented up to this point may be regarded as impractical, but probably will not be opposed as incorrect in principle. The situation is different with my next point, concerning limitations of the right to know, transparency and open government.

The right of the public to know what is going on in governance and the demands for transparency and open government are in principle valid, in terms of democratic values, oversight requirements and, hopefully, because of their potential contribution to an enlightened public opinion.

But the costs of overdoing transparency should be recognized.[2] The need to keep some governance material confidential, even when no issues of security, economic value or privacy are involved, should be recognized. This applies in particular to internal discussion of politically sensitive issues. Frank policy discourse, encouragement of policy iconoclasm and unconventional policy reflection are essential for improving considerations of major choices. But they have no chance if they cannot be kept confidential, sometimes for many years, with due safeguards.

Examples abound, as illustrated by the leaking of a memorandum by the British Prime Minister in July 2000, which cannot but inhibit in the future the writing of frank position papers and policy directives. To take a more serious case, the unification of Germany could not have taken place when it did without very secret talks between a few leaders and their aides (Zelikow and Rice, 1995). *The right of the public to know and the principle of transparent governance, should therefore be balanced with a recognition of the need for some confidentiality of governance processes, including policy reflection and high-level discourse and negotiations. These should be excluded from the public right to know and protected against leaks, subject to judicial review.*

The need to balance oversight with the requirements of capacities to govern is especially pronounced during crises, as discussed next.

NOTES

1. For a fascinating study bringing out the strength of clientelism even in what appear to be centralized and strong states, see Suleiman, 1987. No such studies are available on global organizations, but it seems that clientelism is particularly pronounced and harmful there.
2. On some views, this also applies to anti-corruption measures (Anechiarico and Jacobs, 1996). But the dangers of not doing enough to fight corruption are much greater than short-term costs of doing 'too much'.

21

Gearing Governance for Crises

Crises, breakdowns and traumatization, ranging from large-scale disasters to the collapse of major social institutions and services essential for life, are an ultimate test of capacities to govern. Policy reflection preparations for crises have already been discussed. The question faced now is how institutionally to enable governance to cope with emergencies, including harsh situations that are close to real 'ungovernability'.

To start with 'routine crises': this oxymoronic concept indicates that quite a number of crises occur regularly and can therefore be managed more or less routinely, however different from one another in detail and despite requiring large doses of improvisation. Examples are repetitive natural disasters, minor accidents at nuclear power plants, general strikes and conventional terrorist incidents. This type of crisis is the subject of 'crisis management'. Given that such crises are bound to occur, professional crisis management staffs must be prepared to deal with them. This recommendation is relatively easy to implement, thanks to the increasing stock of pertinent knowledge and experience (Comfort, 1988; Rosenthal, Charles and Hart, 1989; and the *Journal of Contingencies and Crisis Management*, which started in 1993).

Management of war, while never 'routine', is also professionalised within various types of command and control system. This is a subject of profound importance for countries facing possibile wars and similar threats, but I will not discuss it in this book, other than to mention it in the following recommendation: *crisis management should be improved at all levels of governance, by setting up professional units and exercising them constantly among other means. Investments in upgrading crisis management should be proportional to the expected frequency and intensity of crises, with special attention to assuring high-quality command and control systems for countries that may face war-like situations. However, because of the omnipresent likelihood of crises in an epoch of transformations, countries that do not expect crises should also build up at least a core professional staff to deal with crisis management.*

All crisis staff preparations are an exercise in futility if operational capacities are inadequate for implementing their decisions. All crisis management improvements must therefore be accompanied by preparation of appropriate operational abilities. This is difficult because of the involved social, psychological and political costs of visible preparations for crises, and necessary investment in field units and facilities. *Good crisis staff preparation, along with building some skeleton for field operations under crisis conditions, may often, therefore, be the most cost-effective combination.*

These are straightforward recommendations, relatively easy to implement. The weakness of crisis management staffs in nearly all the offices of heads of governments that I studied is thus all the more shocking. This is a clear case of gross delinquency, where relatively simple measures to improve important capacities are neglected. Reasons for this neglect include overload with current problems and an unwillingness to think in advance about unpleasant occurrences. Bureaucratic infighting also blocks the creation of crisis management staffs in the offices of heads of government, which is where they ought to be located.

But more insidious factors are at work and hinder preparations for crises where they really matter: senior policy makers rely on their ability to improvise and do not feel the need to learn how to cope with crises.

Crises are one of the situations when the quality of rulers is of paramount importance. They can serve as immobilizers, 'panic-makers', and 'decision-botchers', being crushed by crises, or as energizers, innovators, and decision-stimulators who ride on the crest of crises towards great achievements.

Especially when crises are very threatening, the behavior of a few top decision-makers can make all the difference between what I diagnose as 'cognitive vertigo' and 'maze behavior', with reckless choice being another disastrous response, on one side, or, on the other, cool evaluation and creative thinking, leading to optimal measures reducing damage and utilizing crises as an opportunity.

The more prevalent situation in the corridors of power during serious crises is that described in the diary of a staff officer in the command centers of the Confederate States, when it became increasingly clear that they would lose the war with the North. They were often 'at their wits end and seem to have no plan, to be drifting along on the current of events' (Younger, 1995, p. 72).

Professional crisis staffs near rulers are a must, and efforts to prepare top decision-makers for crises situations are essential. But in advance of crises, senior politicians usually refuse to participate in crisis exercises, which is the only really effective way to be prepared. The result is that much of the preparatory staff work is in vain, other than in technical matters that are much less important than the quality of top level decisions made under crisis conditions. Therefore, with a few exceptions, even the few crisis staffs set up in offices of heads of government often operate more as briefing rooms instead of professional supports for top-level decisions when the hour of danger-cum-opportunity strikes.

This brings us back to the need for senior politicians constantly to engage in learning. There are sometimes good reasons for senior politicians not to be publicly involved in crisis preparations on sensitive issues, such as the necessity not to reveal prematurely their thinking on sensitive issues. But the real cause of senior politicians usually refusing to participate in crisis exercises is the evaluation which must follow if such exercises are to be useful – and politicians do not like to subject themselves to evaluation, however delicately done.

As the bad performance of some senior Dutch politicians on some crisis games on live television in 1996 showed, they are very badly prepared for one of their more important tasks. However, the political costs of their inept public performance were high, showing that in terms of political calculus senior politicians are right not to put themselves willingly to such tests.[1]

Only in single countries are crisis exercises for high-level decision-makers and feedback sessions accepted. The institutionalization of 'strategic schooling', including crisis exercises on the highest level, in the office of the Swiss Bundeskanzler in 1998 (Carrel, 1999 and http://www.sfa.admin.ch) illustrates the possibilities; but most countries and senior politicians are not ripe for crisis exercises. Indirect surrogates for preparing senior politicians for crises are therefore needed: *senior politicians who will take charge in crises should participate in crisis exercises, followed with learning and evaluation sessions. The experience of Switzerland shows that this may be possible. When not, surrogates must be used, including: very confidential mini-crisis exercises with very few participants; high-quality briefings of top decision-makers on crises exercises; and participation in such exercises by those who would serve in real crises as the main advisers of the decision-makers.*

Even more difficult are the problems posed by crises that are global in their implications, such as large-scale disasters, economic meltdowns, genocide, and large-scale eruptions of violence.

A first step towards improving the ability of global governance to cope with such situations is to upgrade crisis management capacities in emerging global governance. A professional crisis staff should be set up at the highest levels within the United Nations.

Dependence on member states limits the usefulness of United Nations crisis staffs. It is unrealistic in the foreseeable future to propose that country representatives participate in the crisis exercises of the United Nations, though it may prove possible for some to join in informally. Nevertheless, better preparation of senior United Nations officials for crisis is an important step towards making global governance both more resolute and more effective under crises conditions.

More can also be done by non-governmental organizations to help with global crisis management, as demonstrated by The International Crisis

Group (ICG). Independent bodies can organize exercises on global crises in which senior global governance staff as well as country officials can participate without the political sensitivities of United Nations crisis preparations.

In summary, *professional crisis management staffs in the office of the Secretary-General of the United Nations should be strengthened. They should organize exercises, including those on the political handling of international crises, with the participation of top-level United Nations officials and, if possible and not too constraining, country representatives – especially from members of the Security Council. Independent non-governmental bodies should conduct such exercises in less 'sensitive' settings.*

Technical preparations, however essential, are not enough. Global governance needs criteria and norms for taking emergency measures, as illustrated by the debates on NATO actions in Kosovo (Daalder and O'Hanlon, 2000). These should not be left to ad hoc improvisation and a slow accumulation of precedents, however important, but advance agreement on intervention rules is beyond the present capacity of the United Nations. The only feasible way to move ahead until the United Nations becomes much more resolute, as proposed in Chapter Nineteen, is for suitably qualified non-governmental bodies to work on the problem, avoiding impractical proposals while preparing contingency rules for global interventions in crises. *Non-governmental bodies should prepare draft rules, criteria, principles and directives for international crisis interventions. These should be operational, on one hand, and informed by realistic visions on the other. Decision-makers and professionals from global governance bodies and main member states should informally be involved in this work. Its results should serve as a basis for preparations within the United Nations and in member countries.*

A special set of problems is posed by 'transformation breakdowns', in the sense of large-scale social turbulence and collapses associated with radical change, domestic upheavals and external pressures. Some of the resulting incidents and situations are susceptible to the types of crisis management discussed above. But transformation breakdowns can be radical, with the substantial disappearance of law and order, internal warfare, disintegration of social structures, lack of essential supplies, and sometimes aggression against other countries. Circumstances in Africa and the Balkans serve as illustrations of such situations, which can also engulf major countries.

Global transformations inevitably produce many breakdowns in all kinds of social spaces (Almond, Flanagan and Mundt, 1973). Transformation breakdowns will therefore constitute a major challenge to capacities to govern in the foreseeable future.[2] However, their intensity and shape will vary. Much depends on the nature of ongoing transformations, their speed and contents, the elasticity of the cultures in which they take place, the availability of spare resources to dampen some of their painful effects, the ease with which protagonists can acquire weapons, and other variables – including external inter-

ventions. Some 'breakdowns' are but birth pangs of a better future, constituting what Joseph A. Schumpeter called 'creative destruction' (Schumpeter,
1942, ch. 7). But transformation breakdowns may give rise to harsh situations
of ungovernability, requiring extraordinary capacities to govern.

Available knowledge does not provide an adequate understanding of
transformation breakdowns, making them all the more difficult to handle. A
metaphor from chaos theory is again helpful: assuming we have a substance
that can take different shapes, such as water that can become ice or steam;
and assuming we understand well the nature of the relatively stable states of
water as ice, liquid or steam – all of this knowledge provides no insight into
the transformation phases from ice to water and steam. These transitions
are very turbulent and involve a lot of 'breakdowns' on a micro scale, very
different in their dynamics from the relatively stable states of ice, water and
steam. Similarly, we have very little understanding of the transformation
phases from Communist command economies to democratic market-based
economies, from apartheid to political equality, from traditional social structures to modern and post-modern ones, and so on.

But we do know, from limited past experience and from observing ongoing
processes, as well as from theoretical insights, that transformation breakdowns can become very disruptive, with much human suffering and aggressive
behavior. We also know that such processes are not necessarily 'successful' in
the sense of leading in the longer run to desirable social situations, such as
humane democratic regimes and peaceful societies.

Transformation breakdowns may therefore require 'extraordinary' governance and politics. Without going as far as John Stuart Mill – who in *On
Liberty* justified despotism if it created the conditions of liberty and liberalism
– radical transformation processes may require very strong regimes to contain wild breakdowns. Plebiscite democracy with a strong president is risky,
but in some cases this may be the least risky option of all. Even transitional
'constitutional dictatorships', as first developed in the Roman Republic and
also widely used in democracies under serious crisis (very relevant though in
need of updating is Rossiter, 1948), may sometimes be the least bad of all
effective and feasible alternatives.

The need for emergency regimes, which should always be regarded as tran-
sient, must be acknowledged. Carl Schmitt's definition of 'sovereignty' as the
authority to declare a state of emergency (Schmitt, 1963; for context see
Balke, 1996 and McCormick, 2000) rightly recognized the crucial importance
of this power. A delicate balance is required, however, between the risks of
underestimating emergency situations, and thus endangering democracy and
social welfare, and overusing emergency regimes, with similar results.

Modern democratic theory and practice neglect the special needs of
emergency situations. This puts some democracies at risk, even in countries

with long democratic traditions; worse, it results in misreadings of the needs of other countries, where serious emergency measures may be the best option available. *When transformation processes produce dangerous breakdowns, strong emergency regimes may be necessary, based as far as possible on the consent of the population. Sometimes 'constitutional dictatorships' may be the least of all evils. Therefore, countries that adopt emergency regimes for good reasons should be supported, while sanctions should be applied to those that act in an extreme fashion without justification.*

Emergency regimes are dangerous. Many of them adopt unnecessarily harsh policies (Leng, 1990; Gomien, 1993 part III), tend to perpetuate themselves and become aggressive both internally and externally. But also very harmful are situations where no government can be maintained, law and order breaks down, brute force dominates, and societies approach total collapse. Hence the need for global interventions in cases of serious transformation breakdowns, and also against evil regimes thriving on emergency situations.

Events in Bosnia, Somalia and all too many other territories testify not only to the desperate need for effective global crises interventions, but above all to the appalling impotence of existing global governance. Capacities to handle such situations are a major test of global governance and a prerequisite for building up its credibility. Effective emergency arrangements must therefore be instituted, 'run in', and constantly improved in the light of experience. These include upgraded crisis staffs and intervention norms as discussed above, together with the building up of effective forces that can overwhelm any local violence (for some relevant proposals by an international panel of experts see Crossete, 2000).

Global governance capacities to intervene forcefully in extreme emergency situations are an imperative of raison d'humanité, *a main prerequisite of advancing global governance as a whole, and a critical test of its quality. Also required are changes in decision-making rules, with the United Nations Secretary-General being authorized to send forces pending decisions by the Security Council, with a special majority but reduced veto rights (or by its successor Executive Council, as recommended). Suitable staffs, command structures, facilities, instruments, transport and logistics, and well-armed and trained forces should be prepared and kept in a state of readiness.*

Emergencies that require global action can take a number of forms. They may involve relatively clear situations that a country or group of countries cannot handle alone, so that global assistance has to be sought – for example, to cope with famine and natural catastrophes, large-scale epidemics and so on. Or a government may be unable to handle processes that endanger the very fabric of society, such as drug cartel takeovers; or a legitimate government may be overturned by clearly criminal action. States and societies that are obviously disintegrating present an extreme case, as do states controlled by evil rulers.

Such situations often cannot be handled by short-term emergency measures. Instead, it may be necessary to impose and enforce global trusteeship, to satisfy pressing humane values and social needs and lay the foundations for a stable and desirable form of governance while evil rulers are tried before an international court.

However, the dangers of misuse of global emergency interventions must be recognized, as there is sometimes a very thin line between 'neo-colonialist' aggression against countries that are disliked or different, and taking care of essential global and humankind needs. The value of pluralism, subject to *raison d'humanité* imperatives, should make us all the more sensitive to the dangers of hegemonic ideologies and power interests misusing the right to intervene.

Moreover, putting an area under a trusteeship regime involves occupation, impairs the basic political rights of the population and raises many complex problems of implementation. Starting a trusteeship regime is one thing, but bringing it to a successful conclusion, with the establishment of indigenous governments that are supported by the population and develop the country, is quite another

Such risks must be weighed against the high costs of abandoning populations to chaos and death, leaving evil alone and providing free room for manoeuvre to forces which may endanger other countries and seriously imperil *raison d'humanité*.

The Economist published on 4 September 1993 (p. 18) a striking piece of political fiction describing a country in Africa called *Ordinia*. This country is professionally managed for a fixed fee by a team of outsiders, with very little self-government, controlled media and swift justice. The question is posed how many Africans would of their own free will hurry to live in that country if free to do so. This imaginative thought experiment is counterfactual and postulates a situation contravening many globally accepted values. However, the answer to the question is not in doubt: Ordinia would be swamped with immigrants from all over Africa.

Returning to reality, the conclusion is that in extreme conditions of transformation breakdowns, civil warfare, evil rulers and so on, a globally imposed regime may be a good interim solution, on condition that the occupation is successful in meeting the needs of the population for security and amenities of life. However, such action requires large-scale forces and resources, highly committed and well-trained personnel, and – most difficult of all – global resoluteness. If these are not available it is better not to start global interventions that become adventures sure to fail.

Radical measures should not be left to ad hoc decisions alone. Explicit criteria for international interventions should be formulated and widely agreed upon, as suggested above. In addition, major interventions should be subject to judicial review.

Despite all these difficulties, the following recommendation is compelling in terms of alleviating extreme suffering, avoiding serious dangers and advancing *raison d'humanité: when countries disintegrate, evil rulers engage in large-scale crimes against humanity or prepare serious acts of aggression, or populations are subjected to genocide, the United Nations should impose a trusteeship regime, subject to a special decision process and rapid judicial review. Trusteeships should last for a maximum of three years, unless renewed by an extraordinary procedure. Before imposing a trusteeship, conditions for a high probability of success must be satisfied, including clear ideas on goals to be achieved, adequate forces and resources, strong political support by major powers and careful oversight.*

A difficult question is whether the domain for international interventions should be expanded to include potentially explosive situations, and possibly evil rulers perhaps acquiring mass killing weapons. This relates to the problems posed by so-called 'crazy states' (Dror, 1980), 'rogue states' (Litwak, 2000), 'rogue regimes' (Tanter, 1999) and so on. My own tendency is to prefer the risks of global over-intervention to those of under-intervention; but global systems are not yet ripe for coping with the issue.

Even if conducted in the best possible way, interventions of the types discussed above are risky, costly and endanger important values. Furthermore, when transformation breakdowns occur in large or powerful countries, or in states with advanced weapons systems, effective international intervention may be too risky, or even impossible. Helping transformation processes so as to prevent breakdowns is therefore in all respects a better policy, morally as well as in terms of *realpolitik*. However, care must be taken not to 'help' by recommending and even forcing on countries policies that have a high probability to cause more damage. Many of the economic policies recommended by international economic and financial institutes, and also in fact forced upon countries, may accelerate social disintegration rather than put the economy on a way towards equitable growth. *Countries in serious transformation crises should therefore be helped to avoid extreme breakdowns, with special attention given to states having continental and global significance. But care must be taken not to give one-dimensional and dogmatic advice likely to cause serious social harm. Deeper reflection on transformation crises and policies to avoid them is therefore a priority for global think tanks.*

The redesigns developed above place a lot of responsibility and burden on global governance, and especially the United Nations. In the long run this is essential. However, in the foreseeable future the United Nations may not be able adequately to cope with crises and breakdowns. Constant efforts to upgrade the United Nations must therefore be accompanied by effective action being taken by a group of states that operates as a surrogate 'global governance group', with the USA and the European Union at its core, if necessary on their own and even without United Nations authorization.

However undesirable in principle, action taken by self-appointed 'guardian states' may be better than doing nothing in the face of serious societal disintegration and take-over by forces of evil. Every effort should be made to integrate such action into the United Nations, along the lines proposed in Chapter Nineteen. However, *as long as the United Nations is unable to cope with major crises of global significance, the USA and the European Union, together with other willing states, should take appropriate action. But no single country should do so on its own; and such action should be explained and justified before United Nations forums and limited to the minimum necessary to prevent human catastrophes.* ˛

NOTES

1. In 1999, when again a series of crisis games on Dutch television took place, many politicians volunteered to participate. The temptations of being seen, and seeing oneself, on television overcame all other considerations.
2. This also applies to corporations. See Greene, 1982, and Pauchant and Mitroff, 1992.

22

Strengthening the Autonomy of High-Quality Government

The predominant view in contemporary discourse and literature, and also in the minds of large sections of governance elites, is that governments, on which I concentrate in this chapter as distinct from governance as a whole, should not have much autonomy from society. A main reason given for that view is normative, with the value that government should serve society, its present wishes and tastes being regarded as a fundamental norm of democracy. Instrumental arguments lead to the same conclusion, claiming that civil society, markets, grass-roots movements and the like, are more effective in taking care of social needs. The empirical argument is sometimes added that in any case societal forces shape governance, and that democratic governments cannot therefore be autonomous.

These three arguments are faulty. Democratic values require that, ultimately, governments be subordinated to the will of society (in contrast to the 'general will' in the rather mystical sense of Rousseau) as expressed in elections, referenda, civil action and so on. But this does not negate the autonomy of governments as long as they enjoy overall democratic support and legitimacy. Furthermore, much of democratic theory, going back to Edmund Burke, insists on governments exercising their judgment on acting for the good of the people, without being subjected to real-time directives by populations, as long as they enjoy the confidence of a majority as expressed in periodic elections. When the already explored argument of the non-representation of future generations, even in the most democratic of elections, is added, the normative justification of much governmental autonomy, especially in trying to influence the future, seems well supported.

The instrumental argument is even weaker. As discussed, essential higher-order tasks are in critical aspects beyond the legitimate scope and capacity of civil society, markets, grass-roots movements and so on, however important their contributions are. Governments are democratically entitled, and even obliged, to take care of collective futures; and only high-quality government is morally and cognitively able to do so subject to societal oversight and in close partnership with societal actors.

Empirically, history is full of convincing cases of governments, and even individual rulers, making history-shaping decisions with much 'elbow-room' (interesting in this connection is Dennet, 1984). This is well supported by relevant theories and comparative studies (Nordlinger, 1981) as well as writings by insightful insiders (still unsurpassed, despite many imitators, is Crossman, 1975–1977).

The proposed position is therefore as follows: *the autonomy of democratic governments should be increased, especially in 'future-weaving' tasks, subject to democratic legitimation and oversight and substantial participation by a variety of societal actors and processes.*

In order to support the proposed position more strongly, some main inadequacies of societies as a whole, and of most social actors, should be taken into account. For instance:

- The moral characteristics and capacities required for shaping the future, including critical tragic choices, moral education and so on, go far beyond the moral and cultural characteristics of contemporary societies, as further depressed by the mass media, post-modernity and so on. Some social actors are of very high moral stature – much more than any government can be. But dominant social processes and institutions, and in particular market economies, have built-in values that are very different from those appropriate for shaping the future.
- The cognitive requirements of coping with uncertainty and complexity are beyond the currrent and foreseeable capacities of most societies and social actors, with the exception of scarce highly qualified elites and institutions.
- Private power, even when operating at its best, requires oversight and some guidance. This applies also to the very difficult issues of advancing science and technology while containing its dangers. Governments need a great deal of autonomy to perform their irreducible share in such oversight and guidance adequately.

A second line of argument deals in positive terms with the necessity for governments to engage in critical future-shaping tasks: to reiterate three main points that have been discussed throughout this book:

1. Only governments are entitled democratically to make critical authoritative choices trying to shape the future.
2. Only governments can potentially implement many of the critical choices and large-scale interventions in historical processes involved in efforts to influence the future for the better.
3. The second point applies increasingly to global governance, because of the need for global action in coping with the main opportunities and dangers.

The two lines of argument would lead to the conclusion that governments should have much autonomy, subject to democratic oversight, but for a missing term. *The missing term is the assumption that governments have the required moral and cognitive capacities, or at least that there is a good chance they can and will achieve them. However, if governments are incompetent, immoral and perhaps evil, then they should have no autonomy – which they would use for the worse.*

We run here into increasing 'impossibility' situations caused by the non-compatibility of three dynamic curves: one, increasingly complex future-shaping critical choices, with the default decision having a high probability of missed opportunities, and bad or even catastrophic results; two, a growing inability of civil society, markets, non-governmental actors, spontaneous social processes and so on, to cope adequately with these critical choices; and, three, the growing incapacity of governments themselves in coping adequately with critical choices.

If these three curves continue in their present directions the result is an increasing 'impossibility' situation. If so, then one or more of the curves must give way, or some kinds of explosion or implosion will occur which change the dynamics of the system (applicable are the classical 'urban dynamics' models of Jay Forrester, in Forrester, 1969).

Care must be taken with such predictions, as illustrated by the misjudgments of the first famous Report to the Club of Rome, 'Limits to Growth', which relied on such models, but with incorrect premises and parameters (Meadows *et al.*, 1972). Nevertheless, my argument as a whole makes, I think, a strong case for the emergence of an 'impossibility' situation where increasingly crucial choices can be adequately made neither by civil society, markets and the like, nor by governments lacking increasingly essential core capacities.

In the face of such impossibility, two strategies are open. One is to leave resolution to explosive and implosive effects, trusting that after bearable crises and calamities a new and much better dynamic will emerge. Thus, one can hope or assume that the consciousness of large parts of humanity will change under the impact of shocks, providing a good path into the future based on new cultures, civil societies, grass root movements and non-governmental actors, without the need for much governmental intervention. Also, shocks can be expected to bring about radical improvements in governments, making them capable of engaging in high-quality critical choices. Alternatively, one may hope that shocks will produce a 'sustainable' or 'steady-state' future without any need or desire to engage in 'future weaving'.

The second strategy is to try to change the curves so as to steer them away from explosive and implosive 'impossibilities'. This, in turn, can be done by trying to upgrade the capacity of non-governmental actors and of multi-actor processes, such as markets, to engage in adequate 'future weaving'. Upgrading governmental capacities may also achieve this.

Relying on spontaneous recovery after breakdowns that aren't too costly seems to me as too much of a utopian expectation on which to base the future of societies and humanity. As noted, there is no reason whatsoever to assume that the 'cunning of history' or any other hidden meta-dynamic of history assures recuperation without devastating costs, and indeed the long-term existence of the human species.

The self-generated upgrading of societal, non-governmental capacities seems to me to be an unrealistic conjecture. No historic evidence, nor present trends, in either psychology or sociology, provide grounds for thinking that such auto-transformations for the better will occur when needed most.

There remains the difficult issue of how to upgrade capacities to govern. Here, too, evidence does not provide much reason for optimism. Nonetheless, my historical and theoretical studies lead me to the view that the upgrading of governmental capacities is nearly, but not completely, impossible – all the more so after relatively light shocks, which do not change societies for the better but may be sufficient for enabling significant governmental reforms.

Combining all three methods further improves changes to equip humanity with necessary 'future-weaving' capacities. But this depends on the upgrading of governance so it can facilitate societal capacities while containing potentials for the uncontrollable, the bad and the evil. *The overall stance of this book is therefore to emphasize the redesign of governance as a main way to upgrading human future-shaping capacities as a whole. There is no assurance that this will work, but it is worth a maximum effort.*

I unhappily admit that this is a measure of last resort, no better avenues being available, as far as I can estimate ongoing dynamics and their potentials. An additional argument in favor of the adopted approach is that, if carefully executed, the upgrading of governance can do no harm and does not hinder other human capacity-enhancing processes and endeavors, while it may even facilitate them.

Many of the redesigns discussed in this book increase governmental autonomy, while subjecting it to improved oversight. But three requirements deserve further emphasis.

The first is a sense of mission, and a feeling of responsibility for the future on behalf of the higher governance elites, in addition to commitment to the improvement of the current situation. These should be accompanied by some confidence in being able to influence the future for the better and a will to do so, combined with due humility in embarking on so demanding and important a task.

The second is a better understanding by the higher governance elites of the potentials for governmental autonomy provided by modern, post-modern and post-postmodern politics, and the conditions for realizing it. Without such understanding senior politicians feel captive, and are in fact enslaved, to shifting public opinion and the images generated by doubtful opinion polls. Instead, they should educate and enlighten populations and thus enhance the effective democratic autonomy of governments within explainable options. But senior politicians must understand deep social processes to know that they can enhance the autonomy of governments, and do so democratically.

Thirdly, a number of institutional reforms are necessary. Thus, in addition to the already discussed redesigns strengthening rulers, the periods between elections should not be very short, lest there be no hope for needed autonomy other than by a dangerous rule by plebiscite. *Electoral cycles should be lengthened, by holding elections for the main executive and legislative bodies every five to six years; and by clustering elections, such as local and national ones, so as to avoid elections of any kind at less than three-yearly intervals. Concomitantly, procedures for calling special elections should be augmented, so that extraordinary elections can be called by the government, in special circumstances by the symbolic head of state, and via public initiatives supported by a large proportion of voters.*

All social actors bear responsibility for building up human capacities to cope with the challenges posed in the twenty-first century. Creative and educational elites should serve as an avant-garde in doing so, with private powerful actors contributing a large share. But I see no possibility of engaging in essential future-shaping without high-quality governance.

No 'life after politics' (Mulgan, 1997) awaits us. Either politics is revitalized, democracy redirected and capacities to govern radically upgraded, or the likely nature of the future is dismal. Moreover, for upgraded governments to engage successfully in crucial future-shaping endeavors, they need a lot of autonomy, subject to strict democratic oversight and power of veto. Redesign of governments is not an Archimedean fulcrum sure to raise humanity to new heights. But it can serve as an Archimedean screw, for slowly raising the quality of the future and, more importantly, avoiding calamities – until something better comes along.

Finale: Governance Redesign Pending a Quantum Leap

Humanity's deep need for a new beginning was well expressed in the final chorus in Percy Bysshe Shelley's *Hellas* (1821):

> Oh, cease! Must Hate and Death return?
> Cease! Must men kill and die?
> Cease! Drain not to its dregs the Urn
> Of bitter Prophecy.
> The world is weary of the past,
> Oh, might it die or rest at last!

I do not subscribe to the longing for 'rest', in the sense of arriving at some stable 'end of history' or 'sustainability'. Rather, a Promethean or Faustian view fits better the history and nature of humanity, or Imre Madach's vision of humanity,[1] with a lot of risk-taking and struggle and no knowledge of any earthly 'end', but with 'The Principle of Hope' (in the sense of Bloch, 1995). No stable state should be aimed at, nor can any supposed 'equilibrium' be more than a temporary apparition sure to be disrupted by the energy and dynamics characterizing human history and global environments – hopefully for the better, but possibly for the worse. For this reason, as already explained, thinking in terms of 'sustainability' should be rejected, as should all 'endism nonsense', to use an apt phrase by Samuel Huntington (quoted in Ladd, 1993, p. 12).

However, if humanity is to progress, some major elements of human history must be radically altered. Thucydides put well the dangers of history continuing as before. In translation by Hobbes: 'many and heinous things happened ... which ... have been before and shall be ever as long as human nature is the same' (Thucydides, 1989, p. 204). As W. Robert Connor says in summing up Thucydides' views, which were shaped by terrible civil strife in cities thrown into decline after periods of prosperity and good life: because of the constancy of human nature 'the past will recur, but that recurrence has become a threat, not a promise' (Connor, 1984, p. 104).

Humans and humanity are in major respects better off now than ever before. This is a central fact that must not be forgotten in all the warnings about the way in which we are moving and the dangers ahead. But too many unprecedented dangers loom, and too many wholly new opportunities beckon to let us relax and rely on the smooth continuation of some very positive trends, while ignoring the negative ones.

Two historic cases may help further to introduce this Finale. The first is provided by the history of the Maya civilization, and the second by the rupture in the history of the Jewish People and Judaism following the destruction of the Second Temple.

Recent studies (Freidel, Schele and Parker, 1995) of the downfall of the Maya civilization reject environmental explanations, such as overcrowding leading to the depletion of essential resources, changes of climate and so on. Rather, it was profound political failure that 'savaged the Maya back into a simpler society' (*ibid*., p. 323) which, internally weakened, could not withstand the Spanish invasion.

Quite a different dynamic is demonstrated by the history of the Jewish People. During the first centuries of the Christian era the Jewish People were subjected to five catastrophes: the destruction of the Second Temple; the failure of the revolt against the Romans; large-scale genocide; exile of most of the people; and the rise of Christianity. These added up to a total rupture in history of the type that usually annihilates peoples and civilizations.

It was outstanding spiritual creativity that enabled the overcoming of the rupture by providing a new basis for existence enabling the Jewish People to survive and sometimes thrive, in exile. This creativity was epitomized in the so-called 'Mode of Yavneh' in which outstanding religious thinkers and spiritual creators reconstituted religious practice so as to fit the radically different conditions of being dispersed among the nations (Aderet, 1997).

Together these two cases (and my reading of human history and social science as a whole) lead to two main conjectures on the future of humanity. Firstly, in the longer run radical changes in human values, cultures, civilizations, and, probably, in human nature are essential for survival and thriving, given ongoing global transformations. However, secondly, to enable such changes to evolve or be brought about, which may take generations, outstanding governance capacities to govern and 'weave the future' are an essential condition, though far from sufficient by themselves.

Certain human traits and tendencies of belief (Wright, 1994) were useful for human survival and so were preferred by natural selection (and/or creation?) – for example, the 'flight or fight' reflex, with the tendency to react to anything strange with immediate feelings of hostility, then either run away or attack. Our distant ancestors found it helpful to think in linear terms of causes and effects as they learned to manipulate the environment, with the result that this 'frame' came to dominate our modes of thought. But hostility and continuous 'cultivation of hatred' (Gay, 1993) can ultimately lead to genocidal warfare; and simplistic cause-and-effect thinking is an obstacle to coping with increasing complexity. Consequently, humanity needs to learn to be less ready to sense hostility, find new ways of thinking in terms of uncertainty, and much more.

It is the radical transformation in crucial dimensions of life that make traits that generally served humanity well in the past into serious dangers to its future. It is enough to mention the tendencies to 'hate' when under pressure, apparently 'wired' into our brain, in combination with easily available weapons of mass killing, to demonstrate that substantial 'rewiring' is essential for long-term survival and thriving. This conclusion applies to large sets of basic traits of humanity as presently constituted that need to change in order to permit humanity to flourish in what is in many respects a 'new human universe'. *For humanity to thrive in a radically different 'human universe', radical changes are needed in deeply embedded propensities, orientations, values, modes of thinking and behavior patterns.*

Profound philosophical and theological questions are thrown up by the paradox of humanity bringing about a new 'human universe', however conditioned by the laws of the given 'physical universe'.[2] It is a universe in which humanity can only thrive if some of its basic traits change, but these changes can most probably come about only by human action, 'natural' evolutionary processes being either too long-term or too catastrophic.

Here we can reformulate the crucial 'future-weaving' task of governance. *The most fundamental, most difficult, and also most risky task of governance is to facilitate, and partly bring about, the most urgent changes in humanity while preserving the human species, however improved, and improving its conditions; until, hopefully, creative forces in society bring about more fundamental changes – the nature of which is at present inconceivable.*

Let us assume for a moment that humanity had the instruments to change deliberately its basic attributes and create *homo superior* or *homo heinous*. It is hard to imagine a more horrifying power given to an ill-prepared sorcerer's apprentice. Even simple questions are hard to answer.

To take a relatively easy one: Should human beings have habits of obedience and group solidarity? The experience of the *Shoah* shows that if they do, ordinary persons can easily become mass killers.[3] The experiments of Stanley Milgram (Milgram, 1974) suggest that students can easily be induced to cause deliberate pain to others. With these examples in mind, one might well be tempted to eliminate group solidarity and/or (if the two can be separated) obedience habits from the recipe for *homo superior*.

Yet without such habits, human societies as we know or can envisage them would break down. Instead of occasional genocide, however terrible, we may

217

end up with a doomsday technology version of the war of all against all envisaged by Thomas Hobbes, or perhaps a world of monads as discussed by Gottfried Wilhelm Leibnitz, or some other unimaginable and unlivable future.

Fortunately, these are merely nightmares (or utopias?), because our ability to reshape human beings is as yet very limited – albeit increasing and therefore increasingly posing forbidding ethical and political dilemmas. The problem for the foreseeable future is how to use such limited capacities as we have to change ourselves in order to inculcate values and ways of thinking that may be regarded, hopefully with near consensus, as desirable and perhaps essential for human survival.[4] These include, for instance, less self-love, selfishness and readiness to use violence, and a greater sense of human solidarity, empathy with the destitute and suffering, and a dislike of violence. Such transformations are essential not only as compelling moral commands but also as practical prerequisites if humanity is to survive and thrive.

Human values and ways of thinking and behaving have in part, as mentioned, deep roots in evolution (or 'original sin' together with 'creation in the image of God', however literally or metaphorically the reader may wish to understand these profound images). Nevertheless, many of them are susceptible to change by relatively fast-working cultural influences, as history shows.

We do not know, and at present have no way of knowing, which human characteristics are rigidly programmed into our minds, and how far we are capable of learning, adjusting and changing. However, there is no doubt that many areas of behavior can be modified and that certain ways of feeling and reasoning are open to cultural influences. Furthermore, the human race is increasingly able to alter its own biology and psychology, and ultimately perhaps to control its evolution (Anderson, 1987; J. Kingdon, 1993).

As discussed, these needs and possibilities pose what is the most important and fundamental, but also the most problematic and dangerous higher-order task of governance: namely, to facilitate, control, and guide changes in the very bases of human existence, including bio-neurological and psycho-cultural structures, patterns, processes and potentials.

To move, however gingerly, in this direction a major phase transition in capacities to govern is needed. It is towards building up these capacities that the redesign proposals presented in this book are directed.

What is really needed is a quantum jump in the consciousness and values of humanity, but this is beyond deliberate human choice. Thinking that humanity needs a new 'Axial Age' does not make it happen. Given that it is beyond our collective moral and technical capacities to transform global values, we have no choice but to allow some fateful changes to occur, as it were, spontaneously, which is of the essence of the human condition. The earlier discussion of science as being largely beyond the reach of governance or other human guidance mechanisms is a case in point.

But such a fatalistic or deterministic view must be balanced by an understanding of history as opening up many plausible worlds, with deliberate human choice exerting a significant influence on the selection of the one to be realized (Hawthorn, 1991; McCall, 1994; for a different view, see Lloyd, 1993). Governance can and should fulfill main roles in such human choice.

The salient tasks of governance and their contexts can be summed up as follows. *Prophets, value creators, spiritual leaders, scientists and the like are essential for bringing about changes for the better in humanity. But their appearance and products are uncertain, their effects limited by 'hard-wired' attributes of humanity, and some of them may be servants of evil. Guiding and regulating interventions with basic characteristics of humanity therefore constitutes the ultimate 'future-weaving' task of governance, one that is essential but very difficult and dangerous. Some instruments for doing so are available, such as education and mass media. Much more radical instruments, permitting even the revising of human 'wiring' are emerging, and likely to become operational in the foreseeable future. Gearing governance – and societies and humanity as a whole – for this task should therefore start as soon as possible, one of the first and most crucial needs being serious consideration of the moral issues involved.*

Even a little progress toward improving critical capacities to govern is worthwhile, and may be enough to make the difference between self-destruction and survival with progress, until better ideas about what to do emerge or a quantum jump occurs. This is all the more urgent because of many ominous developments in 'post-modern' politics (Good and Velody, 1998). However, assuming the redesigns proposed in this book are useful, the next question is: Are they feasible?

Significant advances in capacities to govern have occurred in human history (as uniquely surveyed in Finer, 1997). Especially interesting for our purposes are the emergence in classical Greece (Meier, 1980, part C) of the idea of politics as a recognized domain of human life susceptible to deliberate shaping, and the development of statecraft in early China (Creel, 1970). In both cases crises provided the impetus to new conceptualizations of politics – the battle of Salamis in Greece (Euben, 1986) and the wars and devastation of the Warrior States in China.

As argued by J. Peter Euben, 'A good argument can be made that political theory was "born" and is reborn in times of cultural crisis; that its raison d'etre is the reconstitution of political discourse and life' (Euben, 1990, p. 127). This thesis can be supported by other instances, such as the reconstitution of law and science and the advent of novel forms of governance following the Black Death (Palmer, 1994, with context provided by Gottfried, 1983, chs 5–7) and the emergence of the modern state system at the 1648 Peace of Westphalia, after the Thirty Years War.

In the words of Merleau-Ponty (quoted in Whiteside, 1988, pp. 183–4), 'political action operates at the ambiguous frontier between freedom and facticity' and 'at certain moments ... nothing is absolutely fixed by the facts, and it is precisely our withdrawal or intervention that history awaits in order to take form'. Hopefully, we are at such an open moment of history, which provides opportunities for implementing radical governance redesigns – or otherwise the opportunity will be supplied by escalating failures and crises.

Grave socio-political and cultural crises may be conducive, and perhaps essential, to radical innovations in politics and governance. But there is no assurance that they will result in beneficial institutions and regimes, as illustrated by the victory of Nazism in the Weimar Republic (Bracher, 1978; Abraham, 1981). To increase the chances that crises will result in desirable innovations, promising ideas have to be prepared well in advance. But crises are only one factor out of many that may make governance redesign practical. Public pressure, visible governance failures and enlightened leaders can also bring about reforms, as was the case in the past and is happening, though inadequately, in the present.

Government redesigns meeting real needs should therefore be prepared, even when they seem not to be feasible, so as to be ready when radical governance restructuring becomes feasible – such as result from crisis or enlightened democratic rulership.

Reforms of government have frequently been proposed – sometimes attempted, occasionally implemented – and have often produced beneficial results, such as improving services for citizens. But ongoing governmental reforms – with some exceptions such as the further construction of the European Union – are too restricted (though high-sounding in rhetoric) to make much difference to governance capacities to shape the future. Hence the need for more innovative and radical redesign ideas and proposals.

Some of the redesigns proposed in this book are rather radical. Nevertheless, I am not satisfied that they are innovative enough to meet requirements. The trouble is that what appears to be practical may not be very useful; what appears to be useful may not be practical. And there is a scarcity of innovative ideas that are both powerful enough to upgrade critical capacities to govern and which may be feasible – either under prevailing conditions, or otherwise in special situations that may be realized in the foreseeable future.

Available experiences and literature, however interesting, contain few sufficiently innovative ideas on governance. Even when feasibility constraints are relaxed, and creative though impractical proposals are sought (with the proviso that they do not falsify human nature) it is very hard to find truly novel ideas on governance in contemporary thinking. Similarly, I failed to identify imaginative redesigns of governance in a rather large sample of futuristic writings, including science fiction. Imagined worlds that presume to be 'new' are in essence nothing more than extreme versions of well-known ideas, or of existing practices.

In pursuing such ambitious undertakings as inventing and developing new designs for capacities to govern, we must bear in mind that the fundamental material out of which governance is composed are human beings – as individuals and in different social configurations. This limits what is possible, but by upgrading the material as far as we can and, especially, by recombining it in new ways (Armstrong, 1989), it is possible to make substantial improvements to capacities to govern. Genuine 'reinvention of governance' and 'political engineering' (Ranney, 1976) are beyond our capabilities. Yet significant redesigns may be possible if we succeed in making a 'conceptual revolution' (Ball, Farr and Hanson, 1989; Thagard, 1992) in our thinking on governance.

The history of art offers a helpful metaphor (as suggested by Jacob Burckhardt's already mentioned discussion of the state and politics in the Renaissance as 'a work of art'), bringing out difficulties and potentials: even the extremes of Italian futurism were strongly influenced by 'primitivism'.[5] Similarly, modern governments have many 'primitive' elements carried over from the past,[6] such as: the importance of Big Men (Maryanski and Turner, 1992, pp. 112–19) and, occasionally, Big Women; relationships between rulers and advisers (Goldhamer, 1978); basic similarities in bureaucratic structures between early Chinese and Middle Eastern empires and modern states; some aspects of group decision processes with their tendency to error (Janis, 1982; Hart, 1990); some principal sources of power (Mann, 1986; 1993); and many more.

Despite constancy in basic human features and continuity of traditions, radical innovations – in the full sense of 'novelty proper' as proposed by Carl R. Hausmann (Hausmann, 1984) – have taken place in art. Similarly, significant innovations have occurred in governance since early states emerged. These include, for instance: mass democracy, empowerment of the people, division of functions, human rights, the rule of law, extensive use of experts,[7] and nowadays the new structures created by the European Union and the emergence of global governance. These examples provide hope for the future, but – taking into account the persistence of primitive elements in governance and the limited elasticity of human beings, groups and collectives that constitute the materials out of which governance is made – redesign, even on the non-revolutionary though partly radical scale proposed in this book, will not come easily. *We should not, therefore, expect too much, even from radical and well-thought-out governance reform. But if we try very hard, enough can probably be achieved to make a significant difference to the future of humanity.*

It is possible to take a darker view of the way in which essential governance redesigns will come about. Thinking, for a moment, the unthinkable (in line with Kahn, 1962), let us imagine that a so-called 'limited' nuclear war takes place, with, say, 50 million dead, many more injured, and large-scale ecological damage, though not such as to endanger human survival. If we picture for a moment such a nightmare, two questions arise: Would such a catastrophe bring about human learning, resulting in a better world, in which no such slaughter would ever happen again? And, assuming such learning does occur and brings about a new and better human world, is this an optimistic or a pessimistic scenario, given the record of human history?

I leave it to the reader to ponder these questions. The aims of governance redesign, as advocated in this book, are to try to provide a way of meeting aspirations and preventing serious damage without depending on such major catastrophe as a 'learning shock'. A second-best aim is to have redesign ideas ready in case serious failures of present governance create effective demand, and search for radical improvements.

There is basis for hope that some necessary governance redesigns may take place without the costs of catastrophe. The description by Tocqueville of the emerging USA written in 1840 fits well the situation of the world today:

> The society of the modern world has but just come into existence. Time has not yet shaped it into perfect form: the great revolution by which it has been created is not yet over: and amid the occurrences of our time it is almost impossible to discern what will pass away with the revolution itself, and what will survive its close. The world which is rising into existence is still half encumbered by the remains of the world which is waning into decay; and amidst the vast perplexity of human affairs, none can say how much of ancient institutions and former manners will remain, or how much will completely disappear (quoted in Commager, 1993, p. 111).

Much work must be done; proposed redesigns have to be evaluated and improved; concrete governance situations have to be studied, so as to identify appropriate needs and possibilities; redesign suggestions have to be put to the tests of different realities; and, most important of all, additional and better governance redesigns must be invented and developed.[8] But these tasks are not impossible.

In a recently published letter C. G. Jung wrote: 'It demands concentrated attention, much mental work and, above all, patience, the rarest thing in our restless and crazy times' (*International Herald Tribune*, 20–21 November 1993, p. 4). He was referring to the search for the meaning of life; but his admonition also applies to upgrading capacities to govern.

I am very frustrated with my own inadequate creativity. But Plato, a genius in all respects who did invent radically new governance ideas, also expressed discouragement: 'All existing states are badly governed and the conditions of the laws practically incurable without some miraculous remedy and the assistance of fortune' (*Seventh Epistle*, quoted in Euben, 1990, p. 240, n. 4).

It is my hope that this book may at least stimulate others to do better in upgrading crucial governance capacities to 'weave the future'. This is a summons that should be taken up by the most creative minds.

NOTES

1. The Hungarian country gentleman Imre Madach published in 1862 a dramatic poem *The Tragedy of Men*, which is regarded by some critics as comparable to works by Milton, Goethe, Byron and Ibsen. It has Adam move through different periods of history with Lucifer, raising issues concerning the meaning of human existence, with its desperation and hopes. For a new English translation, see Madach, 1993.

2. Let me mention the speculation by a leading astrophysicist that in the future a high-tech humanity may be able to produce new physical universes with quite different laws of nature from ours; within the higher-order laws of an all-encompassing 'cosmos' which includes 'multiverses', that is a plurality of very different universes of which ours is only one (Rees, 1999, pp. 130, 150–4). But, if at all, this is in the very distant future.

3. This is dramatically brought out in a study of a reserve police battalion, not an SS 'elite' unit, as described in Browning, 1992, to be read in conjunction with Haas, 1988, which shows the relative ease with which widely held conceptions of 'good' and 'evil' can be reengineered. I leave aside the conjectures on historic propensities in Germany leading to the *Shoah*, as claimed in hotly debated Goldhagen, 1996.

4. For example, see Laszlo, 1977, 1983; Laszlo *et al.*, 1977; and Hans Küng, 1991. Additional value changes that may be desirable are illustrated by the notion of 'euergetism' (that is, a sense of duty to use riches for the public good and public pressure to do so, such as prevailed in Hellenistic and Roman cities, see Veyne, 1990).

5. As demonstrated at the exhibitions at the Palazzo Grassi in Venice in 1986 (see Hulten, 1987) and at the Museum of Modern Art in New York in 1984 (see Rubin, 1984). For another kind of insight into the continuity of human 'wiring' and cultures underpinning social institutions, see Dayagi-Mendels, 1989.

6. It is doubtful how far so-called 'primate politics' is relevant (see Schubert and Masters, 1991). Many treatments of the continuation of our animal heritage in human institutions, including governance, underrate the break between higher primates and human civilizations (Diamond, 1991; Maryanski and Turner, 1992). 'Sociobiological' explanations of human nature are quite simplistic in their essence, despite their impressive scientific apparatus (see Wilson, 1975, 1978). Nonetheless, governance is limited by human nature, as conditioned by evolution, and governance itself is in part shaped by quasi-evolutionary processes (Vanhanen, 1992).

7. Regarded by some scholars as a 'revolution', see MacDonagh, 1958, as further discussed in MacLeod, 1988. Gascoigne, 1998 is also interesting in this context.

8. Despite my best efforts, some of the redesign proposals may be too biased by my Western background to be applicable to governance rooted in other cultures. Asian countries, for example, may require partially different approaches.

References and Further Reading

This list includes all the references given in the text and notes and some closely related publications.

Abraham, D. (1981) *The Collapse of the Weimar Republic: Political Economy and Crisis*, Princeton: Princeton University Press.

Ackoff, R. L. and F. E. Emery (1972) *On Purposeful Systems*, Chicago: Aldine Atherton.

Aderet, A. (1997) *From Destruction to Restoration: The Mode of Yavneh in Re-Establishment of the Jewish People*, Second Revised Edition, in Hebrew. Jerusalem: The Magnes Press.

Ager, D. (1993) *The New Catastrophism: The Importance of the Rare Event in Geological History*, Cambridge, UK: Cambridge University Press.

Akzin, B. (1962) 'The Revival of Monarchy'. *Prognosis*, No. 13, 1 June. First published in French in *Futuribles*, Paris: S.E.D.E.I.S.

Allison, G. T. *et al.* (1996) *Avoiding Nuclear Anarchy: Containing the Threat of Loose Russian Nuclear Weapons and Fissile Material*, Cambridge, MA: MIT Press.

Almond, G. A. and S. Verba. (1963) *The Civic Culture: Political Attitudes and Democracy in Five Nations*, Princeton: Princeton University Press.

Almond, G. A., S. C. Flanagan and R. J. Mundt, eds (1973) *Crisis, Choice, and Change: Historic Studies of Political Development*, Boston: Little, Brown.

Almond, G. A. and S. Verba, eds (1980) *The Civic Culture Revisited*, Boston: Little, Brown.

Amman Jr, A. C. (1992) *Administrative Law in a Global Era*, Ithaca, NY: Cornell University Press.

Anderson, W. T. (1987) *To Govern Evolution: Further Adventures of the Political Animal*, Boston: Harcourt Brace Jovanovich.

Anechiarico, F. and J. B. Jacobs (1997) *The Pursuit of Absolute Integrity: How Corruption Control Makes Government Ineffective*, Chicago: University of Chicago Press.

Angelotti, T. (1993) *Metropolis 2000: Planning, Poverty and Politics*, London: Routledge.

Annan K. A. (2000) *We The People: The Role of the United Nations in the 21st Century*, New York: United Nations. (www.un.org/millennium/sg/report).

Annan, N. (1995) *Changing Enemies: The Defeat and Regeneration of Germany*, London: Harper-Collins.

Apollon, W. (1996) *Lacan, Politics, Aesthetics*, Albany, NY: State University of New York Press.

Archibugi, D. and D. Held, eds (1995) *Cosmopolitan Democracy: An Agenda for a New World Order*, Cambridge, UK: Polity Press.

Argyris, C. (1992) *On Organizational Learning*, Oxford: Basil Blackwell.

Armstrong, D. M. (1989) *A Combinational Theory of Possibility*, Cambridge, UK: Cambridge University Press.

Ashby, W. R. (1957) *An Introduction to Cybernetics*, New York: Wiley.

Asimov, I. (1993) *Forward The Foundation*, New York: Doubleday.

Attfield, R. and B. Wilkins, eds (1992) *International Justice and the Third World: Studies in the Philosophy of Development*, London: Routledge.

Audi, R. ed. (1999) *The Cambridge Dictionary of Philosophy*. Second Edition, Cambridge, UK: Cambridge University Press.

Ayittey, G. B. N. (1992) *Africa Betrayed*, New York: St. Martin's Press.

Backscheider, P. R. (1993) *Spectacular Politics: Theatrical Power and Mass Politics in Early Modern England*, Baltimore, MD: Johns Hopkins University Press.

Ball, T., J. Farr, and R. L. Hanson, eds (1988) *Political Innovation and Conceptual Change*, Cambridge, UK: Cambridge University Press.

Balke, F. (1996) *Der Staat nach seinem Ende: Die Versuchung Carl Schmitts*, München: Wilhelm Fink.

Baron, J. (1998) *Judgment Misguided: Intuition and Error in Public Decision Making*, New York: Oxford.

Bartelson, J. (1995) *The Genealogy of Sovereignty*, Cambridge, UK: Cambridge University Press.

Barzun, J. (2000) *From Dawn to Decadence: 500 Years of Western Cultural Life – 1500 to the Present*, New York: HarperCollins.

Bauer, H. H. (1994) *Scientific Literacy and the Myth of the Scientific Method*, Urbana, IL: University of Illinois Press.

Beardsworth, R. (1996) *Derrida & the Political*, London: Routledge.

Beer, S. (1966) *Decision and Control: The Meaning of Operational Research and Management Cybernetics*, London: Wiley.

Beer, S. (1979) *The Heart of Enterprise*, London: Wiley.

Beer, S. (1981) *Brain of the Firm*, second edition. London: Wiley.

Bekke, H, A. G. M., J. L. Perry, and T. A. J. Toonen (1996) *Civil Service Systems in Comparative Perspective*, Bloomington, IN: Indiana University Press.

Belenky, M. F. *et al.* (1986) *Women's Way of Knowing*, New York: Basic Books.

Bell, D. (1996) *The Cultural Contradictions of Capitalism: With a New Afterword by the Author*, Twentieth Anniversary Edition. New York: Basic Books.

Berry, M. E. (1982) *Hideyoshi*, Cambridge, MA: Harvard University Press.

Bertelsmann Foundation (1993) *Carl Bertelsmann Prize 1993: Democracy and Efficiency in Local Government*, vol. I, *Documentation of the International Research*, Gütersloh, Germany: Bertelsmann Foundation Publishers.

Bicchieri, C. (1993) *Rationality and Co-ordination*, Cambridge, UK: Cambridge University Press.

Binde, J. (1997) 'L'éthique du Futur: Pourquoi Faut-il Retrouver Le temps Perdu?'. *Futuribles*, No. 226. December, pp. 19–40.

Bjoergo, T. and B. Witte, eds (1993) *Racist Violence in Europe*, New York: St. Martin's Press.

Blackstone, T. and W. Plowden (1988) *Inside the Think Tank: Advising the Cabinet, 1971–1983*, London: Heinemann.

Bloch, E. (1995) *The Principle of Hope*, Cambridge, MA: MIT Press. (First published in German in 1959).

Blockmans, W. (1997) *A History of Power in Europe*, Antwerp: Fonds Mercator.

Blondel, J. (1980) *World Leaders: Heads of Government in the Postwar Period*, London: Sage.

Bloom, H. (1995) *The Lucifer Principle: A Scientific Expedition into the Forces of History*, New York: The Atlantic Monthly Press.

Bloom, H. (1995) *The Western Canon: The Books and School of the Ages*, New York: Riverhead Books.

Bloom, H. (1998) *Shakespeare: The Invention of the Human*, New York: Riverhead Books.

Bogdanor, V. (1995) *The Monarchy and the Constitution*, Oxford: Oxford University Press.

Bohman, J. (1996) *Public Deliberation: Pluralism, Complexity, and Democracy*, Cambridge, MA: MIT Press.

Bohrer, K. H. (1983) *Die Ästhetik des Schreckens: Die pessimistische Romantik und Ernst Jüngers Frühwerk*, Frankfurt am Main: Ullstein Materialien.

Boime, A. (1998) *The Unveiling of the National Icons: A Plea for Patriotic Iconoclasm in a Nationalist Era*, Cambridge, UK: Cambridge University Press.

Bok, S. (1979) *Lying: Moral Choice in Public and Private Life*, New York: Vintage Books.

Bourdieu, P. (1996) *The State Nobility: Elite Schools in the Field of Power*, Cambridge: Polity Press. (First published in French in 1989).

Botkin, D. (1990) *Discordant Harmonies: A New Ecology for the Twenty-First Century*, New York: Oxford University Press.

Bovens, M. and P, 'T Hart (1996) *Understanding Policy Fiascoes*, Brunswick, NJ: Transaction.

Bovens, M. (1997) *The Quest for Responsibility: Accountability and Citizenship in Complex Organisations*, Cambridge, UK: Cambridge University Press.

Bracher, K. D. (1978) *Die Auflösung der Weimarer Republik*, Düsseldorf: Droste.

Bramall, C. (1993) *In Praise of Maoist Economic Planning: Living Standards and Economic Development in Sichuan since 1931*, Oxford: Oxford University Press.

Brantlinger, P, (1983) *Bread and Circuses: Theories of Mass Culture as Social Decay*, Ithaca: Cornell University Press.

Braudel, F. (1980) *On History*, Chicago: University of Chicago Press.

Braudel, F. (1988) *The Identity of France. Volume I: History and Environment*, London: Collins.

Braudel, F. (1990) *The Identity of France. Volume II: People and Production*, London: Collins.

Brecht, A. (1978) *Kann die Demokratie Überleben: Die Herausforderungen der Zukunft und die Regierungsformen der Gegenwart*, Stuttgart: Deutsche Verlags-Anstalt.

Breyer, S. (1993) *Breaking the Vicious Circle*, Cambridge, MA: Harvard University Press.

Briggs, A. and D. Snowman, eds (1996) *Fins de Siècle: How Centuries End 1400–2000*, New Haven: Yale University Press.

Brint, M. (1991) *A Genealogy of Political Culture*, Boulder, CO: Westview.

Broder, D. S. (2000) *Democracy Derailed: Initiative Campaigns and the Power of Money*, New York: Harcourt.

Broembsen, F. V. (1999) *The Sovereign Self: Towards a Phenomenology of Self-Experiencing*, Northvale, NJ: Jason Aronson.

Brown, C. (1995) *Serpents in the Sand: Essays on the Nonlinear Nature of Politics and Human Destiny*, Ann Arbor: University of Michingan Press.

Browning, C. R. (1992) *Ordinary Men: Reserve Police Battalion 101 and the Final Solution in Poland*, New York: HarperCollins.

Brunnson, N. and J. P. Olsen (1993) *The Reforming Organization*, London: Routledge.

Bruno, M. (1993) *Crisis, Stabilization, and Economic Reform: Therapy by Consensus*, Oxford: Clarendon.

Buckler, S. (1993) *Dirty Hands: The Problem of Political Morality*, Aldershot, UK: Avebury.

Bückmann, G. (1964) *Geflügelte Worte*, Berlin: Haude & Spener'sche Verlagsbuchhandlung.

Budzieszewski, J. (1986) *The Resurrection of Nature: Political Theory and the Human Character*, Ithaca: Cornell University Press.

Budzieszewski, J. (1988) *The Nearest Coast of Darkness: A Vindication of the Politics of Virtues*, Ithaca: Cornell University Press.

Buisseret, D., ed. (1993) *Monarchs, Ministers, and Maps: The Emergence of Cartography as a Tool of Governance in Early Modern Europe*, Chicago: University of Chicago Press.

Burke, T. P. (1993) *No Harm: Ethical Principles for the Economy*, New York: Paragon House.

Butler, D., A. Adonis and T. Travers (1994) *Failure in British Government: The Politics of the Poll Tax*, Oxford: Oxford University Press.

Buzan, B. and G. Segal (1998) *Anticipating the Future: Twenty Millennia of Human Progress*, London: Simon and Schuster.

Cahill, T. (1999) *Desire of the Everlasting Hills: The World Before and After Jesus*, New York: Nan A. Talese Doubleday.

Calabresi, G. and P. Bobbit (1979) *Tragic Choice*, New York: Norton.

Canetti, E. (1960) *Masse und Macht*, Hildesheim: Claasen.

Carmel, H., ed. (1999) *Intelligence for Peace: The Role of Intelligence in Times of Peace*, London: Cass.

Carnegie Commission on Preventing Deadly Conflict (1997) *Preventing Deadly Conflict: Final Report*, New York: Carnegie Corporation.

Carrel, L. F. (1999) *Strategische Führungsausbildung: Concept 1999–2003*, Bern: Schweizerische Bundeskanzlei.

Cerney, P. G. (1990) *The Changing Architecture of Politics: Agency and the Future of the State*, London: Sage.

Chanteur, J. (1992) *From War to Peace*. Boulder, CO: Westview Press. First published in French in 1989.

Cherniak, C. (1986) *Minimal Rationality*, Cambridge, MA: MIT Press.

Chirot, D. (1996) *Modern Tyrants: The Power and Prevalence of Evil in Our Age*, Princeton: Princeton University Press.

Chomsky, N. (1994) *World Orders Old and New*, New York: Columbia University Press.

Christians, C., J. P. Ferre, and P. M. Fackler. (1993) *A Social Ethics of News*, New York: Oxford University Press.

Chua, B. (1995) *Communitarian Ideology and Democracy in Singapore*, London: Routledge.

CIA (2000) *Global Trends 2015: A Dialogue About the Future With Nongovernment Experts* (IC 20000-02, http://wwwe.cia.gov/publications/globaltrends2015).

Cilliers, P. (1998) *Complexity and Postmodernity: Understanding Complex Systems*, London: Routledge.

Clark, G. and L. B. Sohm (1966) *World Order Through World Law*, 3rd enlarged edition. Cambridge, MA: Harvard University Press.

Cleveland, H. (1993) *Birth of a New World: An Open Moment for International Leadership*, San Francisco: Jossey-Bass.

Clinton, D. (1993) *The Two Faces of National Interest*, Baton Rouge, LA: Louisiana State University Press.

Cobb, R. W. and M. H. Ross, eds (1997) *Cultural Strategies of Agenda Denial*, Lawrence: University Press of Kansas.

Codevilla, A. (1992) *Informing Statecraft: Intelligence for a New Century*, New York: Free Press.

Cohen, A. A. (1993) *The Tremendum: A Theological Interpretation of the Holocaust*, New York: Continuum.

Collini, S., D. Winch and J. Burrow. (1983) *That Noble Science of Politics: A Study in Nineteenth-Century Intellectual History*, Cambridge, UK: Cambridge University Press.

Collins, S. L. (1989) *From Divine Cosmos to Sovereign State: An Intellectual History of Consciousness and the Idea of Order in Renaissance England*, Oxford: Oxford University Press.

Comfort, L. K., ed. (1988) *Managing Disaster: Strategies and Policy Perspectives*, Durham, NC: Duke University Press,.

Commager, H. S. (1993) *Commager on Tocqueville*, Columbia, MO: University of Missouri Press.

Commission on America's National Interests (1996) *America's National Interests*, Cambridge, MA: Center for Science and International Affairs, John F. Kennedy School of Government, Harvard University.

Commission on Global Governance, Report of the (1995) *Our Global Neighbourhood*, Oxford: Oxford University Press.

Connor, W. R. (1984) *Thucydides*, Princeton: Princeton University Press.

Cooper, R. (1996) *The Post-Modern State and the World Order*, London: DEMOS.

Corkey, J. *et al.*, eds (1998) *Management of Public Service Reforms: A Comparative Review of Experiences in the Management of Programmes of Reform of the Administrative Arm of Central Government*, Brussels: International Institute of Administrative Sciences.

Cowen, J. S. (1989) *Kalila Wa Dimna: An Animal Allegory of the Mongol Court*, New York: Oxford University Press.

Creel, H. G. (1970) *The Origins of Statecraft in China. Volume I: The Western Chou Empire*, Chicago: University of Chicago Press.

Creveld, M. V. (1991) *The Transformation of War*, New York: Free Press.

Creveld. M. V. (1999) *The Rise and Decline of the State*, Cambridge, UK: Cambridge University Press.

Crossette, B. (2000) 'Wider Powers Are Urged For Peace Forces of UN', *International Herald Tribune*, August 24, pp. 1 and 4.

Crossman, R. (1975–1977) *The Diaries of a Cabinet Minister*, 3 vols. London: Hamish Hamilton.

Crozier, M., S. P. Huntington, and J. Watanuki (1975) *The Crisis of Democracy: Report on the Governability of Democracy to the Trilateral Commission*, New York: New York University Press.

Daalder, I. H. and M. E. O'Hanlon (2000) *Winning Ugly: NATO's War to Save Kosovo*, Washington, DC: The Brookings Institution.

Dahl, R. A. (1999) *On Democracy*, New Haven, CO: Yale University Press.

Dasgupta, P. (1993) *An Inquiry into Well-Being and Destitution*, Oxford: Oxford University Press.

Davidson, B. (1992) *The Black Man's Burden: Africa and the Curse of the Nation-State*, New York: Times Books.

Davies, A. F. (1980) *Skills, Outlooks and Passions: A Psychoanalytic Contribution to the Study of Politics*, Cambridge, UK: Cambridge University Press.

Dayagi-Mendels, M. (1989) *Perfumes and Cosmetics in the Ancient World*, Jerusalem: The Israel Museum.

Debray, R. (1994) *Charles De Gaulle: Futurist of the Nation*, London: Verso. First published in French in 1994.

deLeon, P. (1993) *Thinking About Political Corruption*, Armonk, NY: M.E. Sharpe.

Dennet, D. C. (1984) *Elbow Room: The Varieties of Free Will Worth Wanting*, Oxford: Clarendon Press.

Dermandt, A. (1978) *Metaphern für Geschichte: Sprachbilder und Gleichnisse im Historisch-Politischen Denken*, Munich: C.H. Beck.

Dery, D. (1984) *Problem Definition in Policy Analysis*, Lawrence: University Press of Kansas.

Descombes, V. (1993) *The Barometer of Modern Reason: On the Philosophies of Current Events*, New York: Oxford University Press. Translated from French.

Deuchler, M. (1993) *The Confucian Transformation of Korea: A Study of Society and Ideology*, Cambridge, MA: Harvard University Press.

Deutsch, C. W. (1969) *The Nerves of Government*, New York: Free Press.

Diamond, J. (1991) *The Rise and Fall of the Third Chimpanzee: How Our Animal Heritage Affects the Way We Live*, London: Radius.

Diamond, J. (1997) *Guns, Germs and Steel: A Short History of Everybody for the Last 13,000 Years*, London: Vintage.

Dietl, H. (1993) *Institutionen und Zeit*, Tübingen: J.C.B. Mohr.

Dilenschneider, R. L. (1992) *A Briefing for Leaders: Communication as the Ultimate Exercise of Power*, New York: HarperBusiness.

Dogan, M., ed. (1989) *Pathways to Power: Selecting Rulers in Pluralistic Democracies*, Boulder, CO: Westview Press.

Doran, C. F. (1991) *Systems in Crisis: New Imperative of High Politics at Century's End*, Cambridge: Cambridge University Press.

Douglas, M. (1987) *How Institutions Think*, London: Routledge and Kegan Paul.

Downs, G. and D. Rocke (1995) *Optimal Imperfection? Domestic Uncertainty and Institutions in International Relations*, Princeton: Princeton University Press.

Drews, R. (1993) *The End of the Bronze Age: Changes in Warfare and the Catastrophe of ca 1200 BC*, Princeton: Princeton University Press.

Dreyfus, H. L. and P. Rabinow (1983) *Michael Foucault: Beyond Structuralism and Hermeneutics*, second edition. Chicago: University of Chicago Press.

Dror, Y. (1980) *Crazy States: A Counterconventional Strategic Problem*, updated edition. Millwood, NY: Kraus Reprints.

Dror, Y. (1983) *Public Policymaking Reexamined*, enlarged edition. Brunswick, NJ: Transaction Books.

Dror, Y. (1984) 'Required Breakthroughs in Think Tanks'. *Policy Sciences*, Vol. 16, pp. 199–225.

Dror, Y. (1988a) 'Advanced Workshops in Policy Analysis for Senior Decision Makers: Lessons from Experience', in: S. Mailick, S. Hobermas and S. J. Wall, eds, *The Practice of Management Development*, New York: Prager, pp. 15–161.

Dror, Y. (1988b) *Policymaking Under Adversity*, paperback edition. Brunswick, NJ: Transaction Books.

Dror, Y. (1988c) 'Uncertainty: Coping With It and With Political Feasibility', in: H. J. Miser and E. S. Quade, eds, *Handbook of Systems Analysis: Craft Issues and Procedural Choices*, pp 247–281. New York: North-Holland.

Dror, Y. (1993) 'School for Rulers', in: K. B. De Greene, ed., *A Systems-Based Approach to Policymaking*, Boston: Kluwer Academic Publisher, ch. 5.

Dror, Y. (1995) 'Israeli Gambles with History: The Lavi Combat Airplane and the Peace Process with the PLO'. In: H. J. Miser, ed., *Handbook of Systems Analysis: Cases*, pp. 239–268. London: Wiley.

Dror Y. (1997a) 'Delta-type Senior Civil Service for the 21st Century', *International Review of Administrative Sciences*, Vol. 63, No. 1 (March), pp. 7–23.

Dror, Y. (1997b) 'Enhancing Professionalism in Public Policy Planning: The Making of Highly Qualified Creative and Conscientious Policy Advisors'. *UN Document, Paper No. 3, Regional Conference on Public Service in Transition*, Thessaloniki, Greece, 17–20 November.

Dror, Y. (in preparation a) *The Superior Ruler: A Mirror for Political Weavers of the Future*.

Dror, Y. (in preparation b) *Policy Reflection: A Workbook In Statecraft Professionalism*.

Duemler, D. G. (1993) *Bringing Life to the Stars*, Lanham, MD: University Press of America.

Dumont, L. (1981) *Homo Hierarchicus: The Caste System and Its Implications*, revised edition, Chicago: University of Chicago Press.

Dunn, D. H., ed. (1996) *Diplomacy at the Highest Level: The Evolution of International Summitry*, London: Macmillan, 1996.

Dunn, J. (1993) *Western Political Theory in the Face of the Future*, second edition. Cambridge, UK: Cambridge University Press.

Dunn, W. N. (1994) *Public Policy Analysis: An Introduction*, second edition. Englewood Cliffs, NJ: Prentice-Hall.

Dustar, F. (1996) *Abschied von der Macht: Demokratie und Verantwortung*, Frankfurt am Main: Fischer.

Dworkin, R. (1996) 'The Curse of American Politics'. *The New York Review of Books*, 17 October, pp. 19–24.

Edelman, M. (1964) *The Symbolic Uses of Politics*, Urbana: University of Illinois Press.

Edelman, M. (1971) *Politics as Symbolic Action: Mass Arousal and Quiescence*, New York: Academic Press.

Edelman, M. (1988) *Constructing the Political Spectrum*, Chicago: University of Chicago Press.

Eden, R. (1983) *Political Leadership and Nihilism: A Study of Weber and Nietzsche*, Gainesville, FL: University Presses of Florida.

Edmunds, L. (1975) *Chance and Intelligence in Thucydides*, Cambridge, MA: Harvard University Press.

Eisenstadt, S. N. (1963) *The Political Systems of Empires: The Rise and Fall of the Historic Bureaucratic Societies*, New York: Free Press.

Eisenstadt, S. N., ed. (1986) *The Origins and Diversity of Axial Age Civilizations*, Albany: State University of New York Press.

Eisenstadt, S. N. (1996) *Japanese Civilization: A Comparative View*, Chicago: University of Chicago Press.

Eisenstadt, S. N. (1999a) *Paradoxes of Democracy: Fragility, Continuity and Change*, Philadelphia: Johns Hopkins University Press.

Eisenstadt, S. N. (1999b) *Fundamentalism, Sectarianism, and Revolution: The Jacobin Dimension of Modernity*, Cambridge, UK: Cambridge University Press.

Elboim-Dror, R. (1993) *Yesterday's Tomorrow: Vol. I: Zionist Utopias; Vol. II: An Anthology of Zionist Utopias*, Jerusalem: Yad Izhak Ben-Zvi Institute and Bialik Institute. In Hebrew, English version in preparation.

Elgie, R. E. (1993) *The Role of the Prime Minister in France, 1981–91*, London: Macmillan.

Elias, N. (1969) *The Court Society*, Oxford: Blackwell.

Elias, N. (1978) *The Civilizing Process. Vol. I: The History of Manners*, Oxford: Basil Blackwell.

Elias, N. (1982) *The Civilizing Process. Vol. II: State Formation and Civilization*, Oxford: Basic Blackwell.

Eliasoph, N. (1998) *Avoiding Politics: How Americans Produce Apathy in Everyday Life*, Cambridge, UK: Cambridge University Press.

Elkins, D. J. (1995) *Beyond Sovereignty: Territory and Political Economy in the Twenty-First Century*, Toronto: University of Toronto Press.

Elster, J. (1984) *Ulysses and the Sirens*, revised edition. Cambridge, UK: Cambridge University Press.

Elster, J. ed. (1986) *The Multiple Self*, Cambridge, UK: Cambridge University Press.

Elster, J. (1993) *Local Justice: How Institutions Allocate Scarce Goods and Necessary Burdens*, Cambridge, UK: Cambridge University Press.

Elster, J., ed. (1998) *Deliberative Democracy*, Cambridge, UK: Cambridge University Press.

Elster, J. (2000) *Ulysses Unbound*, Cambridge, UK: Cambridge University Press.

Elster, J. and J. E. Roemer, eds (1991) *Interpersonal Comparisons of Well-Being*, Cambridge, UK: Cambridge University Press.

Elster, J., C. Offe and U. Preuss (1998) *Institutional Design in Post-communist Societies: Rebuilding the Ship at Sea*, Cambridge, UK: Cambridge University Press.

Ericsson, K. A. and J. Smith, eds (1991) *Towards a General Theory of Expertise: Prospects and Limits*, New York: Cambridge University Press.

Erlanger, S. (2000) 'Hear the "Voices of the People", Havel Implores World Bodies'. *International Herald Tribune*, 23 August, p. 6.

Ester, P., L. Halman and R. de Morr, eds (1993) *The Individualizing Society: Value Change in Europe and North America*, Tilburg, The Netherlands: Tilburg University Press.

Etheredge, L. S. (1985) *Can Governments Learn? American Foreign Policy and Central American Revolutions*, New York: Pergamon.

Etzioni, A. (1968) *The Active Society: A Theory of Societal and Political Processes*, New York: Free Press.

Etzioni, A. (1988) *The Moral Dimension: Toward a New Economics*, New York: Free Press.

Etzioni, A. (1993) *The Spirit of Community: Rights, Responsibilities, and the Communitarian Agenda*, New York: Crown.

Etzioni, A. (1996) *The New Golden Rule: Community and Morality in a Democratic Society*, New York: Basic Books.

Euben, J. P. (1986) 'The Battle of Salamis and the Origins of Political Theory'. *Political Theory*, Vol. 14, No. 3, pp. 359–90.

Euben, J. P. ed. (1986) *Greek Tragedy and Political Theory*, Berkeley: University of California Press.

Euben, J. P. (1988) 'The Political Science of Political Corruption', in T. Ball, J. Farr and R. L. Hanson, eds, *Political Innovation and Conceptual Change*, Cambridge, UK: Cambridge University Press, pp. 220–46.

Euben, J. P. (1990) *The Tragedy of Political Theory: The Road Not Taken*, Princeton: Princeton University Press.

Evans, P. B., H. K. Jacobson and R. D. Putnam, eds (1993) *Double-Edged Diplomacy: International Bargaining and Domestic Politics*, Berkeley: University of California Press.

Fackenheim, E. L. (1994) *To Mend the World: Foundations of Post-Holocaust Jewish Thought*, Bloomington: Indiana University Press.

Fairbanks, M. S. L. (1997) *Plowing the Sea: Nurturing the Hidden Sources of Growth in the Developing World*, Boston: Harvard Business School Press.

Falk, R. A. (1975) *A Study of Future Worlds*, New York: Free Press.

Falk R. (1999) *Predatory Globalization: A Critique*, Oxford: Blackwell.

Falk, R. A., R. C. Johansen, and S. S. Kim, eds (1993) *The Constitutional Foundations of World Peace*, Albany: State University of New York Press.

Featherstone, M., ed. (1990) *Global Culture: Nationalism, Globalization and Modernity*, London: Sage.

Ferguson, N., ed. (1997) *Virtual History: Alternatives and Counterfactuals*, London: Picador.

Ferguson, N. (1998) *The Pity of War*, London: Penguin.

Ferguson, T. (1995) *Golden Rule: The Investment Theory of Party Competition and the Logic of Money-Driven Political Systems*, Chicago: University of Chicago Press.

Fernandez-Santamaria, J. A. (1983) *Reason of State and Statecraft in Spanish Political Thought, 1595–1640*, New York: University Press of America.

Fest, J., ed. (1997) *Die Grossen Stifter: Lebensbilder-Zeitbilder*, Berlin: Siedler.

Fil, T. (1997) *Gestalten des Utopischen: Zur Sozialpragmatik kollektiver Vorstellungen*, Konstanz: Universitätsverlag Konstanz.

Finer, S. E. (1997) *The History of Government*, Three Volumes. Oxford: Oxford University Press.

Fishkin, J. S. (1991) *Democracy and Deliberation: New Directions for Democratic Reform*, New Haven: Yale University Press.

Fleck, D. C. (1993) *Go! Die Eko-Diktatur*, Hamburg: Rasch und Roehring.

Fleisher, C. H. (1986) *Bureaucrat and Intellectual in the Ottoman Empire: The Historian Mustafa Ali (1541–1600)*, Princeton: Princeton University Press.

Foot, P. (1978) *Virtues and Vices and Other Essays in Moral Philosophy*, Berkeley: University of California Press.

Forde, S, (1989) *The Ambition to Rule: Alcibiades and the Politics of Imperialism in Thucydides*, Ithaca: Cornell University Press.

Forrester, J. W. (1969) *Urban Dynamics*, Cambridge, MA: MIT Press.

Freidel, D., L. Schele and J. Parker. (1995) *Maya Cosmos: Three Thousand Years of the Shaman's Path*, New York: Quill.

French, P. A., T. E. Uehling, Jr, and H. Wettstein, eds (1988) *Midwest Studies in Philosophy* Vol. XIII: *Ethical Theory: Character and Virtue*, Notre Dame, IN: University of Notre Dame Press.

Friedman, M. and R. Friedman (1984) *The Tyranny of the Status Quo*, New York: Harcourt Brace.

Friedman, T. L. (2000) *The Lexus and the Olive Tree*, New York: Bantam Doubleday Bell.

Fromm, E. (1960) *The Fear of Freedom*, London: Routledge.

Frost, M. (1996) *Ethics in International Relations: A Constitutive Theory*, Cambridge, UK: Cambridge University Press.

Fukuyama, F. (1992) *The End of History and The Last Man*, New York: Free Press.

Fukuyama, F. (1995) *Trust: The Social Virtues and the Creation of Prosperity*, New York: Free Press.

Fuller, G. E. (1991) *The Democracy Trap: Perils of the Post-Cold War World*, New York: Dutton.

Gamson, W. A. (1993) *Talking Politics*, Cambridge, UK: Cambridge University Press.

Gardner, H. (1993) *Frames of Mind: The Theory of Multiple Intelligences*, New York: Basic Books. First published 1983.

Gardner H. (1995) *Leading Minds: An Anatomy of Leadership*, New York: Basic Books.

Gascoigne, J. (1998) *Science in the Service of Empire: Joseph Banks, the British State and the Uses of Science in the Age of Revolution*, Cambridge, UK: Cambridge University Press.

Gasset, J. O. y. (1985) *The Revolt of the Masses*, Notre Dame, IN: University of Notre Dame Press. First published in Spanish in 1929.

Gaucher, M. (1997) *The Disenchantment of the World: A Political History of Religion*, Princeton: Princeton University Press.

Gay, P. (1993) *The Cultivation of Hatred: The Bourgeois Experience: Victoria to Freud*, New York: Norton.

Geertz, C. (1973) *The Interpretation of Culture*, New York: Basic Books.

Gellman, B. (2000) 'Death Watch: The Belated Global Response to AIDS in Africa' *The Washington Post*, 5 July.

Gellner, E. (1988) *Plough, Sword and Book: The Structure of Human History*, Chicago: University of Chicago Press.

Gelven, M. (1991) *Why Me? A Philosophical Inquiry into Fate*, DeKalb, IL: Northern Illinois University Press.

George, R. P. (1993) *Making Men Moral: Civil Liberties and Public Morality*, Oxford: Clarendon Press.

Gerber, E. R. (1999) *The Populist Paradox*, Princeton: Princeton University Press.

Gernet, J. (1996) *A History of Chinese Civilization*, second edition. Cambridge: Cambridge University Press.

Gershuny, J. (1978) *After Industrial Society? The Emerging Self-service Economy*, Atlantis Highlands, NJ: Humanities Press.

Gharajedaghi, J. (1999) *Systems Thinking: Managing Chaos and Complexity – A Platform for Designing Business Architecture*, Boston: Butterworh Heinemann.

Giddens, A. (1984) *The Constitution of Society: Outline of the Theory of Structuration*, Cambridge: Polity Press.

Giddens, A. (1999) *The Third Way: The Renewal of Social Democracy*, Cambridge: Polity Press.

Giddens, A. (2000a) *The Third Way and Its Critics*, Cambridge: Polity Press.

Giddens, A. (2000b) *Runaway World: How Globalization is Reshaping Our Lives*, London: Routledge.

Gigerenzer G. *et al.* (1989) *The Empire of Chance: How Probability Changes Science and Everyday Life*, Cambridge, UK: Cambridge University Press.

Gilbert, R. (1993) *The Mortal President*, New York: Basic Books.

Gilligan, C. (1982) *In a Different Voice*, Cambridge, MA: Harvard University Press.

Gillis, J. R., ed. (1994) *Commemorations: The Politics of National Identity*, Princeton: Princeton University Press.

Ginzburg, C. (1980) *The Cheese and The Worms: The Cosmos of a Sixteenth-Century Miller*, Harmondsworth, UK: Penguin Books.

Glenn, J. C. and T. J. Gordon. (2000) *State of the Future at the Millennium*, Washington, DC: American Council for the United Nations University.

Glossop, R. J. (1993) *World Federation? A Critical Analysis of Federal World Government*, Jefferson, NC: McFarland.

Godelier, M. (1986) *The Making of Great Men: Male Domination and Power Among the New Guinea Baruya*, Cambridge, MA: Cambridge University Press. First published in French in 1982.

Godet, M. (1985) *Crises Are Opportunities*, Montreal: Gamma Institute Press.

Goldhagen, D. J. (1996) *Hitler's Willing Executionists: Ordinary Germans and the Holocaust*, New York: Knopf.

Goldhamer, H. (1978) *The Adviser*, New York: Elsevier.

Goldman, H. (1988) *Max Weber and Thomas Mann: Calling and the Shaping of the Self*, Berkeley: University of California Press.

Gomien, D., ed. (1993) *Broadening the Frontiers of Human Rights: Essays in Honour of Asbjorn Eide*, Oslo: Scandinavian University Press.

Good, J. and I. Velody, eds (1998) *The Politics of Postmodernity*, Cambridge, UK: Cambridge University Press.

Goode, W. J. (1967) 'The Protection of the Inept', *American Sociological Review*, Vol. 32, No. 1, February, pp. 5–19.

Goodin, R. E. (1992) *Motivating Political Morality*, Oxford: Blackwell.

Goodin, R. E., ed. (1996) *The Theory of Institutional Design*, Cambridge, UK: Cambridge University Press.

Gorbatschow, M., S. Sagladin, and A. Tschernjajew (1997) *Das Neue Denken: Politik im Zeitabler der Globalisierung*, München: Goldman.

Gore, A. (1992) *Earth in the Balance: Ecology and the Human Spirit*, New York: Houghton Mifflin.

Gore, A. (1993) *The Gore Report on Reinventing Government – From Red Tape to Results: Creating a Government that Works Better and Costs Less*, New York: Times Books.

Gottfried, R. S. (1983) *The Black Death: Natural and Human Disaster in Medieval Europe*, New York: The Free Press.

Government of Canada, Privy Council Office. (1997) *Memoranda to Cabinet: A Drafter's Guide*, Ottawa: Privy Council Office.

Gray, J. (1998) *False Dawn: The Delusions of Global Capitalism*, London: Granta Books.

Green, V. (1993) *The Madness of Kings: Personal Trauma and the Fate of Nations*, Far Thrupp, UK: Sutton.

Greene, K. B. D. (1982) *The Adaptive Organization: Anticipation and Management in Crisis*, New York: Wiley.

Grenoble, L. A. and L. J. Whaley, eds (1998) *Endangered Language Loss and Community Response*, Cambridge, UK: Cambridge University Press.

Gress, D. (1998) *From Plato to Nato: The Idea of the West and its Opponents*, New York: The Free Press.

Griffin, J. (1986) *Well-Being: Its Meaning, Measurement and Moral Importance*, Oxford: Clarendon Press.

Group of Thirty (1991) *The Summit Process and Collective Security: Future Responsibility Sharing*, Washington, DC: Group of Thirty.

Guardini, R. (1967) *Tugenden*, Mainz: Matthias-Grönewald-Verlag.

Guiradini, R. (1988 and 1989) *Sorge um den Menschen*, 2 Vols. Mainz: Matthias-Grönewald-Verlag. First published 1966 and 1967.

Haag, E., ed. (1979) *Capitalism: Sources of Hostility*, Washington, DC: The Heritage Foundation.

Haas, P. J. (1988) *Morality After Auschwitz: The Radical Challenge of the Nazi Ethics*, Philadelphia: Fortress Press.

Habermas, J. (1976) *Legitimation Crisis*, London: Heinemann.

Hacking, I. (1975) *The Emergence of Probability*, New York: Cambridge University Press.

Hacking, I. (1990) *The Taming of Chance*, New York: Cambridge Univerisity Press.

Hajib, Y. K. (1983) *Wisdom of Royal Glory: A Turko-Islamic Mirror for Princes*, Chicago: University of Chicago Press. Written in a Turkish dialect in 1069.

Hall, J. A. (1996) *International Orders*, Cambridge, UK: Polity Press.

Hallpike, C. R. (1988) *The Principles of Social Evolution*, Oxford: Oxford University Press.

Hamel, G. and C. K. Prahalad. (1993) 'Strategy as Stretch and Leverage'. *Harvard Business Review*, March-April, pp. 75–84.

Hamel, G. and C. K. Prahalad. (1994) *Competing for the Future*, Boston: Harvard Business School Press.

Hardin, G. (1993) *Living Within Limits: Ecology, Economics, and Population Taboos*, Oxford: Oxford University Press.

Hare, R. M. (1963) *Freedom and Reason*, Oxford: Clarendon.

Hargreaves I. and I. Christie, eds (1998) *Tomorrow's Politics: The Third Way and Beyond*, London: DEMOS.

Hariman, R. (1995) *Political Style: The Artistry of Power*, Chicago: University of Chicago Press.

Harpham, G. G. (1987) *The Ascetic Imperative in Culture and Criticism*, Chicago: University of Chicago Press.

Harre, R. (1993) *Social Being*, second edition. Oxford: Blackwell.

Hart, P. T. (1990) *Groupthink in Government: A Study of Small Groups and Policy Failures*, Amsterdam: Swets & Zeitlinger.

Hausman, C. R. (1984) *A Discourse on Novelty and Creation*, second edition. Albany: State University New York Press.

Hawrylyshyn, B. (1980) *Road Maps to the Future: Towards More Effective Societies. A Report to the Club of Rome*, New York: Pergamon.

Hawthorn, G. (1991) *Plausible Worlds: Possibility and Understanding in History and the Social Sciences*, Cambridge, UK: Cambridge University Press.

Hayek, F. A. (1979) *Law, Legislation and Liberty. Vol. III: The Political Order of a Free People*, London: Routledge & Kegan Paul.

Heclo, H. (1977) *A Government of Strangers: Executive Politics in Washington*, Washington, DC: Brookings Institution.

Heineman Jr, B. W. and C. A. Hessler (1980) *Memorandum for the President: A Strategic Approach to Domestic Affairs in the 1980s*, New York: Random House.

Held, D. ed. (1993) *Prospects for Democracy: North, South, East, West*, Cambridge, UK: Polity Press.

Held, D., (1995) *Democracy and the Global Order: From the Modern State to Cosmopolitan Governance*, Cambridge, UK: Polity Press.

Hennis, W. P., G. Kielmansegg, and U. Matz, eds (1977 and 1979) *Regierbarkeit: Studien zu Ihrer Problematisierung*, 2 vols. Stuttgart: Klett-Cotta.

Hentig, H. v. (1924) *Über den Caesarenwahnsinn: Die Krankheit des Kaisers Tiberius*, Munich: Verlag Von J.F. Bergmann.

Herman, A. (1997) *The Idea of Decline in Western History*, New York: The Free Press.

Hirschman, A. O. (1958) *The Strategy of Economic Development*, New Haven: Yale University Press.

Hirschman, A. O. (1986) *Rival Views of Market Society and Other Recent Essays*, New York: Viking.

Hirst, P. (1993) *Associative Democracy: New Forms of Economic and Social Governance*, Oxford: Polity.

HMSO (1972) *The Reorganisation of Central Government*, Cmnd. 4506, presented to Parliament in October 1970. London: HMSO.

HMSO (1995) *Committee on Standards of Public Life: First Report*. London: HMSO, CM 2850-I HMSO.

Hobsbawm, E. (1994) *The Age of Extremes: A History of the World, 1914–1991*, New York: Pantheon.

Hodgkinson, C. (1983) *The Philosophy of Leadership*, Oxford: Blackwell.

Hoffer, E. (1951) *The True Believer*, New York: Harper & Row.

Holton, R. (1998) *Globalization and the Nation-State*, New York: St. Martin's Press.

Hucker, C. O. (1959) 'Confucianism and the Chinese Censorial System', in D. S. Nivison and A. F. Wright, eds, *Confucianism in Action*, Stanford: Stanford University Press, pp. 182–208.

Hucker, C. O. (1966) *The Censorial System of Ming China*, Stanford: Stanford University Press.

Hulten, P., organizer (1987) *Futurism and Futurisms*, London: Thames and Hudson.

Hunt, E. (1995) *Will We Be Smart Enough? A Cognitive Analysis of the Coming Workforce*, New York: Russell Sage Foundation.

Huntington, S. P. (1996) *The Clash of Civilizations and the Remaking of World Order*, New York: Simon and Schuster.

Hurka, T. (1993) *Perfectionism*, New York: Oxford University Press.

Illich, I. (1973) *Tools for Conviviality*, New York: Harper & Row.

International Bank for Reconstruction and Development and the World Bank. (1997) *The State in a Changing World: World Development Report 1997*, New York: Oxford University Press.

International Commission on Peace and Food, The Report of, (1994) *Uncommon Opportunities: An Agenda for Peace and Equitable Development*. London: Zed Books.

International Monetary Fund (1997) *Corruption and the Rate of Temptation: Do Low Wages in the Civil Service Cause Corruption*, Washington, DC: IMF Working Paper.

International Monetary Fund et al. (2000) *2000 A Better World for All: Progress Towards the International Development Goals*, www.paris21.org/betterworld.

Ishihara, S. (1990) *The Japan That Can Say No: Why Japan Will be First Among Equals*, New York: Simon and Schuster.

Ivy, M. (1995) *Discourses of the Vanishing: Modernity, Phantasm, Japan*, Chicago: University of Chicago Press.

Jackson, R. H. and A. James, eds (1993) *States in a Changing World: A Contemporary Analysis*, Oxford: Clarendon Press.

Jacobs, J. (1992) *Systems of Survival: A Dialogue on the Moral Foundations of Commerce and Politics*, New York: Random.

Jamieson, K. H. (1992) *Dirty Politics: Deception, Distraction, and Democracy*, Oxford: Oxford University Press.

Jänicke, M. (1990) *State Failure: The Impotence of Politics in Industrial Society*, Cambridge, UK: Polity.

Janis, I. L. (1982) *Groupthink: Psychological Studies of Policy Decisions and Fiascoes*, revised edition. Boston: Houghton Mifflin.

Jantsch, E. (1975) *Design for Evolution: Self-Organization and Planning in the Life of Human Systems*, New York: Braziller.

Jaspers, K. (1949) *Vom Ursprung und Ziel der Geschichte*, Munich: Piper Verlag.

Jaspers, K. (1958) *Die Atombombe und die Zukunft des Menschen: Politisches Bewusstsein in Unserer Zeit*, Munich: R. Piper.

Jaspers, K. (1960) *Psychologie der Weltanschauungen*, second edition, Berlin: Springer. First published 1922.

Jay, M. (1984) *Adorno*. London: Fontana.

Jervis, R. (1997) *System Effects: Complexity in Political and Social Life*, Princeton: Princeton University Press.

Jeter, J. (2000) 'Death Watch: S. Africa's Advances Jeopardized by AIDS'. *The Washington Post*, 6 July.

Johnson, L. E. (1993) *A Morally Deep World: An Essay on Moral Significance and Environmental Ethics*, Cambridge, UK: Cambridge University Press.

Johnson, L. M. (1993) *Thucydides, Hobbes, and the Interpretation of Realism*, DeKalb, IL: Northern Illinois University Press.

Jonas H. (1984) *The Imperative of Responsibility: In Search of an Ethics for the Technological Age*, Chicago: University of Chicago Press.

Jordan, G. and C. Weedon. (1995) *Cultural Politics: Class, Gender, Race and the Postmodern World*, Oxford: Blackwell.

Jouvenel, B. de (1967) *The Art of Conjecture*, New York: Basic Books.

Joy, B. (2000) 'Why the Future Doesn't Need Us', *Wired*, April, pp. 238–262.

Judis, J. B. (2000) *Paradox of American Democracy: Elites, Special Interests, and the Betrayal of the Public Trust*, New York: Pantheon.

Kaase, M. and K. Newton. (1995) *Beliefs in Government*, Oxford: Oxford University Press.

Kahn, H. (1962) *Thinking the Unthinkable*, New York: Horizon Press.

Kahnemann, D., P. Slovic, and A. Tversky, eds (1982) *Judgement Under Uncertainty: Heuristics and Biases*, Cambridge, UK: Cambridge University Press.

Kaplan, R. D. (1996) *The Ends of the Earth: A Journey at the Dawn of the 21st Century*, New York: Random House.

Kaplan, R. D. (2000) *The Coming Anarchy: Shattering the Dreams of the Post Cold War*, New York: Random House.

Kapstein, E. (1996) 'Workers and the World Economy', *Foreign Affairs*, May/June, pp. 16–37.

Karplus, W. J. (1992) *The Heavens Are Falling: The Scientific Prediction of Catastrophes in Our Time*, New York: Plenum.

Kaufman, H. (1985) *Time, Chance, and Organizations: Natural Selection in a Perilous Environment*, Chatham, NJ: Chatham House.

Kaufman-Osborn, T. V. (1991) *Politics/Sense/Experience: A Pragmatic Inquiry into the Promise of Democracy*, Ithaca: Cornell University Press.

Kaus, M. (1992) *The End of Equality*, New York: Basic Books.

Keegan, J. (1993) *A History of Warfare*, London: Hutchinson.

Keegan, J. (1995) 'Better at Fighting: How the "Martial Races" of the Raj still Monopolize Service in the Indian Army'. *Times Literary Supplement*, 24 February, pp. 3–4.

Kegan, R. (1994) *In Over Our Heads: The Mental Demands of Modern Life*, Cambridge, MA: Harvard University Press.

Kekes, J. (1990) *Facing Evil*, Princeton: Princeton University Press.

Kekes, J. (1993) *The Morality of Pluralism*, Princeton: Princeton University Press.

Keller, D. (1990) *Television and the Crisis of Democracy*, Boulder, CO: Westview.

Kelsen, H. (1961) *General Theory of Law and State*, New York: Russell and Russell. First published in German in 1945.

Kennan, G. F. (1993) *Around the Cragged Hill: A Personal and Political Philosophy*, New York: W.W. Norton.

Kennedy, P. (1987) *The Rise and Fall of the Great Powers*, New York: Random House.

Khalilzad, Z. and I. O. Lesser, ed. (1988) *Sources of Conflict in the 21st Century: Regional Futures and U.S. Strategy*, Santa Monica, CA: The RAND Corporation.

King, A. and B. Schneider. (1991) *The First Global Revolution: A Report by the Council of The Club of Rome*, London: Simon & Schuster.

Kingdon, J. (1993) *Self-Made Man*, New York: Wiley.

Kingdon, J. W. (1995) *Agendas, Alternatives, and Public Policies*, second edition. New York: HarperCollins College Publishers.

Kirdar, U., ed. (1992) *Change: Threat of Opportunity*, five volumes. New York: UNDP.

Kissinger, H. (1994) *Diplomacy*, New York: Simon & Schuster.

Klein, R. (1994) 'Creatures of the Short Cut', *Times Literary Supplement*, 11 February, p. 12.

Klitgaard, R. (1991) *Controlling Corruption*, Berkeley: University of California Press.

Klitgaard, R. (1995) *Institutional Adjustment and Adjusting to Institutions*, World Bank Discussion Paper. Washington, DC: The World Bank.

Knoblock, J. (1990) *Xunzi: A Translation and Study of the Complete Works*, three volumes. Stanford: Stanford University Press.

Kosslyn, S. M. and O. Koenig (1992) *Wet Mind: The New Cognitive Neuroscience*, New York: Free Press.

Kossoy, E. and A. Ohry. (1992) *The FELDSHERS: Medical Sociological and Historical Aspects of Medicine with Below University Level Education*, Jerusalem: Magnes Press.

Kuhn, T. S. (1970) *The Structure of Scientific Revolutions*, second edition. Chicago: University of Chicago Press.

Kuhn, T. S. (1977), *The Essential Tension: Selected Studies in Scientific Traditions and Change*, Chicago: University of Chicago Press.

Küng, H. (1991) *Global Responsibility: In Search of a New World Ethics*, New York: Crossroad.

Küng, H., ed. (1995) *Ja zum Weltethos: Perspektiven für die Suche nach Orientierung*, Munich: Piper.

Küng, H. and K. J. Kuschel (1993) *A Global Ethic: The Declaration of the Parliament of the World's Religions*, London: SCM Press.

Kupperman, J. J. (1991) *Character*, Oxford: Oxford University Press.

Ladd, E. C. (1993) 'The End of Endism?', *Times Literary Supplement*, 10 December.

Lange-Eichbaum, W. and W. Kurth. (1967) *Genie Irrsinn und Ruhm: Genie-Mythus und Pathographie des Genies*, Sixth edition. Munich: Ernest Reinhardt. First published 1927.

Langston, T. S. (1992) *Ideologues and Presidents: From the New Deal to the Reagan Revolution*, Baltimore: Johns Hopkins University Press.

Lapham, L. H. (1993) *The Wish for Kings: Democracy at Bay*, New York: Grove/Atlantis Press.

Lash, J. (1995) *The Hero: Manhood and Power*, London: Thames & Hudson.

Lasswell, H. (1911) *Politics: Who Gets What, When and How*, New York: Peter Smith.

Laszlo, E. (1977) *Goals in a Global Community*, Oxford: Pergamon.

Laszlo, E. (1983) *Systems Sciences and World Order: Selected Studies*, Oxford: Pergamon.

Laszlo, E. *et al.* (1977) *Goals for Mankind: A Report to the Club of Rome on the New Horizons of Global Community*, New York: Dutton.

Lechner F. and J. Boli, eds (2000) *The Globalization Reader*, Oxford: Blackwell.

Ledeneva, A. V. (1998) *Russia's Economy of Favours: Blat, Networking and Informal Exchange*, Cambridge: Cambridge University Press.

Leeuw, F. L., R. C. Rist and R. C. Sonnichsen, eds (1993) *Can Governments Learn? Comparative Perspectives on Evaluation and Organizational Learning*, Brunswick, NJ: Transaction.

Lehrer, K. (1990) *Metamind*, Oxford: Clarendon Press.

Leng, S., ed. (1990) *Coping with Crises: How Governments Deal with Crises*, Lanham, MD: University Press of America.

Lewin, L. (1991) *Self-Interest and Public Interest in Western Politics*, Oxford: Oxford University Press.

Lewin, L. C. (pseudonym) (1967) *Report from Iron Mountain on the Possibility and Desirability of Peace*, New York: Dell.

Lewis, B. (1988) *The Political Language of Islam*, Chicago: The University of Chicago Press.

Lijphard, A. (1999) *Patterns of Democracy: Government Forms and Performance in Thirty-Six Countries*, New Haven: Yale University Press.

Lindblom, C. E. (1965) *The Intelligence of Democracy*, New York: Free Press.

Lindblom, C. E. (1968) *The Policy-Making Process*, Englewood Cliffs, NJ: Prentice-Hall.

Linstone, H. A. *et al.* (1984) *Multiple Perspectives for Decisionmaking: Bridging the Gap Between Sciences and Action*, New York: Elsevier.

Lipson, L. (1993) *The Ethical Crises of Civilization: Moral Meltdown or Advance?* London: Newbury Park, CA: Sage.

Little, W. and E. Posada-Carbó, eds (1996) *Political Corruption in Europe and Latin America*, London: Macmillan.

Litwak, R. S. (2000) *Rogue States and U.S. Foreign Policy: Containment After the Cold War*, Washington, DC: The Woodrow Wilson Center Press.

Lloyd, C. (1993) *The Structure of History*, Oxford: Blackwell.

Longford, E. (1993) *Royal Throne: The Future of the Monarchy*, London: Hodder & Stoughton.

Lowi, T. J. (1979) *The End of Liberalism: The Second Republic of the United States*, second edition. New York: Norton.

Lucas, J. R. (1993) *Responsibility*, Oxford: Oxford University Press.

Lui, A. Y. (1981) *The Hanlin Academy: Training Ground for the Ambitious 1644–1850*, Hamden, CO: Archon Books.

Lukacs, J. (1999) *Five Days in London: May 1940*, New Haven: Yale University Press.

Lummis, C. D. (1996) *Radical Democracy*, Ithaca. NY: Cornell University Press.

Lupia, A. and M. D. McCubbins (1998) *The Democratic Dilemma: Can Citizens Learn What They Need to Know?* Oxford: Oxford University Press.

Luttwak, E. N. (1987) *Strategy: The Logic of War and Peace*, Cambridge, MA: Harvard University Press.

Luttwak, E. N. (1994) *The Endangered American Dream*, New York: Simon & Schuster.

Macalpine, I. and R. Hunter. (1991) *George III and the Mad-Business*, London: Pimlico. First published in 1969.

MacDonagh, O. (1958) 'The Nineteenth Century Revolution in Government: A Reappraisal'. *Historical Journal*, Vol. I, No. 1, pp. 52–67.

Macdonald, D. J. (1992) *Adventures in Chaos: American Intervention for Reform in the Third World*, Cambridge, MA: Harvard University Press.

MacIntyre, A. (1978) *After Virtue*, Notre Dame, IN: University of Notre Dame Press.

Maclean, V. (1993) *Crowned Heads. Kings, Sultans and Emperors: A Royal Quest*, London: Hodder & Stoughton.

MacLeod, R., ed. (1988) *Government and Expertise: Specialists, Administrators and Professionals, 1860–1919*, Cambridge, UK: Cambridge University Press.

MacMahon, E. B. and L. Curry (1987) *Medical Cover Ups in the White House*, Washington, DC: Farragut.

Madach, I. (1993) *The Tragedy of Man*, Edinburgh: Canongate. Originally published in Hungarian in 1862.

Maddison, A. (1991) *Dynamic Forces in Capitalist Development: A Long-Run Comparative View*, Oxford: Oxford University Press.

Madsen, D. and P. G. Snow. (1991) *The Charismatic Bond: Political Behavior in Time of Crisis*, Cambridge, MA: Harvard University Press.

Mann, M. (1986) *The Sources of Social Power. Vol. I: A History of Power from the Beginning to A.D. 1760*, Cambridge, UK: Cambridge University Press.

Mann, M. (1993) *The Sources of Social Power. Vol. II: The Rise of Classes and Nation States, 1760–1914*, Cambridge, UK: Cambridge University Press.

Mancuso, M. (1995) *The Ethical World of British MPs*, Montreal: McGill-Queen's University Press.

Mansfield, H. C. (1996) *Machiavelli's Virtue*, Chicago: University of Chicago Press.

March, J. G. (1988) *Decisions and Organizations*, Oxford: Blackwell.

March, J. G. and J. P. Olsen. (1989) *Rediscovering Institutions: The Organizational Basis of Politics*, New York: The Free Press.

Margalit, A. (1995) *The Decent Society*, Cambridge, MA: Harvard University Press.

Margolis, H. (1992) *Paradigms and Barriers: How Habits of Mind Govern Scientific Beliefs*, Chicago: University of Chicago Press.

Márquez, G. G. (1990) *The General in his Labyrinth*, New York: Knopf.

Maryanski, A. and J. H. Turner. (1992) *The Social Cage: Human Nature and The Evolution of Society*, Stanford: Stanford University Press.

Mass-Borgese, E. (1998) *The Ocean Circle: Governing the Sea as a Global Resource: A Report to the Club of Rome*, Tokyo: United Nations University Press.

May, E. R. (1972) *'Lessons' of the Past: The Uses and Misuses of History in American Foreign Policy*, New York: Oxford University Press.

May, E. R. and P. D. Zelikow, eds (1997) *The Kennedy Tapes: Inside the White House During the Cuban Missile Crisis*, Cambridge, MA: Harvard University Press.

McCall S. (1994) *A Model of the Universe: Space-Time, Probability, and Decision*, Oxford: Clarendon Press.

McCormick, J. P. (2000) *Carl Schmitt's Critique of Liberalism: Against Politics as Technology*, Cambridge, UK: Cambridge University Press.

McDougall, W. A. (1997) *Promised Land, Crusader State: The American Encounter with the World Since 1776*, Boston: Houghton Mifflin.

McIntyre, A., ed. (1988) *Aging and Political Leadership*, Albany: State University of New York Press.

McNamara, R. S. (1995) *In Retrospect: The Tragedy and Lessons of Vietnam*, New York: Times Books.

McNeill, D. and P. Freiberger. (1993) *Fuzzy Logic*, New York: Simon & Schuster.

McNeill, P. M. (1993) *The Ethics and Politics of Human Experimentation*, Cambridge, UK: Cambridge University Press.

Meadows, D. L. *et al.* (1972) *The Limits to Growth*, New York: New American Library.

Meadows, D. H., D. L. Meadows, and J. Randers (1992) *Beyond the Limits: Global Collapse or a Sustainable Future*, London: Earthscan.

Meier, C. (1980) *Die Entstehung des Politischen bei den Griechen*, Frankfurt am Main: Suhrkamp.

Meier, C. (1980) *Die Ohnmacht des Allmächtigen Dictators Caesar*, Frankfurt am Main: Suhrkamp.

Meinecke, F. (1957) *Die Idee der Staatsräson in der Neuen Geschichte*, Munich: Oldenbourg. First published 1924/5.

Meinecke, F. (1969) *Weltbürgertum und Nationalstaat*, Munich: R. Oldenbourg, 1969. First published 1907.

Meisami, J. S., translator and editor (1991) *The Sea of Precious Virtues: A Medieval Islamic Mirror for Princes*, Salt Lake City: University of Utah Press. Written in Persian in the mid-twelfth century.

239

Mennell, S. (1992) *Norbert Elias: An Introduction*, Oxford: Blackwell.

Mestrovic, S. G. (1991) *The Coming Fin De Siècle*, London: Routledge, 1991.

Mestrovic, S. G. (1993) *The Barbarian Temptation: Towards a Postmodern Critical Theory*, London: Routledge.

Michael. D. N. (1997) *On Learning to Plan – and Planning to Learn*, new enlarged edition, Alexandria, VA: Miles River Press.

Micklethwait, J. and A. Wooldridge (2000) *A Future Prefect: The Challenge and Hidden Promise of Globalization*, New York: Times Books.

Milbrath, L. W. (1989) *Envisioning a Sustainable Society: Learning Our Way Out*, Albany: State University of New York Press.

Milgram, S. (1974) *Obedience to Authority*, London: Tavistock.

Miller, J. B. (1976) *Towards a New Psychology of Women*, Boston: Beacon Press.

Miller, J. H. (1995) *Topographies*, Stanford, CA: Stanford University Press.

Miller, R. W. (1993) *Moral Differences: Truth, Justice and Conscience in a World of Conflict*, Princeton: Princeton University Press.

Miser, H. J., ed. (1995) *Handbook of Systems Analysis: Cases*, London: Wiley.

Miser, H. J. and E. S. Quade, eds (1985) *Handbook of Systems Analysis: Overview of Uses, Procedures, Applications, and Practice*, New York: North-Holland.

Miser, H. J. and E. S. Quade. (1988) *Handbook of Systems Analysis: Craft Issues and Procedural Choices*, New York: North-Holland.

Mohammad, M. and S. Ishihara. (1995) *The Voice of Asia: Two Leaders Discuss the Coming Century*, Tokjo: Kodansha International.

Mommsen, W. J. and W. Schluchter, eds (1992) *Wissenschaft als Beruf/Politik als Beruf, Max Weber Gesamtausgabe*, (Vol. 17) Tübingen: J.C.B. Mohr.

Montaigne, M. (1991) *The Essays of Michel de Montaigne*, Translated and edited by M. A. Screech. London: Allen Lane.

Moore, M. H. (1995) *Creating Public Value: Strategic Management in Government*, Cambridge, MA: Harvard University Press.

Moorthy, S. and S. Hawkins (1998) *Advertising Repetition and Quality Perception*, University of Rochester Business School, Working Paper.

Morris, C. W. (1998) *An Essay on the Modern State*, Oxford: Oxford University Press.

Morris, D. (1997) *Behind the Oval Office: Winning the Presidency in the Nineties*, New York: Random.

Morris, D. (1999a) *Vote.com: How Big-Money Lobbyists and the Media are Losing their Influence, and the Internet is Giving Power to the People*, Los Angeles: Renaissance Books.

Morris D. (1999b) *The New Prince: Machiavelli Updated for the Twenty-First Century*, Los Angeles: Renaissance Books.

Moscovici, S. (1985) *The Age of the Crowd: A Historical Treatise on Mass Psychology*, Cambridge, UK: Cambridge University Press. First published in French in 1981.

Moselley, C. and R. E. Asher, eds (1994) *Atlas of the World's Languages*, London: Routledge

Mosiek, U. (1978) *Verfassungsrecht der Lateinischen Kirche*, three volumes. Freiburg: Rombach.

Mulgan, G., ed. (1997) *Life After Politics: New Thinking for the Twenty-First Century*, London: Fontana.

Münz, C. (1995) *Der Welt ein Gedächnis geben: Geschichtstheologisches Denken im Judentum nach Auschwitz*, Gütersloher: Chr. Kaiser.

Murray, W., M. Knox and A. Bernstein. (1994) *The Making of Strategy: Rulers, States and War*, Cambridge, UK: Cambridge University Press.

Murray, F. and J. Lane, eds (1996) *South Africa: Designing New Political Institutions*, Newbury Park, CA: Sage.

Nardin, T. and D. R. Maple, eds (1992) *Traditions of International Ethics*, Cambridge, UK: Cambridge University Press.

Naville-Sington P. and D. Sington. (1993) *Paradise Dreamed: How Utopian Thinkers have Changed the Modern World*, London: Bloomsbury.

Nelson, R. H. (1991) *Reaching for Heaven on Earth: The Theological Meaning of Economics*, Savage, MD: Rowman & Littlefield.

Neustadt, R. E. (1980) *Presidential Power: The Politics of Leadership from FDR to Carter*, revised edition. New York: Wiley.

Neustadt, R. E. and E. R. May. (1986) *Thinking in Time: The Uses of History for Decision Makers*, New York: Free Press.

Nichols, J. (1992) *Linguistic Diversity in Space and Time*, Chicago: University of Chicago Press.

Nicolis, G. and I. Prigogine (1989) *Exploring Complexity*, New York: Freeman.

Nietzsche, F. (1874) *Vom Nutzen und Nachteil der Historie für das Leben*, Giorgio Colli und Mazzino Montinari, Kritische Studienausgabe. Munich: Deutscher Taschenbuch Verlag, 1988. Band 1, pp. 243–334.

Nisbet, R. (1993) *History of the Idea of Progress*, new edition. Brunswick, NJ: Transaction.

Nolte, E. (1991) *Geschichtsdenken im 20. Jahrhundert: Von Max Weber bis Hans Jonas*, Frankfurt am Main: Propylaen.

Nolte, H. (1993) *Die Eine Welt: Abriss der Geschichte des Internationalen Systems*, revised edition. Hanover: Fackelträger-Verlag.

Nordlinger, E. A. (1981) *On the Autonomy of the Democratic State*, Cambridge, MA: Harvard University Press.

North, D. C. (1990) *Institutions, Institutional Change and Economic Performance*, Cambridge, UK: Cambridge University Press.

Nozick, R. (1974) *Anarchy, State and Utopia*, New York: Basic Books.

Nussbaum, M. C. (1986) *The Fragility of Goodness: Luck and Ethics in Greek Tragedy and Philosophy*, Cambridge, UK: Cambridge University Press.

Nussbaum, M. C. (1995a) *The Therapy of Desire: Theory and Practice in Hellenistic Ethics*, Princeton: Princeton University Press.

Nussbaum, M. C. (1995b) *Poetic Justice: The Literary Imagination and Public Life*, Boston: Beacon Press.

Nussbaum, M. C. and A. Sen, eds (1993) *The Quality of Life*, Oxford: Clarendon Press.

Oakeshott, M. (1996) *The Politics of Faith and the Politics of Scepticism*, New Haven: Yale University Press.

Oberal, A. S. (1993) *Population Growth, Employment and Poverty in Third-World Mega-Cities: Analytical and Policy Issues*, London: Macmillan.

O'Brien, M. D. (1996) *Father Elijah: An Apocalypse*, San Francisco: Ignatius Press.

OECD (1986) *Innovation Policy: France*, Paris: OECD.

OECD (1998) *21st Century Technologies: Promises and Perils of a Dynamic Future*, Paris: OECD.

OECD (1999) *The Future of the Global Economy: Towards a Long Boom?* Paris: OECD.

OECD (In publication). *21st Century Governance: Power in the Global Knowledge Economy and Society*, Paris: OECD.

Oestreich, G. (1982) *Neostoicism and the Early Modern State*, Cambridge, UK: Cambridge University Press. First published in German.

Ohmae, K. (1995) *The End of the Nation State: The Rise of Regional Economies*, New York: The Free Press.

Olson Jr, M, L. (1982) *The Rise and Decline of Nations: Economic Growth, Stagflation, and Social Rigidities*, New Haven: Yale University Press.

O'Neill, M. J. 1993. *The Roar of the Crowd: How Television and People Power Are Changing the World*, New York: Times Books.

Ophulus, W. (1997) *Requiem for Modern Politics: The Tragedy of the Enlightenment and the Challenge of the New Millennium*, Boulder, CO: Westview.

Osborne, D. and T. Gaebler (1992) *Reinventing Government: How the Entrepreneurial Spirit is Transforming the Public Sector*, Reading, MA: Addison Wesley.

Ostrom, E. (1990) *Governing the Commons: The Evolution of Institutions for Collective Action*, Cambridge, UK: Cambridge University Press.

Ostry, S., ed. (1991) *Authority and Academic Scribblers: The Role of Research in East Asian Policy Reform*, San Francisco: ICS Press.

Ottolenghi, E. (1998) *A Matter of Conflict: The Place of Judicial Review in a Democracy*, Doctoral Thesis submitted at the Hebrew University of Jerusalem.

Pagden, A. (1995) *Lords of All the World: Ideologies of Empire in Spain, Britain and France c. 1500 – c. 1800*, New Haven: Yale University Press.

Page, B. (1995) *Who Deliberates? Mass Media in Modern Democracy*, Chicago: University of Chicago Press.

Painter, M. (1998) *Collaborative Federalism: Economic Reform in Australia in the 1990s*, Cambridge, UK: Cambridge University Press.

Palmer, R. C. (1994) *English Law in the Age of the Black Death, 1348–1381*, Raleigh, NC: University of North Carolina Press.

Paquet, G. (1999) *Governance Through Social Learning*, Ottawa: University of Ottawa Press.

Parker, G. and L. M. Smith, eds (1978) *The General Crisis of the Seventeenth Century*, London: Routledge and Kegan Paul.

Parker, R. D. (1994) *'Here, the People Rule': A Constitutional Populist Manifesto*, Cambridge, MA: Harvard University Press.

Pauchant, T. C. and I. I. Mitroff. (1992) *Transforming the Crisis Prone Organization: Preventing Individual, Organizational, and Environmental Tragedies*, San Francisco: Jossey-Bass.

Paulos, J. A. (1988) *Innumeracy: Mathematical Illiteracy and its Consequences*, New York: Hill and Wang.

Paulos, J. A (1991) *Beyond Numeracy: Ruminations of a Number Man*, New York: Knopf.

Paz, O. (1985) *One Earth, Four or Five Worlds: Reflections on Contemporary History*, San Diego: Harcourt Brace Jovanovich.

Pears, D. (1984) *Motivated Irrationality*, Oxford: Clarendon Press.

Pettit, P. (1991) 'Consequentialism', in P. Singer, ed., *A Companion to Ethic*, Oxford: Basic Blackwell, ch. 19.

Pfaff, W. (1993) *The Wrath of Nations: Civilization and the Furies of Nationalism*, New York: Simon & Schuster.

Phillips, L. (1993) *Looking Backward: A Critical Appraisal of Communitarian Thought*, Princeton, NJ: Princeton University Press.

Pimm, S. (1991) *The Balance of Nature? Ecological Issues in the Conservation of Species and Communities*, Chicago: University of Chicago Press.

Plato (1995) *Statesman*, Edited by J. Annas and R. Waterfield. Cambridge: Cambridge University Press.

Platt, R. J. (1966) *The Step to Man*, New York: Wiley.

Platt, R. J. (1981) 'Research and Development Needs for Solving Global Problems', in: UNESCO, *Social Implications of the Scientific and Technological Reproduction*, Paris: UNESCO, pp. 341–52.

Polanyi, M. (1974) *Personal Knowledge: Towards a Post-Critical Philosophy*, Chicago: University of Chicago Press.

Porritt, J. (1993) 'Sustainable Development: Panacea, Platitude, or Downright Deception?', in: B. Cartledge, ed., *Energy and the Environments: The Linacre Lectures 1991–2*, Oxford: Oxford University Press, ch. 2.

Porter, M. R. (1990) *The Competitive Advantage of Nations*, London: Macmillan.

Post, J. M. and R. S. Robins. (1993) *When Illness Strikes The Leader: The Dilemma of the Captive King – From George III to Ronald Reagan*, New Haven: Yale University Press.

Postrel, V. (1999) *The Future and Its Enemies: The Growing Conflict Over Creativity*, New York: Touchtone.

Powell Jr, G. B. (1982) *Contemporary Democracies: Participation, Stability, and Violence*, Cambridge, MA: Harvard University Press.

Przeworksi, A. (1999) *Democratic Accountability, and Representation*, Cambridge, UK: Cambridge University Press.

Puhl, L. J. (1951) *The Spiritual Exercises of St. Ignatius: Based on Studies in the Language of the Autograph*, Chicago: Loyola University Press.

Putman, R. D. (1993) *Making Democracy Work: Civic Traditions in Modern Italy*, Princeton: Princeton University Press.

Pye, L. W. and S. Verba, eds (1965) *Political Culture and Political Development*, Princeton: Princeton University Press.

Quade, E. S. (1989) *Analysis for Public Decisions*, revised edition by G. M. Carter, New York: North-Holland.

Raadschelders, C. N. (1998) *Handbook of Administrative History*, New Brunswick, NJ: Transaction.

Raiffa, H. (1968) *Decision Analysis*, Reading, MA: Addison-Wesley.

Ranney, A. (1976) '"The Divine Science": Political Engineering in American Culture'. *American Political Science Review*, vol. 70, no. 1, March, pp. 140–8.

Rawls, J. (1993) *Political Liberalism*, New York: Columbia University Press.

Rawls, J. (1999) *A Theory of Justice*, revised edition. Oxford: Belknap Press.

Rees, M. (1999) *Just Six Numbers: The Deep Forces That Shape the Universe*, New York: Basic Books.

Regan Jr, B. T., and E. Z. Williams, eds (1992) *Re-creating Authority in Revolutionary France*, New Brunswick, NJ: Rutgers University Press.

Reich, R. B. (1998) *Locked in the Cabinet*, New York: Vintage Books.

Reid, A. (1996) *Shakedown: How the New Economy is Changing Our Life*, Toronto: Doubleday Canada.

Reinicke, W. H. (1998) *Global Public Policy: Governing without Government?* Washington, DC: The Brookings Institution.

Reno, W. (1995) *Corruption and State Politics in Sierra Leone*, Cambridge, UK: Cambridge University Press.

Rescher, N. (1993) *Pluralism: Against the Demand for Consensus*, Oxford: Oxford University Press.

Richter, H. (1997) *Der Gottes-komplex: Die Geburt und die Krise des Glaubens an die Allmacht des Menschen*, Munich: Econ.

Riddell, P. (1993) *Honest Opportunism: The Rise of the Career Politician*, London: Hamish Hamilton.

Ridley F. F. and D. Wilson, eds (1996) *The Quango Debate*, Oxford: Oxford University Press.

Riezler, K. (1954) 'Political Decisions in Modern Society', *Ethics*, vol. 64, no. 2, part 2 (January), pp. 1–55.

Rifkin, J. (1995) *The End of Work: The Decline of the Global Labour Force and the Dawn of the Post-Market Era*, New York: Warner Books.

Robertson, R. (1992) *Globalization: Social Theory and Global Culture*, London: Sage.

Robson, W. A. (1964) 'The Reform of Government'. *The Political Quarterly*, vol. 35, no. 2, April–June, pp. 193–211.

Roetz, H. (1993) *Confucian Ethics of the Axial Age: A Reconstruction Under the Aspect of the Breakthrough Toward Postconventional Thinking*, Albany: State University of New York Press.

Röhl, J. C. G. (1994) *The Kaiser and His Court: Wilhelm II and the Government of Germany*, Cambridge, UK: Cambridge University Press.

Rokeach, M. (1960) *Open and Closed Mind*, New York: Basic Books.

Rokeach, M. (1973) *The Nature of Human Values*, New York: Free Press.

Rokeach, M. (1979) *Understanding Human Values: Individual and Societal*, New York: Free Press.

Root, H. L. (1996) *Small Countries Big Lessons: Governance and the Rise of East Asia*, Hong Kong: Oxford University Press.

Rose, N. (1990) *Governing the Soul: The Shaping of the Private Self*, London: Routledge.

Rose, R. (1993) *Lesson-Drawing in Public Policy: A Guide to Learning Across Time and Space*, Chatham, NJ: Chatham House.

Rosecrance, R. (1986) *The Rise of the Trading State: Commerce and Conquest in the Modern World*, New York: Basic Books.

Rosecrance, R. and A. A. Stein, eds (1993) *The Domestic Bases of Grand Strategy*, Ithaca: Cornell University Press.

Rosell, S. A. *et al.* (1992) *Governing an Information Society*, Montreal: Institute for Research in Public Policy.

Rosell, S. A. (1999) *Renewing Governance: Governing by Learning in the Information Age*, Oxford: Oxford University Press.

Rosen, S. (1998) *Plato's Statesman: The Web of Politics*, New Haven: Yale University Press.

Rosenau, J. N. (1990) *Turbulence in World Politics: A Theory of Change and Continuity*, Princeton: Princeton University Press.

Rosenau, J. N. and E. Czempiel, eds (1992) *Governance Without Government: Order and Change in World Politics*, Cambridge, UK: Cambridge University Press.

Rosenhead, J., ed. (1989) *Rational Analysis for a Problematic World: Problem Structuring Methods for Complexity, Uncertainty and Conflict*, Chichester, UK: Wiley.

Rosenthal, U., M. T. Charles and P. 't Hart, eds (1989) *Coping with Crisis: The Management of Disasters, Riots and Terrorism*, Spingfield, IL: Charles C Thomas.

Rositter, C. L. (1948) *Constitutional Dictatorship: Crisis Government in Modern Democracies*, Princeton: Princeton University Press.

Roussel, E. (1995) *Jean Monnet, 1888–1979*, Paris: Fayard.

Rowen, H. H. (1978) *John de Witt, Grand Pensionary of Holland, 1625–1672*, Princeton: Princeton University Press.

Roy, O. (1994) *The Failure of Political Islam*, Cambridge, MA: Harvard University Press.

Royal (Swedish) Ministry for Foreign Affairs. 1974. *To Choose a Future: A Basis for Discussion and Deliberation on Future Studies in Sweden.* In Cooperation with the Secretariat for Future Studies. Stockholm: Royal Ministry for Foreign Affairs.

Rubin, W., ed. (1984) *'Primitivism' in 20th Century Art: Affinity of the Tribal and the Modern*, two vols. New York: The Museum of Modern Art.

Rufin, J. (1991) *L'empire et les nouveaux barbares*, Paris: Jean-Claude Latt's.

Ruh, H. (1996) *Anders, Aber Besser: Die Arbeit Neu Erfinden – Für Eine Solidarische und Überlebensfähige Welt*, Frauenfeld, Switzerland: Waldgut.

Ruh, H. (1997) *Störfall Mensch: Wege aus der Ökologischen Krise*, Gütersloh: Chr. Kaiser.

Russet, B. (1993) *Grasping the Democratic Peace*, Princeton: Princeton University Press.

Saage, R. (1997) *Utopie Forschung: Eine Bilanz*, Darmstadt: Primus.

Sachedina, A. A. (1988) *The Just Ruler in Shi'ite Islam: The Comprehensive Authority of the Jurist in Imamite Jurisprudence*, Oxford: Oxford University Press.

Sagan, C. (1997) *Billions and Billions: Thoughts on Life and Death at the Brink of the Millennium*, New York: Random House.

Said, E. W. (1979) *Orientalism*, New York: Vintage Books.

Said E. W. (1993) *Culture and Imperialism*, New York: Alfred Knopf.

Samuels, A. (1993) *The Political Psyche*, London: Routledge.

Sandhu, K. S. and P. Wheatley, eds (1989) *Management of Success: The Moulding of Modern Singapore*, Singapore: Institute of Southeast Asian Studies.

Sandoz, E. (1981) *The Voegelinian Revolution: A Biographical Introduction*, Baton Rouge: Louisiana State University Press.

Sartori, G. (1996) *Comparative Constitutional Engineering: An Inquiry into Structure, Incentives and Outcomes*, 2nd ed. London: Macmillan.

Sartre, J. (1992) *Notebooks for an Ethics*, Chicago: University of Chicago Press. First published in French in 1983.

Saul, J. P. (1992) *Voltaire's Bastards: The Dictatorship of Reason in the West*, New York: Vintage Books.

Scharfstein, B. (1995) *Amoral Politics: The Persistent Truth of Machiavellism*, Albany: State University of New York.

Schauer, F. (1991) *Playing by the Rules: A Philosophical Examination of Rule-Based Decision-Making in Law and in Life*, Oxford: Clarendon Press.

Scheid, J. and J. Svenbro (1996) *The Craft of Zeus: Myths of Weaving and Fabric*, Cambridge, MA: Harvard University Press.

Schell, J. (1982) *The Fate of the Earth*, New York: Knopf.

Schelling, T. C. (1978) *Micromotives and Macrobehavior*, New York: Norton.

Schelling, T. C. (1984) *Choice and Consequence*, Cambridge, MA: Harvard University Press.

Schick, A. (1990) *The Capacity to Budget*, Washington, DC: The Urban Institute Press.

Schlesinger, A, Jr (1993) 'The Radical'. *The New York Review of Books*, vol. 40, no. 4 (February).

Schmidt, H. (1998) *Auf der Suche nach einer öffentlichen Moral: Deutschland vor dem neuen Jahrhundert*, Stuttgard: Deutsche Verlags-Anstalt.

Schmitt, C. (1963) *Der Begriff des Politischen*, Berlin: Duncker & Humblot. Shorter version first published 1927.

Schmitt, C. (1970) *Politische Theologie II: Die Legende von der Erledigung jeder Politischen Theologie*, Berlin: Duncker & Humblot.

Schmitt, C. (1975) *Theorie der Partisanen: Zwischenbemerkung zum Begriff des Politischen*, second edition. Berlin: Duncker & Humblot.

Schmitt, C. (1979) *Politische Theologie: Vier Kapitel zur Lehre von der Souveränität*, Berlin: Duncker & Humblot. Reprint of second edition, 1934.

Schmitt, C. (1982) *Politische Romantik*, Berlin: Duncker & Humblot. Reprint of second edition. 1925.

Schmookler, A. B. (1993) *The Illusion of Choice: How the Market Economy Shapes Our Destiny*, Albany, NY: State University of New York Press.

Schon, D. A. (1971) *Beyond the Stable State: Public and Private Learning in a Changing Society*, London: Temple Smith.

Schubert, G. and R. D. Masters, eds (1991) *Primate Politics*, Carbondale: Southern Illinois University Press.

Schulman, P. R. (1980) *Large-Scale Policy Making*, New York: Elsevier.

Schumacher, E. F. (1973) *Small is Beautiful*, New York: Harper Torchbooks.

Schumpeter, J. A. (1942) *Capitalism, Socialism and Democracy*, New York: Harper & Row.

Schwab, K., ed. (1995) *Overcoming Indifference: Ten Key Challenges in Today's Changing World: A Survey of Ideas and Proposals for Action on the Threshold of the 21st Century*, Albany: University Press of New York.

Schwartz, B. (1986) *The Battle for Human Nature*, New York: Norton.

Seldon, A. and D. Collings. (1999) *Britain under Thatcher*, London: Longman.

Selznick, P. (1992) *The Moral Commonwealth: Social Theory and the Promise of Community*, Berkeley: University of California Press.

Senge, P. M. (1990) *The Fifth Discipline: The Art and Practice of The Learning Organization*, New York: Doubleday Currency.
Sennett, R. (1978) *The Fall of Public Man: On the Social Psychology of Capitalism*, New York: Vintage.
Sharpe, L. J., ed. (1993) *The Rise of Meso Governance in Europe*, London: Sage.
Sheffer, G., ed. (1993) *Innovative Leaders in International Politics*, Albany, NY: State University of New York Press.
Shehadi, K. S. (1994) *Ethnic Self-determination and the Break-up of States*, London: Brassey's, International Institute of Strategic Studies, Adelphi Paper 283.
Shermer, M. (1997) *Why People Believe Weird Things: Pseudoscience, Superstition and Other Confusions of Our Time*, New York: Freeman.
Shonfield, A. (1982) *The Use of Public Power*, Oxford: Oxford University Press.
Shugart, M. S. and J. M. Carey. (1993) *Presidents and Assemblies: Constitutional Design and Electoral Dynamics*, Cambridge, UK: Cambridge University Press.
Sikora, R. I. and B. Barry, eds (1978) *Obligations to Future Generations*, Philadelphia: Temple University Press.
Silberman, B. S. (1993) *Cages of Reason: The Rise of the Rational State in France, Japan, the United States and Great Britain*, Chicago: University of Chicago Press.
Simenton, D. K. (1984) *Genius, Creativity, and Leadership: Historiometric Inquiries*, Cambridge, MA: Harvard University Press.
Simma, B., ed. (1994) *The Charter of the United Nations: A Commentary*, Oxford: Clarendon Press.
Simon, H. A. (1981) *The Sciences of the Artificial*, revised edition. Cambridge, MA: MIT Press.
Simon, H. A.. (1983) *Reason in Human Affairs*, Stanford: Stanford University Press.
Simon, J. L. (1980) *The Ultimate Resource*, London: M. Robertson.
Simon, J. L. (1995) *The State of Humanity*, Oxford: Blackwell.
Simon, J. L. (1996) *The Ultimate Resource 2*, Princeton: Princeton University Press.
Singer, M. and A. Wildavsky (1996) *The Real World Order: Zones of Peace / Zones of Turmoil*, revised edition. Chatham, NJ: Chatham House.
Singer, P. (1993) *Practical Ethics*, Cambridge University Press.
Singer, P. (1995) *How are We to Live? Ethics in an Age of Self-Interest*, Amherst, NY: Prometheus Books.
6, P. (1997) *Holistic Government*, London: DEMOS.
Sklair, L. (1991) *Sociology of the Global System: Social Change in Global Perspective*, New York: Harvester Wheatsheaf.
Slaton, C. D. and T. Becker. (2000) 'Democracy Beyond the Information Age: 21st Century Political Communication'. *Foresight*, April. Vol. 2, No. 2., pp. 199–209.
Slobodkin, L. B. (1992) *Simplicity and Complexity in Games of the Intellect*, Cambridge, MA: Harvard University Press.
Smiley, M. (1992) *Moral Responsibility and the Boundaries of Community: Power and Accountability from a Pragmatic Point of View*, Chicago: University of Chicago Press.
Sniderman, P. M., R. A. Brody, and P. E. Tetlock. (1991) *Reasoning and Choice: Explorations in Political Psychology*, Cambridge, UK: Cambridge University Press.
Sobhan, R. (1993) *Bangladesh: Problems of Governance*, New Delhi: Konark Publishers.
Solzhenitsyn, A. (1995) '*The Russian Question': At the End of the Twentieth Century*, NY: Farrar, Strauss and Giroux.
Sorensen, R. A. (1992) *Thought Experiments*, Oxford: Oxford University Press.
Sorokin, P. A. (1942) *Man and Society in Calamity: The Effects of War, Revolution, Famine, Pestilence Upon Human Mind, Behavior, Social Organization and Cultural Life*, New York: Dutton.

Soros, G. (1998) *The Crisis of Global Capitalism: Open Society Endangered*, New York: Public Affairs Press.

Soros, G. (2000) *Open Society: The Crisis of Global Capitalism Reconsidered*, New York: Public Affairs Press.

Soto, H. de (1989) *The Other Path: The Invisible Revolution in the Third World*, New York: Harper & Row.

South Commission, The (1990) *The Challenge to the South*, Oxford: Oxford University Press.

Sprangens Jr, T. (1990) *Reason and Democracy*, Durham, NC: Duke University Press.

Spiaerenburgh, P. (1984) *The Spectacle of Suffering*, Cambridge University Press.

Springborg, P. (1981) *The Problem of Human Needs and the Critique of Civilisation*, London: Allen and Unwin.

Spruyt, H. (1994) *The Sovereign State and its Competitors*, Princeton: Princeton University Press.

Spybey, T. (1995) *Globalization and World Society*, Oxford: Polity.

Stacey, R. (1992) *Managing the Unknowable: Strategic Boundaries Between Order and Chaos in Organizations*, San Francisco: Jossey-Bass.

Stares, P. B. (1996) *Global Habit: The Drug Problem in a Borderless World*, Washington, DC: The Brookings Institution.

Starn, R. and L. Partridge (1992) *Arts of Power: Three Halls of State in Italy, 1300–1600*, Berkeley: University of California Press.

Statman, D., ed. (1993) *Moral Luck*, Albany: State University of New York Press.

Steinberger, P. J. (1993) *The Concept of Political Judgment*, Chicago: University of Chicago Press.

Steinbruner, J. D. (1974) *The Cybernetic Theory of Decision: New Dimensions of Political Analysis*, Princeton: Princeton University Press.

Stemlau, J., ed. (1996) *Sharpening International Sanctions: Towards a Stronger Role for the United Nations*, New York: Carnegie Corporation.

Stephanopoulos, G. (1999) *All Too Human: A Political Education*, Boston: Little, Brown.

Sternberg, R. J. and R. K. Wagner, eds (1986) *Practical Intelligence: Nature and Origins of Competence in the Everyday World*, Cambridge, UK: Cambridge University Press.

Sternhall, Z. (1994) *The Birth of Fascist Ideology: From Cultural Rebellion to Political Revolution*, Princeton: Princeton University Press.

Sternhall, Z., ed., (1996) *The Intellectual Revolt Against Liberal Democracy 1870–1945*, Jerusalem: The Israel Academy of Sciences and Humanities.

Stone, D. (1996) *Capturing the Political Imagination: Think Tanks and the Policy Process*, London: Cass.

Streich, J. (1997) *30 Jahre Club of Rome: Anspruch – Kritik – Zukunft*, Basel: Birkhäuser Verlag.

Struyk, R. J., M. Ueno and T. Suzuki. (1993) *A Japanese Think Tank: Exploring Alternative Models*, Washington, DC: The Urban Institute.

Suleiman, E. N. (1987) *Private Power and Centralization in France: The Notaries and the State*, Princeton: Princeton University Press.

Susser, B. and C. Liebman (1999) *Choosing Survival: Strategies for a Jewish Future*, New York: Oxford University Press.

Suter, K. (1993) *Global Change: Armageddon and the New World Order*, Sutherland, N. S. W., Australia: Albatross Book.

Sutton, B. (1993) *The Legitimate Corporation: Essential Readings in Business Ethics and Corporate Governance*, Oxford: Blackwell.

Sztompka, P. (1991) *Society in Action: The Theory of Social Becoming*, Chicago: University of Chicago Press.

Tainter, J. A. (1988) *The Collapse of Complex Societies*, Cambridge, UK: Cambridge University Press.

Talmon, J. (1952) *The Origins of Totalitarian Democracy*, London: Secker & Warburg.

Tamames, R. (1991) *A New World Order*, working paper. Madrid: Castellana Cien.

Tamir, Y. (1993) *Liberal Nationalism*, Princeton: Princeton University Press.

Tanter, R. (1999) *Rogue Regimes: Terrorism and Proliferation*, updated edition. London: Macmillan.

Task Force on the Future of Public Television (1993) *Reinventing Public Television*, Washington, DC: The Brookings Institution.

Taylor, C. (1989) *Sources of the Self: The Making of the Modern Identity*, Cambridge, MA: Harvard University Press.

Taylor, C. (1992) *Multiculturalism and 'The Politics of Recognition'*, Princeton: Princeton University Press.

Tedlock, P. and A. Belkin, eds (1996) *Counterfactual Thought Experiments in World Politics*, Princeton: Princeton University Press.

Temking, L. S. (1993) *Inequality*, New York: Oxford University Press.

Tennsje, T. (1992) *Populist Democracy: A Defence*, London: Routledge.

Tester, K. (1992) *Civil Society*, London: Routledge.

Teubner, G. (1992) *Law as an Autopoietic System*, Oxford: Blackwell.

Thackston, W. M., translator and editor (1996) *The Baburnama: Memoirs of Babur, Prince and Emperor*, New York: Oxford University Press.

Thagard, P. (1992) *Conceptual Revolutions*, Princeton: Princeton University Press.

Thomas, R. M., ed. (1993) *Teaching Ethics. Vol. I: Government Ethics*, Cambridge, UK: Centre for Business and Public Sector Ethics.

Thompson, J. (1992) *Justice and World Order: A Philosophical Inquiry*, London: Routledge.

Thompson, J. (1987) *Evolution and Escalation: An Ecological History of Life*, Princeton: Princeton University Press.

Thompson, M., R. Ellis and A. Wildavsky. (1990) *Cultural Theory*, Boulder, CO: Westview.

Thompson, M., R. Ellis and A. Wildavsky. (1992) 'Political Culture', in: M. Hawkesworth and M. Kogan, eds, *Encyclopedia of Government and Politics*, 2 vols. London: Routledge, pp. 507–20.

Thompson, W. C. (1980) *In The Eye of the Storm: Kurt Riezler and the Crises of Modern Germany*, Iowa: University of Iowa Press.

Thucydides (1989) *The Peloponnesian War. The Complete Hobbes Translation*, Reprint. Chicago: The University of Chicago Press.

Toffler, A. (1971) *Future Shock*, New York: Bantam.

Toffler, A. (1995) *Creating a New Civilization: The Politics of the Third Wave*, Atlanta: Turner Publishing.

Tomlinson, J. (1991) *Cultural Imperialism*, Baltimore: Johns Hopkins University Press.

Tomlinson, J. (1999) *Globalization and Culture*, Chicago: University of Chicago Press.

Tonn, B. (1996) 'A Design for Future-oriented Government'. *Futures*, vol. 28, no. 5, June, pp. 413–431.

Tuchman, B. W. (1984) *The March of Folly: From Troy to Vietnam*, New York: Knopf.

Tufte, E. R. (1978) *Political Control of the Economy*, Princeton: Princeton University Press.

Tulis, J. K. (1987) *The Rhetorical Presidency*, Princeton: Princeton University Press.

Tully, J. (1995) *Strange Multiplicity: Constitutionalism in an Age of Diversity*, Cambridge, UK: Cambridge University Press.

UNESCO (1994) *World Science Report*, Paris: UNESCO.

Unger, R. M. (1987a) *Part I of Politics, a Work in Constructive Social Theory: False Necessity – Anti-Necessitarian Social Theory in the Service of Radical Democracy*, Cambridge, UK: Cambridge University Press.

Unger, R. M.. (1987b) *Plasticity into Power: Comparative-Historical Studies on the Institutional Conditions of Economic and Military Success*, Cambridge, UK: Cambridge University Press.

Union of International Associations (1991) *Encyclopedia of World Problems and Human Potential*, two volumes, 3rd edition, Munich: K.G. Saur.

United Nations Development Programme (1999) *Human Development Report 1999*, Los Angeles: Getty Center for Education in the Arts.

United Nations Development Programme (2000a) *Overcoming Human Poverty: Poverty Report 2000*, New York: UNDP.

United Nations Development Programme (2000b) *Human Development Report 2000: Human Rights and Human Development*, Oxford: Oxford University Press.

United Nations Environmental Programme (1995) *Global Diversity Assessment*, Cambridge, UK: Cambridge University Press.

Urquhart, B. (1993) *Ralph Bunche*, New York: Norton.

Urquhart, B. and E. Childers (1990) *A World in Need of Leadership: Tomorrow's United Nation*, Uppsala, Sweden: Dag Hammarskjold Foundation.

Urquhart, B. and E. Childers (1996) *A World in Need of Leadership: Tomorrow's United Nations – A Fresh Appraisal*, Uppsala, Sweden: Dag Hammarskjold Foundation.

Vanhanen, T. (1992) *On the Evolutionary Roots of Politics*, New Delhi: Sterling Publishers.

Vayrynern, R., ed. (1999) *Globalization and Global Governance: Canadian–U.S. Conference on Governance*, Lanham, MD: Rowlman and Littlefield.

Verheijen, T. (1995) *Constitutional Pillars for New Democracies: The Cases of Bulgaria and Romania*, Leiden: DSWO Press.

Vertzberger, Y. Y. (1990) *The World in Their Minds: Information Processes, Cognition, and Perception in Foreign Policy Decisionmaking*, Stanford: Stanford University Press

Veyne, P. (1990) *Bread and Circuses: Historical Sociology and Political Pluralism*, London: Allen Lane.

Vick, K. (2000) 'Disease Spreads Faster Than the Word', *The Washington Post*, 7 July.

Viroli, M. (1993) *From Politics to Reason of State: The Acquisition and Transformation of the Language of Politics 1250–1600*, Cambridge, UK: Cambridge University Press.

Voegelin, E. (1952) *The New Science of Politics: An Introduction*, Chicago: University of Chicago Press.

Voegelin, E. (1974) *The Ecumenic Age*. vol. IV of *Order and History*, Baton Rouge: Louisiana State University Press.

Volcansek, M. L., ed. (1992) *Judicial Politics and Policy-Making in Western Europe*, London: Frank Cass.

Wade, R. (1990) *Governing the Market: Economic Theory and the Role of Government in East Asian Industrialization*, Princeton: Princeton University Press.

Wakeman Jr, F. (1985) *The Great Enterprise: The Manchu Reconstruction of Imperial Order in Seventeenth-Century China*, two vols. Berkeley: University of California Press.

Waldrop, M. M. (1992) *Complexity: The Emerging Science at the Edge of Order and Chaos*, New York: Simon & Schuster.

Waley, A. (1982) *Three Ways of Thought in Ancient China*, Stanford: Stanford University Press.

Wallace, J. F. (1978) *Virtues and Vices*, Ithaca: Cornell University Press.

Wallerstein, I. (1974) *The Modern World-System*, New York: Academic Press.

Walton, D. N. (1986) *Courage: A Philosophic Investigation*, Berkeley: University of California Press.

Walton, D. N. (1992) *Slippery Slope Arguments*, Oxford: Clarendon.

Walzer, M. (1977) *Just and Unjust Wars: A Moral Argument with Historical Illustration*, New York: Basic Books.

Walzer, M. (1983) *Sphere of Justice: A Defence of Pluralism and Equality*, New York: Basic Books.
Warnke, M., ed. (1984) *Politische Architektur in Europa: Vom Mittelsalter bis Heute – Repräsentation und Gemeinschaft*, Cologne: DuMont.
Watson, A. (1992) *The Evolution of International Society*, London: Routledge.
Weaver, R. K. and B. A. Rockman, eds (1993) *Do Institutions Matter? Government Capabilities in the United States and Abroad*, Washington, DC: The Brookings Institution.
Weber, E. (1986) *France Fin de Siècle*, Cambridge MA: Harvard University Press.
Weidenfeld, W., ed. (1996) *Demokratie am Wendepunkt: Die Demokratische Frage als Project des 21. Jahrhunderts*, Berlin: Siedler.
Weimer, D. L and A. R. Vining. (1992) *Policy Analysis: Concepts and Practice*, second edition. Englewood-Cliffs, NJ: Prentice-Hall.
Weir, S. and W. Hall. (1994) *Ego Trip: Extragovernmental Organizations in the UK and Their Accountability*, London: Charter 88.
Weisberg, J. (1996) *In Defence of Government*, New York: Scribners.
Weizsäcker, E. von, A. B. Lovins and L. H. Lovins. (1997) *Factor Four: Doubling Wealth, Halving Resources – The New Report to the Club of Rome*, London: EarthScan.
Welch, D. A. (1993) *Justice and the Genesis of War*, Cambridge: Cambridge University Press.
Wells, H. G. (1967) *A Modern Utopia*, Lincoln: University of Nebraska Press. First published 1905.
Werlen, B. (1993) *Society, Action and Space: An Alternative Human Geography*, London: Routledge.
Whiteside, K. H. (1988) *Merleau-Ponty and the Foundations of an Existential Politics*, Princeton: Princeton University Press.
Wildavsky, A. (1988) *Searching for Safety*, New Brunswick, NJ: Transaction.
Will, G. F. (1983) *Statecraft as Soulcraft: What Government Does*, New York: Simon & Schuster.
Willetts, P., ed. (1996) *The Conscience of the World: The Influence of Non-Governmental Organizations in the UN System*, Washington, DC: The Brookings Institution.
Williams, B. (1981) *Moral Luck: Philosophical Papers 1973–1980*, Cambridge, UK: Cambridge University Press.
Williams, B. *et al.* (1985) *Politics, Ethics and Public Service*, London: Royal Institute of Public Administration.
Williams, T. A. (1982) *Learning to Manage Our Future: The Participative Redesign of Societies in Turbulent Transition*, New York: Wiley.
Williams, W. (1988) *Washington, Westminster and Whitehall*, Cambridge, UK: Cambridge University Press.
Williams, W. (1990) *Mismanaging America: The Rise of The Anti-Analytic Presidency*, Lawrence, KS: University Press of Kansas.
Williamson, J. (1993) *The Political Economy of Policy Reform*, Washington, DC: Institute for International Economics.
Williamson, O. E. (1996) *The Mechanisms of Governance*, Oxford: Oxford University Press.
Willner, A. R. (1984) *The Spellbinders: Charismatic Political Leadership*, New Haven: Yale University Press.
Wilson, E. O. (1975) *Sociobiology: The New Synthesis*, Cambridge, MA: Harvard University Press.
Wilson, E. O. (1978) *On Human Nature*, Cambridge, MA: Harvard University Press.
Wilson, E. O. (1998) *Consilience: The Unity of Knowledge*, New York: Knopf.
Wiseman, T. P. (1971) *New Men in the Roman Senate 139 B.C. – A.D. 14*, Oxford: Oxford University Press.
Wittrock, B., ed. (1983) *Governance in Crisis*. special issue of *Policy Sciences*, Vol. 15 (April).

Wolf Jr, C. (1996) *Markets or Governments: Choosing between Imperfect Alternatives*, second edition. Cambridge, MA: MIT Press.

Wood, E. M. (1995) *Democracy Against Capitalism: Renewing Historical Materialism*, Cambridge, UK: Cambridge University Press.

World Bank, The (1993) *The East Asia Miracle: Economic Growth and Public Policy*, Oxford: Oxford University Press.

World Bank, The (2000) *Entering the 21st Century: World Development Report 1999/2000*, New York: Oxford University Press.

World Commission on Environment and Development (1987) *Our Common Future*, Oxford: Oxford University Press.

World Energy Council (1993) *Energy for Tomorrow's World*, New York: St. Martin's Press.

World Health Organization (1999) *The World Health Report 1999: Making a Difference*, Rome: WHO.

Wormald, B. H. G. (1993) *Francis Bacon: History, Politics and Science 1561–1626*, Cambridge, UK: Cambridge University Press.

Wriggins, H. W. (1969) *The Ruler's Imperative: Strategies for Political Survival in Asia and Africa*, New York: Columbia University Press.

Wright, A. F. and D. Twitchett, eds (1962) *Confucian Personalities*, Stanford: Stanford University Press.

Wright, R. (1994) *The Moral Animal: Evolutionary Psychology and Everyday Life*, New York: Pantheon Books.

Yergin, D. and J. Stanislaw (1998) *The Commanding Heights: The Battle between Government and the Marketplace that is Remaking the Modern World*, New York: Simon & Schuster.

Yew, L. K. (1998) *The Singapore Story: Memoirs of Lee Kuan Yew*, Singapore: Prentice-Hall.

Young, M. (1958) *The Rise of the Meritocracy (1870–2033)*, London: Thames & Hudson.

Younger, E., ed. (1995) *Inside the Confederate Government: The Diary of Robert Garlick Hill Kean*, Baton Rouge, LA: Louisiana State University Press.

Zakaria, F. (1997) 'The Rise of Illiberal Democracy'. *Foreign Affairs*, November/December, pp. 22–43.

Zaller, J. R. (1992) *The Nature and Origins of Mass Opinion*, Cambridge, UK: Cambridge University Press.

Zeckhauser, R. J., ed. (1991) *Strategy and Choice*, Cambridge, MA: MIT Press.

Zelikow, P. and C. Rice (1995) *Germany Unified and Europe Transformed*, Cambridge, MA: Harvard University Press.

Zolo, D. (1992) *Democracy and Complexity: A Realistic Approach*, Cambridge, UK: Polity.

Zuboff, S. (1990) *In the Age of the Smart Machine: The Future of Work and Power*, New York: Basic Books.

Index